THISTLE SO

'A lively autobiographical account of one family's
laughter and tears... a roller-coaster ride...'
The Scots Magazine

SNOWBALL ORANGES

'Peter Kerr writes with a combination of nice observation and gentle humour'
The Sunday Times

'an affectionate and amusing tale on Majorca and its inhabitants'
Sunday Express

'Peter Mayle's *A Year in Provence* saw Brits flock to the area in their
droves and *Snowball Orange*'s author, Peter Kerr, could well end up
being responsible for a new tide of Brits thronging, pesetas in hand,
to the island of Mallorca!...For anyone heading out to the island in the
near future, Snowball Oranges is almost as good as going there!'
World of Property magazine

'Fabulously evocative'
Spanish Homes magazine

'With prose as elegant as this, Snowball Oranges is one travel book that needs
no illustrations. In fact it reads more like a novel, brimming with charming
characters and good humour... By the time you reach the last page, you feel
as though you are in the Mediterranean... and you don't want to go home'
Amazon.co.uk

MAÑANA MAÑANA

'Ever dreamt of a new life in the sun? This is the story of one
couple who tried it… with hilariously unexpected results…
a warm-hearted mixture of disaster and hilarity'
Daily Mail

'A wealth of funny stories about a large circle of local eccentrics'
The Sunday Times

'Hilarious'
Spanish Homes magazine

FROM
PAELLA TO
PORRIDGE

Summersdale Publishers Ltd
46 West Street
Chichester
West Sussex
PO19 1RP
UK

www.summersdale.com

Printed and bound in Great Britain

ISBN 10: 1 84024 506 9
ISBN 13: 978-1-84024-506-6

Illustrations by Peter Kerr

FROM
PAELLA TO
PORRIDGE

A Farewell to Mallorca and a Scottish Adventure

PETER KERR

summersdale

CONTENTS

'But pleasures are like poppies spread:
You seize the flow'r, its bloom is shed;
Or like the snow falls in the river,
A moment white – then melts forever.'

From Tam o' Shanter by Robert Burns (1759–96)

– ONE –

OUT FOR A DUCK

'The smallest pot always contains the sweetest jam,' said old Maria.

'*Sí*,' old Pep grunted, 'but an empty sack cannot stand upright.'

'Better to own a little that is dear to you than have all the potato fields of Sa Pobla,' Maria countered.

Pep inclined his head backwards and squinted at her from beneath the overhang of his black beret. With the work-gnarled little finger of his right hand delicately raised, he plucked a misshapen *cigarrillo* from the corner of his mouth, remained ominously silent for a few moments, then drawled, 'Women have long hair and short brains!'

Maria gave a little snort of umbrage, then came back with, 'When a man's teeth fall out, his tongue wags loose!'

The self-satisfied smirk that had been wrinkling Pep's scraggy features since delivery of his last riposte was promptly converted into a pucker of pique. This, I suspected, was just as much to hide his generously-spaced graveyard of dental tombstones as to convey his annoyance at what Maria doubtless felt had been her *coup de grâce*. Pep's little black eyes narrowed as he replaced his hand-rolled cigarette in the corner of his mouth. He took care, I noticed, not to open his lips any more than was absolutely necessary to accommodate the *cigarrillo*'s soggy butt. Applying the same technique to the opposite corner of his mouth, he muttered, ventriloquist-style, 'And when a woman's teeth fall out, her brains soon follow.'

I could sense that Maria was about to take a swipe at Pep with her trusty mattock hoe, being sensitive, no doubt, to the fact that her own surviving teeth were arranged in a neat two-up, three-down formation. I had always thought that this gave her the appearance of a mischievous little elf when she smiled, but the look on her face now was more akin to that of a homicidal hobgoblin in a straw hat and black frock.

Pep continued to eyeball her inscrutably as sparks began to pop and crackle from the end of his cigarette. Time for a peace-making interjection, I reckoned.

'*Buen tiempo para el campo ayer, no?*' I said with a nervous little laugh. 'Good weather for the fields yesterday, no?'

But the British custom of bringing up the subject of the weather during any conversational hiatus cut no ice with this pair of crotchety old Mallorcan worthies – despite my picking a saying often used in rural Spain after unseasonable downpours like the one we'd experienced the previous day.

'*Y tambien para los patos*. And for the ducks as well,' Pep mumbled disinterestedly. His eyes remained fixed on Maria, and on her cocked hoe in particular.

'Anyway, Pep and Maria, about the price of land,' I said in an effort to steer the conversation back to where it had started before they'd engaged in their battle of Mallorcan proverbs. 'Is it still possible to buy good farmland at a fair agricultural value on a holiday island like this?'

'I am one duck short,' Maria piped up. She glowered accusingly at Pep.

'That's all right, Maria,' I quickly put in, before Pep could grab the opportunity to continue his female-brains theme by telling her that a duck wasn't all she was short of. 'I'll give you a hand to look for it, never fear.'

Maria had this quirky little habit of conducting her conversations in backflips – picking up on the last-but-one topic being discussed. You had to keep your wits about you when she was in this mode, which was almost permanently these days. Knee-high to a fruit fly and ninety if she was a day, Maria still had a mind as sharp as a razor, however – no matter what Pep suggested to the contrary. And there wasn't a single detail of the day-to-day state of the orchards, crops and livestock on her little *finca* of which she wasn't totally aware, as Jaume, her long-suffering son-in-law and general farm factotum, would ruefully affirm.

Maria's *finca*, given over mainly to lemon trees, was the next one up the valley from our own, on which oranges were the main crop. The two little farms were separated by a crumbling drystone wall. Along its base grew tall clumps of wild fennel, intertwined here and there by rambling grapevines growing from stubby, contorted rootstock that had been planted there who knows when and by who knows whom. Maria once told me that they'd been there for as long as she could remember, and, despite her diminutive size, she had the memory of an elephant. Even now, though, those old vines, with the encouragement of a little pruning, produced enough plump grapes to fill the fruit bowl on our kitchen table for many an autumn week.

Pep and Maria had known each other all of their lives, as both were natives of the valley, and Pep's *finca* was located just over the lane from hers and ours. The apparently hostile attitude that they showed towards each other was, I suspected, a bit of a sham – something of an act that, for reasons known only to themselves, they liked to carry out in front of anyone they thought might be taken in by it. As I was, in their eyes, a *loco extranjero* – a crazy foreigner – I fitted the bill just fine. But, despite both of them being capable of genuinely cantankerous behaviour at times, we'd come to know Pep and Maria as good, kind and generous neighbours.

We (that's my wife Ellie and I, along with our two sons – Sandy, now nineteen, and Charlie, seven years his junior) had come to live in this lush valley, hidden away in the Tramuntana Mountains of Mallorca, almost two years earlier. We'd bought the small orange farm of Ca's Mayoral on an impulse, after stumbling upon it as a result of taking a wrong turn on a holiday drive through the mountains. No doubt, if we'd spared the time to think seriously about what we were doing, we'd never have risked committing ourselves, our sons and everything we had to a type of farming we knew nothing about – and in a foreign land to boot. But, enchanted by the place almost as soon as we set eyes on it, Ellie and I had decided to sell up back home and take the plunge.

'Home' was the agricultural county of East Lothian in the south of Scotland, where we'd been growing barley and raising beef cattle on a fifty-acre spread near the historic market town of Haddington. We loved the area, justifiably known as the Garden of Scotland, not so much for its pastoral beauty – stunning though it is – as for the fertility of its gently rolling landscape. We also loved our home, the little farm of Cuddy Neuk, set on a hillside with uninterrupted views over the wide waters of the Firth of Forth and beyond to the chequered fields and undulating skyline of the ancient Kingdom of Fife.

In truth, I suppose we would never have dreamed of leaving that place, given a choice. However, in the big-is-beautiful and bigger-still-is-even-more-beautiful climate that had been developing over the years in British farming, we were facing a future in which fifty acres just wasn't going to be enough to provide us with a living any more. A farm of ten times that size would have been needed to profitably sustain the type of agriculture we were involved in. But that would have required the investment of a serious amount of capital, and a serious amount of capital we neither had nor were ever likely to have.

So, when we stumbled upon the opportunity to start afresh on an even *smaller* farm in a far-off land and involving totally unfamiliar skills of husbandry, we blithely fell into the role of *locos extranjeros* and bought the place. And 'crazy foreigners' is how the native Mallorcan farmers in the valley must have regarded us at first. They were all fairly elderly, their own offspring having left their little family *fincas* one by one over the years to seek a more lucrative and 'easier' living in the island's burgeoning tourist industry. And here was this greenhorn couple from far-away *Gran Bretaña*, arriving with two young sons in tow to plunge themselves into a way of life that was completely alien to them. *Locos extranjeros* indeed – and not only, as we were soon to find out, because of the 'brave' migratory move we had made.

'Your orchards are riddled with disease, Don Pedro,' was how old Jaume, Maria's rotund and avuncular son-in-law, had broken the news to me shortly after our arrival. The trees had been neglected for years, he'd added, before telling me that, as a retired waiter, his knowledge of fruit trees was fairly limited. However, even someone as inexperienced as he could tell a mile away that our orange groves needed urgent and extensive tree-doctoring if they were ever to be restored to reasonable productivity. Such treatment by a tree maestro would cost us, but the alternative, he predicted, would be to face ruination – and soon.

Even the quiet kick I'd got from being addressed as *Don* Pedro, no matter how waggishly Jaume had used this most deferential of Spanish handles, couldn't allay the feeling of panicky disillusionment that swept over me then. In our starry-eyed ignorance, we'd been sold a lemon of an orange farm by Francisca and Tomàs Ferrer, the charming but wily Mallorcan couple who were the previous owners of Ca's Mayoral. But there could be no going back now, so we simply had to make the best of it, roll up our sleeves and try, somehow, to turn the little farm's fortunes around. And, thanks to the ungrudging advice and help of good people like Maria, Pep and other kind-hearted Mallorcan country folk, we'd succeeded in doing just that. We were making ends meet, though only just. But at least all the hard work and money that we'd invested in Ca's Mayoral was showing signs of paying off. The gamble we'd taken in turning our backs on everything we were familiar with in order to start a new life in a Mediterranean 'paradise' had turned out to be worth it after all – even after such a potentially disastrous start.

Then Spain joined the European Union. It wasn't long before rumours of a glut of citrus fruit were rife. Forecasts were being made of an orange surplus to rival the wheat mountains and wine lakes that already existed in Europe's ever-growing community of free-trading countries. There were even reports of thousands of tons of the fruit being bulldozed into the sea in the Valencia area of mainland Spain, as a mark of protest by growers who were seeing their already modest profit margins being squeezed even further by a rise in bureaucratic regulations and a fall in prices. And, as Valencia is one of the leading orange-producing regions in Europe, these were growers with much larger enterprises than ours. 'Big is beautiful' and 'bigger still is even more beautiful' were going to be the maxims for this type of farming in Spain, just as they'd already become for cereal and beef producers in Britain. The writing was on the wall for little *fincas* like Ca's Mayoral, and, with the benefit of hindsight gained from our previous experience in Scotland, we could read the words clearly. We'd have to expand to survive. Hence my enquiry to Pep and Maria about the availability of sensibly priced farmland here in Mallorca.

But Maria was more immediately interested in finding her lost duck, while Pep was more interested in using Maria's concern for its welfare as a means of getting one up on her.

We were standing in the lane outside the gate to Pep's ramshackle farmstead. It was a late August evening, and the sun had just begun to dip behind the Serra d'es Pinotells, the pine-fringed ridge that rises high above the western flanks of the Sa Coma valley. The day had been searingly hot, and the humidity which is a permanent feature of the island's summer climate was even heavier than normal following the recent rains. It had been one of those oppressively sultry days, when even the sparrows in the little pine grove at the side of the Ca's Mayoral farmhouse couldn't be bothered to summon up the energy to chirp. Now, as dusk sent welcome shadows creeping over the valley floor, the warm, musty air became heady with the scent of wild flowers refreshed by the falling dew.

Though dressed only in shorts and a baggy cotton shirt, I still felt as if I was standing fully-clothed in a sauna. Two years of exposure to the temperatures that turn such enclosed Mallorcan valleys into ovens in the height of summer hadn't really helped me acclimatise much at all. I was still a northern *extranjero*, with a metabolism more suited to coping with chilblains than heat exhaustion.

My two venerable Mallorcan neighbours, on the other hand, couldn't have appeared more comfortable, despite their attire. Maria, as already mentioned, was dressed in the 'uniform' of elderly ladies in rural Spain – a long, black frock that covered everything except her hands and head. And she wore no accessories, apart from the wide-brimmed straw hat that she donned whenever venturing outdoors during the hottest months of summer. Oh, and of course she had her trusty mattock hoe, which she employed to knock out any weed that had the temerity to grow between the rows of her precious lemon trees, to act as a kind of walking stick and, as on this occasion, to threaten physical damage to anyone who got up her nose.

For his part, Pep was sporting the same clobber that he wore all year round. Scruffy as he was, though, there was still a certain dash about his presence, and he knew it. Beneath the ever-present black beret, his wiry frame was clad in a scuffed leather bomber jacket and baggy grey trousers, the latter's frayed hems bound by a liberal splattering of dried mule shit. Doubtless, beneath this outer layer, he would have been wearing what he described as his 'summer-weight' combinations, a one-piece arrangement of long-armed undervest and ankle-length drawers that he claimed never parted company with his hide ('except in emergencies') from the onset of spring until the first storms of autumn. But what the eye doesn't see, the heart doesn't grieve, and Pep's outward appearance was all that mattered to him. A little red neckerchief tied jauntily below his left ear completed his unique interpretation of 'style'.

'I am a duck short,' Maria repeated.

Pep gave a guttural chortle, flashed me a wink, then proceeded to tell me how he had been assembling his little herd of sheep in his yard a few minutes earlier when he heard frantic quacking sounds coming from the lane.

'Maria's missing duck?' I asked rhetorically.

Pep arched an eyebrow, smirked, then shook his head. '*Hombre*, when did you last see a duck wearing a black dress and a straw hat – *sí*, and toting a hoe as well? *Coño*,' he laughed, 'if there had been a telephone in my house, I would have sent for the men in white coats!'

I glanced at Maria, fully expecting her to exact instant revenge on Pep for this affront, but, curiously, she totally ignored it. Instead, she opted to tell me how the duck had slipped past her when she was opening her gate to let Jaume drive through in his little car. Two of its ducklings had died as a result of a soaking they'd got in yesterday's storm, she explained. Ducklings, she sagely added, were susceptible to being fatally chilled by soakings like that. However, small as they were, they would still make a tasty stock. So, she had plucked and cleaned them right away and plopped them into the pot before going to open the gate for Jaume. It was then that the mother duck, being a stupid creature and unable to understand what had really happened, had decided to go in search of her missing babies.

I struggled to suppress a smile as the ensuing scene unfolded in my mind's eye. 'And that's why you were making quacking noises as you came down the lane,' I said as solemnly as I could. 'You were just trying to attract your runaway duck, *correcto*?'

'You will never be able to buy more land in this valley,' was Maria's response. She'd done another of her conversational backflips. 'The *fincas* here are small enough as it is, and no farmer can afford to sell off even one square metre of his land.'

I knew this well enough already, and I understood it too. Although the younger generations had left and would never return to adopt the way of life of their forebears, the custom of parents automatically leaving their small farms to their offspring still persisted. Very often the *finca* would then be used only as a weekend retreat by its new owners and *their* offspring. The land, and any fruit trees that it supported, would be maintained in as good heart as was feasible within the limitations of a hobby-farming regime. At least, though, the tradition of working the small family farm was being carried on, albeit on a part-time basis.

Only on the rare occasions when there was no one for the old folks to leave their property to, or if the inheritors had left the island for good, would little farms like those in the Sa Coma valley be put on the market. Then, inevitably, prices far above their agricultural value would be paid by foreigners, whose interest was limited to upgrading the house for either retirement or holiday use. Consequently, much of the land and its trees would be left to fall into a state of neglect.

That was the trend, and although I was already well aware of it, it didn't help me solve the problem of how to increase the size and long-term profitability of our own farm.

Maria, conversely, couldn't understand why I would ever want to buy more land, if to do so meant having to leave her beloved valley. Hence her quotation of the Mallorcan sayings about smallest pots containing the sweetest jam, and about the folly of coveting the wide, productive fields surrounding the town of Sa Pobla, so far away (for an immovable valley-dweller like her) on the island's central plain.

Pep's proverb, stating that an empty sack can't stand upright, was his way of showing that he at least understood that such blinkered sentiments as Maria's, no matter how cosy, wouldn't pay the bills.

Although the expression of their conflicting, though equally well-intentioned, philosophies had then degenerated into a contest of insults, it didn't disguise the fact that both of our old neighbours were now aware of the problem I was grappling with. And, I suppose, that had really been the main reason I'd asked their advice on the subject in the first place. Neither of them, after all, would have had much knowledge, and probably less interest, in the availability and value of agricultural land anywhere beyond the valley in which their lives were cocooned – and contentedly so at that.

But our needs as a comparatively young family were different from theirs. Much as we would have preferred it to be otherwise, we either had to play the survival game according to the current rules, or risk going bust. That was the harsh reality of things. However, there was no point in labouring the subject, so I elected to change it back to the one that concerned Maria most.

'Tell you what,' I said to her, 'I'll get Sandy and Charlie to help me find that wandering duck of yours. It won't have waddled that far. Probably hasn't even ventured beyond that wet patch where the *torrente* crosses the lane just around the bend there.'

But Maria was having none of that, and she eschewed her customary verbal backflip to emphasise the fact. 'I am certain that it scurried in there.' She pointed with her hoe towards Pep's farmstead. 'She would have headed towards the sound of *his* ducks, thinking that her babies were with them.'

I could see Pep bristling, his hackles rising. Another peace-making interjection was called for. 'Well, I see what you mean,' I said, 'but, ehm, don't you think, Maria, that Pep would have noticed your duck coming into his yard when he was gathering his sheep there?'

Maria sniffed a dismissive sniff. 'Puh, there is none so blind as he who will not see.'

'*And*,' Pep indignantly snapped, 'there are three things not to be trusted – a goat's horn, a mule's hoof and a woman's tongue!'

I groaned inwardly. Not another battle of the proverbs, surely! But my concern was premature, as Pep was about to demonstrate…

He pulled himself up to his full height and puffed out his chest, his bomber jacket bursting open to expose the yellowed fabric of his upper combinations. 'I have many sheep, many goats, many geese, many hens *and* I have many ducks.' Pep was right on his high horse now. 'In fact,' he declared, 'I have more ducks than any one man could ever wish to have. Six!' With that, he turned and walked his sauntering, John Wayne walk back across the lane towards his *finca*.

I watched his deliberately stagy exit in silence, while Maria muttered a string of oaths in *mallorquín*. No sooner had Pep disappeared into the shambles of tumbledown shacks and jerry-built sheds that comprised his farmstead than a cacophony of cackling, quacking, honking, flapping, bleating, braying and barking rose into the limpid, twilight air. Normal silence was resumed as Pep reappeared, ambling back towards us with a hessian sack dangling heavily from his hand.

The sack was moving. It was also quacking. He handed it to Maria.

'Here,' he said with a casual air, 'this prize bird should more than compensate for the miserable bundle of feathers and bones that you have mislaid.' He winked at me again. '*Hombre*, no one can ever say that Pep is not a generous man, eh!' Feeling patently pleased with himself, he then bade us *adéu* and swaggered unhurriedly back towards his farm. He had more important things to do than replace escapee ducks for senile old women, he called back over his shoulder. *Sí claro*, now that the sun had set, he had his herd of sheep to take up to the *bancales altos*, the high mountain terraces, on which he had grazing rights.

'Well,' I said to Maria, 'all's well that ends well, as the saying goes. Oh, and by the way, my offer still stands. The boys and I will go and look for your stray duck now, if you want.'

Maria looked up at me and her mouth opened into that impish, gap-toothed grin of hers. 'And what duck would that be, *muchacho?*'

I started to laugh. 'You don't mean that there never was a –'

'A lost duck?' she tittered.

I nodded my head.

Maria released a wheezy giggle. '*Hombre*, nothing was lost around here tonight but Pep's marbles.' Delighted with herself, she thumped the blade of her hoe on the ground. 'Me senile?' she chuckled. '*Bueno*, who is a duck up and who is a duck down, eh? Just answer me that, *guapo*. *Sí*, just answer me that.'

Her laughter echoed round the valley like a chipmunk on helium as she heaved the duck-laden sack over her shoulder and shuffled off homeward. 'And who needs all the potato fields of Sa Pobla?' she shouted back. '*Sí*, just answer me that as well, *guapo*. Just answer me that.'

★ ★ ★ ★ ★

Ellie was setting the table for our evening meal when I returned from my meeting with our two old *vecinos* out in the lane. 'It's easy for Maria to come out with nice, homespun sayings like that,' she smiled after I'd given her the highlights of the powwow. 'Yes, and it's really touching to know that she doesn't want us to leave this valley, but…'

There was no need for her to say more. We had talked about it over and over again since assessing our financial prospects at the end of our first year in Ca's Mayoral the previous winter. To allow ourselves to be lulled into a false sense of security now that the punishing grind of restoring the run-down *finca* was over would have been short-sighted in the extreme. Things weren't standing still in farming – far from it – and if we didn't keep up, we'd be trampled underfoot soon enough.

For all that this knowledge had been in the back of our minds since the day we arrived at Ca's Mayoral, we had never let it dampen our enthusiasm for the new life we'd chosen. Even Jaume's crushing revelation about the poor state of our orchards had been unable to do that, although it had come perilously close to it for a while. But there's nothing like having to keep busy – and a good sense of humour – for tempering worries. Certainly, we'd had no shortage of hard work, particularly during that first year, when there was so much to do in improving the condition and productivity of the fruit trees. Coping with the summer heat and getting used to conducting conversations, both social and commercial, in a foreign language had been just two of the many other things we'd had to struggle with. There had also been a few dark moments, like when we arrived home one day to find that the house had been broken into and ransacked, or when a violent storm had threatened to turn our first Christmas in the valley into a nightmare. But we ultimately managed to see the funny side of most of the mishaps that befell us and we could now look back on our first two years at Ca's Mayoral as a period dominated by enjoyable and exciting times.

In retrospect, we could see that it was just as well that we'd been down-to-earth enough to realise that embarking on an all-or-nothing adventure like this wouldn't be all plain sailing. True, there had been a few setbacks that might have been avoided *if* we'd looked into everything in a bit more detail first. A duff septic tank, for example; dodgy plumbing and electrics in the house; furniture that we *thought* we'd bought with the property, but which the previous owners had spirited away before we took possession of the place; and various domestic appliances that they *had* left for us, but which turned out to be clapped-out junkyard fodder. Again, though, most of these things produced humorous spin-offs, no matter how bizarre at times, and we could blame nothing but our own naivety for whatever financial cost resulted. The only positive way to look at it was that we'd learned the hard way, and those are lessons you never forget.

Even Ellie's gift of coming out with some classic linguistic clangers had brought about a marked improvement in her Spanish vocabulary, which had been fairly limited before we came to the island. Only once do you ask a waiter for his testicles when you really want rabbit, or a butcher for his penis when you mean a chicken. But at least she was *trying* to communicate in the language of her adopted country. We all were, because we had never forgotten that *we* were the foreigners in someone else's land, so the onus was on us to adapt to their ways and to converse with them in their tongue.

Standing shouting in English at a Spaniard in the way that a certain type of Brit holidaymaker is noted for won't get you far in a close-knit rural community like the one we'd settled in. Nor would a patronising attitude towards the native country folk have contributed to our becoming accepted by them. Bad enough to be regarded as *loco* without coming across as being *condescendiente* as well. After all, we were hands-on, mud-on-our-boots small farmers just like them, and we had to depend on their infinitely greater knowledge of their land, climate and age-old local ways to help us learn, adapt and survive. We'd made a point of keeping ourselves right in those departments, no matter how many mistakes we made in others.

One of those mistakes, at least in old Pep's opinion, had been our decision, at the end of that first traumatic year, to have a swimming pool built in front of the house. In fairness to him, it did seem, on the face of it, a recklessly extravagant item for rookie fruit farmers on a tight budget to be splashing out on. Pep's judgement had been that the money spent on this 'unnecessary luxury and waste of precious water' would have been put to better use in the purchase of more orange-growing land. And no one could fault his logic. But there are invariably two ways of looking at any one thing, and our view on this one had been that adding value to the property we already owned would be a more prudent investment for us at that particular time. We'd applied the same line of thought to the building of a barbecue area, and also to converting the large *almacén* (workroom-cum-store) on the ground floor of the house into a games room, complete with bar and snooker table.

Admittedly, there had been times when I'd doubted the wisdom of committing our limited financial resources to these projects, particularly when signing the contract agreeing the pool-builder's estimate! But we'd offset that considerable expense, to some extent at least, by tackling most of the work on the other two schemes ourselves. A combination of good luck and a need to make-do-and-mend also helped us furnish and equip both for surprisingly little cost. And, now that everything was done and dusted, the transformation to what had been a charming but essentially basic old farmhouse was spectacular. The boost to its value would certainly far outstrip the expenditure involved in its upgrading, and that had been the object of the exercise. We would now have substantially increased collateral available, should the need arise to raise money for buying more land.

That aside, however, it would be less than honest to deny that the prospect of enjoying these new 'leisure facilities' had added a certain self-indulgent element to what we had tried to convince ourselves was a purely *business* plan. But I suppose we felt that we deserved to spoil ourselves a bit after all the hard graft we'd put into improving the farm. After all, we work to live, as the Mallorcans say, not vice versa, and we were determined to take some pleasure from the fruits of our labours – while the opportunity existed, for there was no way of telling just how long it would.

It being a hot and muggy evening, Ellie had decided that eating outdoors would be the thing. The table she was setting, therefore, was the one in the barbecue area, located on the edge of the little pine grove between the house and the ancient, high wall that bordered the lane. Candles flickering lazily on the chunky wooden table set shadows weaving through the overhanging branches of an almond tree, while the scattering of concealed lights the boys and I had installed between the pines lent a warm and welcoming glow to the entire scene. What had originally been a fairly nondescript and seldom visited corner of the garden had become a quite delightful setting for al fresco eating. Although I said it myself, we had created, with minimal outlay, something that looked a million dollars. And even if that was taking self-congratulation a bit too far, the drousy chirruping of crickets now starting up in the nearby pines *did* add a truly priceless touch of Mediterranean magic to the results of our efforts, no matter how modest they may have been.

It never fails to amaze how the smell of a barbecue attracts boys and dogs. Bonny, our young boxer bitch, was first on the scene, quickly followed by Sandy and Charlie. The three of them had been in the new games room. The boys had been playing snooker and, I hoped, keeping their hands off the contents of the little bar I'd built out of old window shutters salvaged from outside the workshop of the local *carpintero*. Bonny liked to 'referee' snooker games by standing with her front paws resting on the edge of the table, closely watching the movement of the balls and resisting the temptation, though only just, to clamp her jaws round any that happened to roll in her direction.

'Gee, the smell of those chops is truly *awe*some!' Charlie enthused in the mid-Atlantic accent common to most of the pupils at his international school. Not that there was a predominance of American kids there, just that their way of speaking seemed to have an infectious attraction for the others.

'You're sounding like Catherine Zeta Jones again,' I told him. This was a comment I'd made so often that it came out almost of its own volition now.

'Yeah, well,' Charlie shrugged, 'I guess we all speak like somebody.' He gave me a playful nudge with his elbow, then added, 'I mean, the kids at school think *you* sound like Sean Connery.'

'Hmm,' Ellie mused, 'it's just a pity he doesn't look like him as well.'

'At least Dad hasn't lost his own accent,' Sandy said, firing a critical glance at his younger brother. 'None of us have. Just you, Charlie.' He shook his head and taunted, 'Aye, your old school chums back home would have a *right* laugh if they could hear you now, eh!'

Charlie let that pass without comment. No matter how much fun his brother poked at him, he was happy with the way he spoke now. It was part of the normal order of things in the laid-back scholastic environment he'd become part of, just as T-shirts, jeans and sneakers formed the accepted code of the school dress. While Charlie probably didn't like his new school, in an academic sense, any more than he would any other seat of learning, he had certainly taken to the informal classroom regime and open-air lifestyle its pupils enjoyed. Moreover, the wide circle of friends of various nationalities and backgrounds he'd made there had broadened his outlook noticeably. All to the good, except for the slightly worrying fact that the friends he seemed keenest on just happened to be the offspring of a few of the richest expat families on the island. Yes, Charlie had developed a taste for the money's-no-object lifestyle that such privileged folk luxuriate in. It was a trait that

Ellie and I knew we'd have to keep in check, and we'd started by making sure that if Charlie wanted to spend time at weekends in such hedonistic company, he'd also have to muck in with the rest of us on the farm work as often as was reasonable for a kid of his age. It's fair to say that he accepted the prerequisite more stoically than cheerfully, but the important thing was that we were making an effort to keep his feet on the ground. Unlike one of his affluent young chums, for instance, it was highly improbable that Charlie would be given his own speedboat for his thirteenth birthday. Not unless I won the *Lotería Nacional* pretty damn soon, that is, and probably not even then.

Nevertheless, Charlie couldn't have been happier with his life in Mallorca now, which was in marked contrast to how he'd felt about coming to the island initially. On his very first night in Ca's Mayoral, he'd been all for going back to Scotland and his grannies right there and then. Conversely, Sandy had been filled with enthusiasm about our move – at first. It hadn't been long before life for him in the valley began to pall, however. Working with us on the farm day after day, with no people of his own age in the vicinity to mix with, was not the most stimulating of environments. Also, having to do the field work wrestling with the handlebars of a tiny, two-wheeled 'tractor', while ducking under the low branches of fruit trees, wasn't his idea of true farming. Although our little Barbieri diesel really was the only type of tractor suitable for the tight confines of an orange grove, Sandy regarded it as nothing but a motorised donkey. He missed the big, four-wheel-drive monsters he'd been used to back home. He longed for the wide, arable fields of East Lothian, where you could sit atop your *real* tractor in air-conditioned, stereo-listening comfort, with every conceivable type of hydraulic and electronic gismo at your fingertips, and not a single fruit tree in sight.

In contrast to Charlie's new life, then, Sandy's had turned out to be a disappointment, and it hadn't come as a complete surprise when he eventually broke the news to us that he'd decided to go back to Scotland and to agricultural college at the start of the forthcoming autumn term. He'd also reasoned that having one less mouth to feed would ease the financial pressure on us at Ca's Mayoral, and while we appreciated his thoughtfulness, Ellie and I both knew that the pull of 'home' was the primary reason for Sandy deciding to draw a line under this chapter of his life.

Ellie would miss him. We all would – even Charlie, despite their perpetual brotherly ribbing. But all fledglings must leave the nest sooner or later, and Sandy's time to test his wings had come. All we could do as parents was give him every encouragement and promise our support. Meanwhile, we'd make the most of his company for the few hours that remained before he left home. We'd be driving him to the airport first thing in the morning.

He sniffed the air while following his nose towards the barbecue. 'I've never heard pork chops described as awesome before,' he said, 'but, for once, I've got to agree with Charlie. If these ones taste as good as they smell…'

He knew full well that the best Mallorcan pork is in a class of its own. It's all about how the pigs are fed on the little *fincas*. A diet rich in fallen figs and all the other bits and pieces of fruit and vegetables that are considered unfit for human consumption results in a taste and texture of meat that can never be replicated on a factory farm, no matter how 'scientifically nourishing' the pelleted pig feed served to the inmates. You won't find such orchard-reared Mallorcan pork in many butchers' shops, of course – simply because there isn't enough of it available.

At one time, a pig was kept on every *finca*. Its slaughter, locally known as the *matances* (literally 'the killing'), was a celebratory occasion that could last for a couple of days as the various processes of butchering, curing and sausage-making were carried out with the help of neighbours. The *matances*, complete with accompanying songs and dances, was an annual event that was keenly looked forward to – except, naturally, by the pig. With the gradual demise of the small family farm, however, such truly organic grunters were becoming something of a rarity.

Old Maria still kept one, though. Being a staunch upholder of everything relating to the 'old days', the thought of not rearing a pig every year would never have entered her mind. I had always resisted her insistence that we should follow suit. No matter how eco-friendly they might be, a pig to gobble up the windfalls of our orchards, and a dung-making donkey to replace the diesel-guzzling tractor were relics of Maria's precious old days that I wasn't about to adopt. One result was that we had nothing to feed our fallen figs to. And Maria's reward to us for giving her pig free access to them had been those very 'awesome' pork chops now sizzling on the barbecue.

Ellie had purposely saved them in the freezer since the previous winter's *matances*. They were her version of the fatted calf, brought out now to mark not the return of a prodigal son, but the impending departure of a pragmatic one.

'Yeah, the chops do smell fantastic, Sandy,' I agreed. 'Makes me wonder if I should give in to Maria's bullying after all – you know, keep a pig ourselves.'

'You already have one,' Sandy replied. He motioned with a flick of his head towards Charlie, who was standing at the table stuffing fistfuls of pickled olives and chunks of crusty bread into this face. 'A fat lot of good paying fees to that fancy school is doing,' Sandy went on. 'He may talk like a movie star, but he eats like a pig, and I can tell you for nothing that he still pees out of his bedroom window at night. Honest, if I were you, I'd save the money and send him to the state school down the road there in Andratx.'

'Hey, just 'cos I thrashed you at snooker, big brother, doesn't mean you can come out with a load of balls like that!' Charlie gobbled another few olives. 'And for the record, I only peed out the bedroom window that once, when the lightning zapped the electric pump and there wasn't any water to flush the john. It's called hygiene. Yeah,' he smirked, 'and it was good for Mum's roses as well.'

'Hmm, remind me never to sniff *them* again,' Sandy muttered.

And so our evening meal progressed, the boys' customary banter temporarily suspended to make way for the more immediately important task of munching their way through those delicious pork chops and all the trimmings. Bonny sat and watched them intently. Her big, soulful eyes envied their every bite, while little dribbles of saliva gathered at the end of her tongue and plopped like forlorn raindrops onto the ground. Although she was forbidden to actually *beg* at the table, she knew – and Ellie and I knew – that one or both of the boys would eventually slip her a surreptitious titbit. It was a safe bet that she wouldn't be spared much, if any, of their pork chops, however. A scrap of buttered bread or a morsel of barbecue-baked potato would be her lot.

A full moon was already rising above the mountains by the time the meal was being rounded off with fruit cocktails that Ellie had made from plums, pears, cherries and apricots, picked that evening from trees dotted here and there throughout the orange groves.

Sandy stood up, patted his stomach, glanced up at the sky, then grinned, 'Harvest moon, eh? Yep, if they've got a moon like that back home, things'll be looking good for cutting the barley.'

'Don't look at that full moon too long, big brother,' Charlie advised. 'It'll only give you a hairy face again. Yeah, and all that howling frightens the hell outa Bonny.'

While the boys, still ribbing each other, made their way back to the games room for another game of snooker, Ellie and I sat on at the table, relaxing over a coffee.

The night was still extremely warm, but a gentle breeze drifting down from the north had taken some of the mugginess out of the air. The chirruping of the crickets had been augmented now by the croaking of a chorus of frogs in the almost waterless *torrente* down beyond our farthest field, and somewhere in the wooded mountainsides a nightingale started to pour out his plaintive song. It was one of those magical Mediterranean nights that we used to dream about before coming to live here. Yet Sandy's instinctive thought when seeing that big Mallorcan moon come up had been one of Scotland – of 'home'.

'Maybe he'll come back here some day,' Ellie murmured after a while.

'Sandy?'

'Yes – you know, if we manage to build a more viable farming business.'

'Yeah, maybe he will at that,' I said with as much conviction as I could.

Ellie was already starting to feel the pangs of missing the bigger of her two 'wee laddies', and I guessed that even my encouraging words weren't enough to convince her that the possibility of Sandy ever returning permanently to Mallorca amounted to only wishful thinking. The chances of our finding more land to buy in the valley fell into the same category, if old Maria knew anything about it – and if she didn't, then no one did.

'Tomorrow we start the search for more land in earnest,' I said, making an effort to appear as positive as I could.

'How about asking the Ferrers if they'll sell us the piece they kept when they sold us this place? They said they'd give us first refusal, and it's only just over the wall. Couldn't be handier.'

Ellie was referring to the little field that Tomàs and Francisca Ferrer had retained for their own use. Unlike Francisca's parents, who had made their living on Ca's Mayoral like many generations of *campesinos* before them, Francisca and Tomàs had had no inclination to carry on the tradition after Francisca's mother passed away. Her broken-hearted old father's interest in the farm had died with his wife, and so he'd gone to live with his daughter and son-in-law in Palma city, where Tomàs held an important position in the local government. But Tomàs came from a small-farm background himself, and despite his rise to the upper echelons of the civil service, there were still traces of the soil flowing in his veins.

Hence their decision to keep that one little field. It would be their weekend hobby farm, on which he could grow beans, potatoes, onions, peppers, aubergines and tomatoes between the fruit trees in the traditional Mallorcan way.

On the day we signed the papers to buy the rest of Ca's Mayoral, the Ferrers had led us to believe that there would be a good chance of their ultimately selling us that little field as well. However, when we took possession of the farm a few months later, they had already employed builders to convert an old mill that stood on the same land into a *casita fin de semana*, their weekend country cottage. There was no way that the Ferrers would sell us that field as long as Tomàs enjoyed working on it with his little tractor, and as long as Francisca took delight in pottering about in her flowerbeds round the *casita*'s door. The fact was that we'd probably go bankrupt first.

Ellie nodded resignedly when I told her. 'So, what's Plan B?' she asked.

'I didn't know there had been a Plan A.'

'That was to try and buy more land here in the valley, but it seems as if old Maria has got it right. It's a non-starter.'

'Yeah, looks like it,' I agreed, feigning nonchalance. I downed the dregs of a shot of *hierbas*, Mallorca's herb-infused green liqueur and a perfect accompaniment to a postprandial coffee. 'But it's a big island,' I shrugged, 'so we'll just have to cast our net a bit wider, that's all.'

Ellie made no comment, but I knew she was thinking plenty. There was a look of foreboding in her eyes when she finally said, 'You think we'll have to leave Ca's Mayoral, don't you?'

I shook my head and gave what I hoped would be a reassuring little laugh. 'Nah, don't you worry. As long as we can find some land within tractor-driving distance of here, there'll be no need for that.'

Even Ellie's brave attempt at a smile couldn't hide her lack of confidence about that. She knew as well as I did that we lived in a part of the island in which land was becoming ever more sought after by property developers. There was even talk of a golf course being built on the outskirts of Andratx, less than a couple of miles down the road from where we were in the Sa Coma valley. If that came about, it would attract potential foreign residents to the area, which in turn would spawn the demand for expensive new houses. This would push up land prices even more, and so the inflationary snowball would continue to grow. It had happened in other parts of Mallorca already.

She looked over to the barbecue, which we'd built into the base of the old wall with rocks collected up the mountain. It was in the form of a sideboard that might have come from Fred Flintstone's house, but it matched the aged rubble and mortar of the wall perfectly.

'Nice how the lanterns on the wall highlight the rough bits of the stone,' she said. 'And the thick clumps of climbing ivy on either side as well. Sort of like nice, leafy curtains in this light, aren't they? And the smell of the smoke from the orange-wood logs. Nice.' Her sigh was a mix of contentment and misgiving. 'Yes, it would be a pity to leave all this – now that we've got it so nice.'

I was spared the need to answer by a whoop and a holler and an almighty splash coming from round the corner of the house.

'That'll be the boys cooling off after a strenuous game of snooker,' I said.

Ellie sighed again. 'Yes, it's nice having the pool now too.'

'Tut, tut! That's five times you've said "nice" in less than a minute,' I scolded schoolmaster-style in an attempt to lighten up her mood. 'I'll have to get you a thesaurus for your birthday if you don't try harder.'

Ellie's smile was a genuine one this time. 'A fat lot of good one of them would be to me.'

'How come?'

'Well, you know I'm useless at playing musical instruments.' Her smile broadened. 'A nice, emerald-encrusted, gold ring would be a nice surprise instead, though.' She stood up. 'Come on – we'll join the boys. It's the last night we'll all be together for a while. Sandy's leaving tomorrow, don't forget.'

Just then, we heard a faint noise coming from somewhere along the lane. A strange noise for this time of night. We both strained our ears, then looked at each other.

'Are you thinking what I'm thinking?' Ellie asked.

I nodded my head, still listening hard. 'I think so.'

'But *they're* not nocturnal creatures!'

The noise was getting closer. There was now no mistaking what it was.

'It's quacking all right,' I said. 'Strange, but true.'

Then other sounds came within earshot. Tinny bells clanking; bleating; an occasional bark and a gruff voice growling curses in *mallorquín*.

'It's Pep,' I said, 'bringing his flock home from nibbling weeds up on the *bancales*. That's him swearing at that dim-witted dog of his, as usual.'

More quacking.

'Maria's duck!' Ellie beamed. 'One must have escaped from her place after all. And Pep found it, and he's bringing it back to her. 'Aw-w-w,' she crooned all mushy-like, 'isn't that nice?'

'Not if you listen carefully to the curses and the quacks,' I cautioned.

'How do you mean?'

'They never happen simultaneously, do they?'

Ellie frowned. 'You mean it's...?'

'Yeah, it's Pep doing the quacking – unless it's a duck that smokes the same amount of coffin-nail roll-ups as he does.'

A puzzled look came over Ellie's face. 'But why would Pep walk along the lane impersonating a duck, for heaven's sake?'

'I have my suspicions,' I laughed. 'Yeah, he'll have noticed these lights of ours shining up through the pine trees, so he knows we're here.'

'So what?'

'So, he's trying to fool us into believing he's found Maria's duck.'

'But why on earth would he want to do that?'

'Because *he* doesn't know that no such duck exists, remember?'

Ellie frowned again. She shook her head. 'I still don't get it.'

'After two years here, I think I know pretty well now how that old rascal's mind works. He'll have had plenty of time to think about things while he was watching his sheep tonight, and I reckon he'll have had second thoughts about the wisdom of showing off by donating that duck of his to Maria in front of me. He'll be worried in case I see that as a sign of weakness – of him being soft to a woman, of all things.'

Ellie responded with a sigh of dismay. 'So, he makes quacking noises to prove that he's Mr Macho Man. Pathetic.'

I laughed at the thought. 'Well, it's just his way of taking a rise out of his old sparring partner Maria.'

Ellie saw the whole episode from another angle entirely, however. 'Or,' she said, looking at me as if I had 'gullible' writ large on my forehead, 'maybe Maria's duck did escape, maybe Pep did see it waddling into his yard, and maybe the duck he gave her in the sack was actually her own.'

I pursed my lips as I pondered these possibilities.

'So maybe,' Ellie concluded, 'your two old chums are *both* taking a rise out of *you!*'

I listened to Pep's croaky quacking fade into the confines of his farmyard, followed by a chesty guffaw.

'Hmm, I never thought about that,' I meekly confessed.

It was Ellie's turn to laugh now. She took me by the elbow. 'Come on,' she giggled, 'let's join the boys by the pool… and watch you don't trip over your bottom lip on the way.'

– TWO –

'SE VENDE'

For parents, a nineteen-year-old son leaving home can be likened to having a tooth pulled – painful at the time, but a relief when it's all over. You hurt at the severing of a part of yourself, yet, once the healing process starts, there's comfort in the realisation that you will ultimately be the better for the parting. That's usually true as far as gums and parents go, but not necessarily so for the son, and certainly never for the pulled tooth. However, in Sandy's case, it all worked out fine.

Back in Scotland, he now 'lived in' during the week at the agricultural college he was attending. Every Friday evening, he'd drive to my parents' house, just thirty miles away in his native East Lothian, where he'd found weekend work on one of the large farms. Life for Sandy couldn't have been more enjoyable, or secure. He was studying the things he was naturally drawn to in life, he was revelling in the easy-going company of like-minded lads of his own age, and he had the security of his grandparents' home to enjoy – and (although he'd never admit it) to be pampered in mercilessly for a couple of days a week. Grannies are like that when it comes to visiting grandsons. His weekend earnings also meant that, without relying on handouts from us, he had enough money in his pocket to spend in the pub in the company of his old mates during the little spare time that remained in his busy schedule.

Meanwhile, the house at Ca's Mayoral did seem unusually quiet without him. It wasn't that he'd ever been a particularly obstreperous or extroverted kid. Quite the opposite, in fact. He'd always been fairly well behaved and he tended to keep himself to himself much of the time. However, as gregarious and fun-loving as he could be when the time and company were right, he also valued family life, but in such an undemonstrative way that it was only now that we had come to realise just how effectual his presence had been. He'd been a great help to me on the farm, no matter how much he railed at having to work with that little 'diesel donkey' of a tractor. But his help had been more than simply manual. He had an old head on young shoulders. Although I'd probably taken it for granted at the time, he had always quietly but confidently offered his opinion, or even advice, on any problem that cropped up, or on any decision that had to be made. I missed him in my own way, just as Ellie did in hers, albeit that her overriding feelings would have been of a less practical, more motherly nature.

We knew that Charlie missed him as well, although he never actually said so. His frequent, out-of-the-blue remarks about 'that big nerd having his nuts frozen off in Scotland these days' or simply 'I wonder what that grumpy brother of mine is getting up to today' gave the game away, however.

Bonny also knew how Charlie felt at such times, even if she didn't understand the words he spoke. Dogs have that uncanny, telepathic way of recognising the moods of their human companions – some more so than others, perhaps. But, of all the dogs who'd owned us (for that's the way round it is to a dog's way of thinking in a happy home), Bonny was by far the most gifted in this respect. As young as she was, I had witnessed her, to give one example, comforting our neighbour, old Jaume, on the occasion of a bereavement in his family, when I – a creature supposedly in possession of much more sophisticated skills of communication than a dog – could only stand and watch him grieving alone without being able to find the words to console him.

Bonny's technique for alleviating Charlie's big-brother blues turned out to be just as sensitive, though tinged with a definite element of self-interest this time. Since buying her as a pup some twenty months earlier, we had trained Bonny to sleep in her basket in the kitchen, and despite some yowled bedtime pleadings at first, she had soon come to accept the situation, even if she didn't particularly like it. Now, however, she decided that the place to be – as a duty to her sad sibling, as she doubtless would have expected us to understand – was in his bedroom, and right there on his bed beside him, during the hours of darkness. Although her move from the kitchen always took place after she thought Ellie and I were safely asleep, and although she'd always returned to her basket before we got up in the morning, we knew what was going on, but said nothing. Bonny, after all, was only doing her 'little mother' thing, just as she had for old Jaume.

We mentioned this to Sandy during one of our regular phone calls to him, and Ellie made the point that it was Charlie's room and not ours in which Bonny had elected to act as night watchdog. This, Ellie suggested, was proof of Bonny's sense of compassion. She knew that Charlie needed her companionship when he was feeling lonely, whereas Ellie and I had each other for company.

Sandy's take on that was notably less romantic. 'Nah,' he pooh-poohed, 'it's more likely just that Charlie's room will *smell* a lot more attractive to her, that's all. I mean, you know where dogs stick their noses when they're checking out each other's ID, for example.'

He had a point there, we had to admit. Nevertheless, we preferred to think otherwise when Bonny eventually decided to divide her nocturnal duties between Charlie's bedroom and our own. I still wasn't fully asleep on her first visit. Squinting through one half-closed eye, I watched her bed-mounting technique with interest and amusement. First having made sure that our heads were on their pillows and that no sign of waking life was apparent, she raised one front paw tentatively onto the duvet, then paused, looked towards our heads again and listened. When she was satisfied that she hadn't been rumbled, the other forepaw delicately followed suit. The same slow-motion procedure was employed with one hind leg then the other. Finally, with a sigh of relief, she settled down between our feet and went to sleep.

The silent chuckle that I'd allowed myself following that masterful exhibition of stealth was replaced by a muted groan when I awoke during the night to hear a soft purring noise emanating from the bottom of the bed – or, to be absolutely accurate, from the bottom of the dog. Yes, Bonny was farting in her sleep. Although the pong may well have blended with the general ambience of Charlie's room without too much notice being taken, its detrimental effect on the potpourri freshness that Ellie ensured always pervaded our bedroom was marked. Fortunately, though, Ellie didn't stir from her slumbers, and I was too tired to bother taking remedial action by giving Bonny her marching orders. 'Let sleeping dogs lie' was the wee-small-hours motto I decided to adopt. I covered my nose with the duvet and went back to sleep.

Thus, life at Ca's Mayoral continued in Sandy's absence. The social order of things had changed a bit, certainly, but we'd grown accustomed to it, content in the knowledge that he had made the correct decision by taking his first steps towards independence. He, the metaphorical pulled tooth, was happy, and we, the metaphorical healing gums, were happy that he was.

★ ★ ★ ★ ★

'It's almost two months since we started the search for more land,' Ellie reminded me one late October day, while walking with me through the orchards to check the ripening oranges ahead of the approaching harvest, 'and we're still no further ahead. It isn't looking too promising, is it?'

While I totally empathised with the realistic nature of what she said, I felt that I had to keep the mood upbeat. 'Yeah, but you know how it is,' I shrugged. 'We're in Spain, and things don't happens that fast. Two months is nothing. The main thing is that we've put the word about in all the right quarters, so we'll just have to be patient and see what turns up. Be *tranquilo* – that's the name of the game here.'

Ellie tutted impatiently. 'You and your "be *tranquilo*" stuff. It's the bane of my life at times, it really is. Honestly, I often wish I hadn't let you abandon your old northern work ethic of getting things done as quickly as possible – to*day!*'

'Listen, it took me long enough to master the art of *mañana*ness after we came all the way south here, so I'm not about to try swimming against the tide again now. The when-in-Rome policy, right?' I gave Ellie a case-dismissed look, before adding, 'This is Mallorca, everything gets done in its own time, and nobody's bursting any blood vessels in the process. That'll do for me, OK?'

Ellie had heard many such examples of the 'logic' of procrastination from me since the day I'd finally proclaimed myself a fully-fledged maestro of Mallorcan *mañana*ness. She called them excuses. She'd never accepted any of them before, and I could tell she wasn't about to buy this one either. In fairness to myself, though, I was just as anxious to find that elusive piece of land as she was, but my paramount wish was to discourage any element of panic from creeping into our search, no matter how futile it had been so far. My view was that we were still managing to get by on the land we had, which meant that time was on our side. Ellie didn't quite see eye-to-eye with me on that, however…

'If you wait for all the old farmers you spoke to in the local bars to come up with something for us, we'll run out of *mañana*s. That's all I'm saying.'

Ellie was right, as usual. Even if the bush telegraph did eventually get the news to one of these old *campesinos* that so-and-so was thinking about selling such-and-such piece of land, the chances were slim of our being told about it before any potentially interested member of his own tight-knit *fraternidad*. The exception, of course, would be if the land had development potential, which would pitch its value well beyond what would be practical for us anyway. *Locos extranjeros* we may have been, but not so *loco* as to pay over the odds for the basic component of our business.

Nevertheless, these old codgers in the bars amounted to our best bet of finding what we were looking for before any Palma estate agents got wind of it and propelled the asking price into orbit. As we knew, the corner of Mallorca where we had chosen to farm was on the brink of a development boom, and the big city estate agents were hovering like vultures.

One essential that we had learned as small farmers in Britain was that, when things get tough, diversification from your core business can be the key to survival. A farm shop to be tended by the wife and a bit of agricultural contracting for larger farmers by the husband had been two of the most favoured enterprises in this regard. As neither of these options would have been feasible for us in our off-the-beaten-track Mallorcan location, I had decided to think about things laterally instead. If, as seemed certain, orange-growing was going to be unprofitable in future except on a large scale, why not branch out into something for which there was a growing demand in Mallorca and of which we just happened to have a fair amount of experience?

Cattle breeding, and in particular the production of quality Aberdeen Angus beef, could be the way ahead for us. There was a growing demand for such premium meat in the more upmarket hotels and restaurants now flourishing on the island, and no one was satisfying that demand locally. Moreover, we wouldn't need much land. All that would be required was sufficient to set up an American-style feedlot, on which the animals are kept and fed in sun-shaded corrals, instead of being allowed to graze freely. Then we'd be in business, provided there was a reliable well to enable the production of fodder using the latest hydroponic techniques – a method of quickly chain-producing 'grass' from seeds sown on indoor gravel trays fertilised by nutrient-enriched water. It seemed like a great idea, and it gave me the necessary spur to get on with the search for land – and *pronto*.

Upcountry from the Sa Coma valley, the terrain is mountainous, with much of it cloaked in forests of pine and evergreen oak. The only farming ever undertaken in such a rugged landscape had been essentially of a subsistence nature. In times past, families had scratched a living from the narrow, terraced *bancales* that are a relic of the Moors' three-century occupation of the island a thousand years earlier. But even the hardiest of native Mallorcans had abandoned all but the largest of such remote places long ago. Their only use now was to diehard, old-time shepherds and goatherds like Pep, whose little flocks were walked up there occasionally to nibble the weeds growing between what remained of the *bancales*' long-untended stands of almond, olive and carob trees.

Consequently we had steered our search in the other direction – seawards from the nearby market town of Andratx, through the gently-undulating countryside that stretches from there to the town's satellite port, some five kilometres farther south.

Huddled round the steep flanks of a spectacular horseshoe bay, Port d'Andratx is no longer the sleepy fishing village it once was. Flotillas of millionaires' yachts and motor cruisers now share the wide waters of the harbour with the local fleet – a clutch of brightly-painted, sea-going trawlers and some pristine-white *llauds*, those beautiful little boats that have been used for centuries to fish the coastal waters of the Balearic Islands for sardines. But gone are the humble fishermen's shacks that used to skirt the shore in peaceful solitude. In their place, trendy restaurants, shops and bars have proliferated in recent years. Exclusive villas now dot the wooded greenery of the encircling mountains like a scattering of white confetti. And the building goes on and on. Port d'Andratx, we were told, was rapidly becoming the Saint Tropez of Mallorca.

Our reconnoitring had been directed well inland from the vicinity of this property developing frenzy, of course. Whenever we could spare the time, we'd travel the country lanes and byways between the Port and Andratx town with our eyes peeled for a '*Se Vende*' sign that would tell us that a field was for sale. But our searches had proved fruitless so far. The only piece of land that had such a notice on its gate was located on the brow of a rise known locally, because of its distinctive profile, as Turtle Mountain. What was for sale was a mere postage stamp of thin soil, enclosed within low, crumbling walls at the end of a donkey track. A *casita de aperos*, a tiny, stonebuilt implement shed typical of Mallorca, stood forlorn and neglected in one corner. The property looked as though it had been devoid of human attention for years. Even the phone number painted along the foot of the faded

'*Se Vende*' board was missing a few digits, suggesting that the seller was in no hurry to find a buyer.

Deep down, I knew that Ellie's diagnosis of our predicament on that October day in the orange grove was correct. Prospects of finding what we were looking for within tractor-driving distance of Ca's Mayoral looked pretty bleak. But before I gave up hope completely, there was one last source of information I wanted to tap.

'Bloody 'ell, man! Is no wonders you no being find no baster land for the buying there! Is the measles, I telling you! Is forking ridickliss!'

It was the authoritative voice of Jordi Beltran, a wiry little Andratx character, who was, in his own words, 'carpenter the boats and many expert'. Jordi's gregarious habits ensured that there was never anything going on around Andratx that he didn't know about, and his local expertise had been a boon to us on many occasions. Although a boat builder by trade, Jordi was also a farmer. His *finca* was tiny, even compared to the modest area of Ca's Mayoral, but it was big enough to allow him to be fairly self-sufficient in vegetables, fruit, eggs and chicken meat. The rest of his income came from clandestine, cash-in-hand, boat-repair work for foreign yachties down at the Port, and from a small pension that he had managed to wangle from the state for an alleged shoulder injury that had rendered him 'unfit for physical work' – permanently. Jordi had it made.

His fractured English had been learned during years of working in factories in the Midlands of England, and his Coventry-cum-Karachi accent owed its idiosyncracies – and high swear word content – to the ethnic mix of the people he had lived among there. I'd traced him down to his customary market-day station, seated at a pavement table outside the Bar Nuevo in Andratx's main square, the Plaza de España. Accustomed though I was to Jordi's improvised English vocabulary, he had me stumped this time.

'Measles?' I said, just to make sure I hadn't picked him up wrongly. 'Did you say... *measles*?'

Jordi nodded his grey-thatched head, crossed his boney legs, took a puff of his cigarette, sat back in his chair, and looked at me as if I was a half-wit. 'You damn-bugger Scotchmens no being understand the Queen's baster English, eh?'

He had me on the back foot already. 'No – I mean, yes. But, well, what have *measles* got to do with it being difficult to find farmland for sale in that area?'

'Is the forking Germings!'

'Germings?'

'Yes, the peoples what being live in Germingy. Jordi been being there one time. Peoples being eat the many sossingers and much baster beer drinking, oh yes.'

'You – you mean Germany?'

'*Yes*, this exackaly what Jordi being bloody tell you, man. Germingy!'

'Measles... Germany... measles... German.' I pondered this for a few moments before the penny finally dropped. 'Oh, right, I understand now. Or, rather, I don't.' I scratched my head. 'I mean, what have German measles got to do with it?'

'Damn-bloody British measles also as well,' Jordi added impatiently. 'They been being all over the forking place down there them days too.'

After several minutes of convoluted explanations, Jordi eventually managed to make me understand what he was getting at. The measles he was referring to were the local folks' description of the rash of holiday homes (mainly German- and British-owned) that were mushrooming on the hillsides on either side of the road to Port d'Andratx. No matter how poor the piece of land, if there was a *casita de aperos* on it, as there invariably was, planning permission would probably be given for its extension to form a large dwelling, with all the fancy trappings that foreigners wanted. So, Jordi said in conclusion, no farmer in his right mind would sell such bits of land for their bare agricultural value.

He gave the air a dismissive swipe. 'Pah! You been being waste your baster time, man!' He then drew my attention to a scruffily dressed old man easing his leg over a battered moped on the other side of the street. That, he told me, was Bartomeu, a farmer who, despite his down-at-heel appearance, was now one of the richest men in south-west Mallorca – a multi-millionaire who had struggled to make a living off his land before the tourist boom changed his fortunes dramatically. Most of his land had been on the steep, wooded hillsides overlooking the bay at Port d'Andtrax – originally good for nothing except grazing a few goats, but now worth a king's ransom to Bartomeu as more and more developers vied to buy individual plots on which to build luxury homes. Why, Jordi revealed, Bartomeu even owned that impoverished little field that was for sale on the slopes of Turtle Mountain, and he could afford to let it lie unused until some *loco extranjero* came along with enough money to convert the *casita* into another pimple in the rash of British and German 'measles'. Oh yes,

Jordi confirmed, I was wasting my baster time trying to buy farmland anywhere between Andratx and the Port. With that, he bade me a laughing farewell, and ambled off to give the benefit of his encyclopaedic local knowledge to someone who had caught his eye on the opposite side of the square.

Doubtless, he'd have laughed even louder if I'd admitted to him that old Bartomeu was actually one of those very *campesinos* in the Andratx bars who had promised to tip me off about any parcels of land that came on the market locally.

Jordi had spoken the truth. I had been wasting my baster time.

I related all of this to Ellie when she joined me after she'd had a rummage round the stalls in the street market. She showed no sign of surprise. We'd both known all along that we were probably on a wild goose chase trying to find land to buy at an affordable price in this area. Our reluctance to face the inevitable had merely prevented us from admitting it. But the time to own up had now arrived. Our net would need to be cast wider still, and that meant only one thing. We would have to move away from the Sa Coma valley.

★ ★ ★ ★ ★

I tied the same '*Se Vende*' sign on the Ca's Mayoral gate that had been there on the fateful day we stumbled across the farm just two years earlier. Strangely, I experienced little of the remorse I thought I'd feel about putting the property up for sale. We had reversed the declining fortunes of the farm by restoring the health and productivity of its trees, and we had transformed the house by completing a comprehensive series of improvements that included a fine swimming pool, games room and barbecue area. A lot of satisfaction had been derived from seeing the results of our work evolve and reach fruition, but the long-term prospects of earning a reasonable living from such a small farm remained unchanged. It was time to move on, and the sooner we started our search for a prospective buyer, who could afford to live there without having to worry about the price of oranges, the better.

One negative thought I did have, though, was that our old neighbours would feel disappointed that we, as members of a later generation, had abandoned our aim of injecting young farming blood into the valley. I did feel bad about having let them down in that respect, even though our decision to sell was rooted in common sense. We had added value to our biggest asset, and we had to capitalise on that now for the sake of our own future survival.

As it happened, neither Pep nor Maria were to make any comment at all about the posting of the 'Se Vende' sign. They would have gathered from what I'd said to them on the evening of Maria's missing duck that our tenure of Ca's Mayoral was likely to be nearing its end. Whatever their innermost feelings on the matter, they made a point of never showing them. So, it seemed that, underneath their sometimes crusty exteriors, considerate old hearts were quietly beating away.

★ ★ ★ ★ ★

The ripples in the pond of reality that had been created by Jordi's frankness spread outwards from Andratx along with our quest to find the block of land that would allow us to carry forward our 'ongoing Mallorcan adventure'.

Fortunately for me, Ellie was used to such euphemisms. A less long-suffering mate would have told me to 'venture' on alone long before then. But our life together had always been something of a roller-coaster ride, with a few unscheduled diversions and near derailments along the way. Luckily, however, Ellie actually got a buzz from tackling one challenge after another.

When she married me, I was a keen-as-mustard, young jazz musician, playing clarinet and leading a band called the Clyde Valley Stompers, based in London, but forever on the road. And the itinerant lifestyle didn't change just because I had a wife. It couldn't. The band was in demand, and our agent made sure the demand was met by filling our date sheet with engagements which often kept us on tour for anything up to three months without a break. Accordingly, the day after our wedding in Scotland, Ellie was whisked four hundred miles south and deposited in a flat I'd rented in the London suburb of North Finchley, there to fend for herself while I went back on my clarinet-playing travels.

For a country girl from a little town like Haddington in East Lothian, the culture shock of suddenly having to pick up the threads of a new life in a huge city that she'd never even visited before must have been daunting. But, despite the lonely times that she'd had to endure, she smiled her way through without a word of complaint. It was the start of a life of such 'adventures' that we were to share as she followed me along what was destined to be a fairly tortuous career path.

After the Beatles-driven Merseybeat juggernaut snow-ploughed just about every other type of popular music off the scene in the mid-sixties, we made our way back home to Scotland, where I started a new career as a record producer. Ironically, it was the experience gained while recording with the Clyde Valley Stompers for George Martin, the producer who later went on to help the Beatles on their way to worldwide superstardom, that provided me with the basic knowledge needed to open a way into this fresh avenue within the music business. With my record production activities to be based in an Edinburgh studio, the outlook for a 'normal' home life seemed set fair at last.

Yet I was to discover that the life of a freelance record producer can be just as nomadic as that of a touring jazz musician. Consequently, Ellie was often left on her own again – except that she now had the infant Sandy to keep her busy as well. Also, as opposed to having the problem of establishing social contacts in what can so often be the isolation of a busy city, she now had to do the same in the real solitude of the remote country cottage that we'd moved into twenty miles from Edinburgh. She didn't have much time to cross that bridge, though, because fate had yet another change of direction prepared for us, and it guaranteed that there would be *no* time for boredom or loneliness in Ellie's life from then on.

★ ★ ★ ★ ★

The little farm of Cuddy Neuk had been in the family since my grandfather took the tenancy of it on moving to East Lothian from the Orkney island of Sanday in the late thirties. He'd prospered there and subsequently bought a larger farm, Hopefield, close to the town of Bonnyrigg in neighbouring Midlothian. His son Jim, my uncle, had stayed on at Cuddy Neuk, helping to run both farms as one business. On his father's death, however, Jim decided to get out of farming, which he'd never particularly liked, and he offered to pass on the tenancy of Cuddy Neuk to me. Although my record production work was flourishing, I grabbed this chance to do what I'd always wanted – to farm on my own account.

And so Ellie, the London-deposited clarinettist's wife, and subsequently the back-of-beyond-domiciled record producer's wife, now became Ellie the farmer's wife. However, as Cuddy Neuk was only a couple of miles from our original home town of Haddington, Ellie was back within easy visiting and shopping distance of everyone and everything familiar to her. Besides, she loved the little Cuddy Neuk farmhouse, particularly as she could do most of the things that needed to be done to bring it up to date herself. She relished the prospect.

She also had to get used to the idea that, from now on, she'd be kept busier than she'd ever imagined, tackling tasks that were completely new to her. Driving tractors, stacking straw bales in hot and dusty harvest fields, manning a grain-sowing drill on exposed hillsides in howling March winds, cutting kale and lifting turnips for livestock fodder on frosty winter mornings, mucking out cattle yards, and acting as a surrogate mother to dozens of bucket-fed calves at all hours of the day *and* night. These were just a few of the new 'skills' that adaptable Ellie would have to master and keep on top of in her latest role.

She probably wasn't too surprised to learn, though, that there was to be even more to her new life than that. She'd also have a second baby son to raise, while being left behind yet again when I went off on even more frequent record producing trips. Not that there wasn't more than enough work for me to cope with in restoring the fairly run-down farm to optimum productivity, and I had all the required enthusiasm and energy for that. It was simply that the one essential in short supply was capital.

Enter fate once again – this time in the form of a record I produced with the Pipes and Drums and Military Band of the Royal Scots Dragoon Guards, a record which turned out to be one of the most unexpected hits ever. 'Amazing Grace' became a bestseller all over the globe, notching up multi-million sales and going on to become the biggest-selling instrumental single of all time.

If only I'd had the foresight, when signing the original contract with the American record company, to ensure that I was on a royalty percentage that would be commensurate with its eventual success. Nevertheless, we were thankful for all mercies, even modest ones, and the income that we did derive from 'Amazing Grace' came in extremely handy at the time when we needed it most to invest in the development of Cuddy Neuk. The windfall even allowed us to make a down-payment on buying the farm.

Such rare strokes of good fortune are sometimes balanced out by the equally unexpected, however. The downside of this one was that, paradoxically, it brought in even more record production work. We couldn't afford to turn down the potential earnings, but the time and travelling involved in fulfilling the contracts meant that I'd be away from home more than ever. Ellie, as a result, would have to shoulder even more of the farm-running and family responsibilities than she had before. Another daunting task that she cheerfully accepted. If this was the direction in which my wayward career path was leading us, then so be it. She'd be right there, working away at whatever was necessary to help keep us on track.

As one of our more cynical friends said at the time, she either deserved a medal or a certificate of insanity!

But hard work seems a lot easier if you're heart's in what you're doing, and Ellie had taken to the farming life as if born to it. Together, we took great delight in seeing our little farm and family thrive and progress. We could hardly have been more content with our lot. Then, unexpectedly again, fate dealt us a blow that nullified all the good luck that we'd recently been granted.

Muir, our younger son, was tragically killed in a road accident while walking to school with Sandy one chill November morning. He was only five.

Suddenly, our world was turned upside down, our emotions turned inside out. All the material things that we had struggled to achieve over the years were as nothing. Indeed, we gladly would have forfeited them all and more to have had wee Muir back. But fate brooks no such covenants. Life must and does go on, regardless of the cards fate deals you. No matter how hard it was to come to terms with this at first, we were thankful that the results of such a devastating accident hadn't been even worse. Sandy's life had also hung by a thread as a result of the injuries he'd sustained, but, miraculously, he'd pulled through. His survival, together with the support of family and friends, helped restore our will to carry on.

The following year, Charlie was born, and with his birth a new feeling of optimism entered our lives. We were learning that, for the fortunate few, the pain of loss, although permanent, can sometimes be allayed by nature's benevolence. Fate had smiled kindly on us once again.

When, some ten years later, the big-is-beautiful trend in farming dictated that an end of an era had come, we left Muir's Neuk and all that it meant to us with heavy hearts, yet with a sense of gratitude for the exciting opportunities that finding Ca's Mayoral had afforded us.

And now we were resigned to leaving that much-loved place, too.

★ ★ ★ ★ ★

'Well, nobody can ever accuse you of making me lead a dull life,' Ellie sighed as she straightened up the '*Se Vende*' sign I'd just tied to the gate.

'Aw, think nothing of it,' I replied. 'You're worth it.'

Ellie had been gathering quinces from a tree down by the well, and I only just managed to duck out of the way of the big, nobbly one that she plucked from her basket and aimed at my head. 'What I'm worth,' she said, raising an impish eyebrow, 'is a nice, consolation treat.'

'Yeah, well, if you're thinking of that nice, emerald-encrusted gold ring again,' I came back, playing her along, 'you're barking up the wrong tree. You're looking at a potentially failed orange farmer here, you know, and don't you forget it!'

'Hmm, maybe. But if we do nicely out of selling this farm, that ring is going to be my bonus, and don't *you* forget that!' She handed me her basket, took me by the arm and led me towards the house. 'But in the meantime,' she added archly, 'a nice dinner of chargrilled rabbit at the Celler Ca'n Renou in Andratx will do nicely, thank you very much.'

Ellie never needed much of an excuse to eat out, so it had grown into a habit of ours in Mallorca, where it's part of the way of life anyway and needn't cost very much, *if* you go where the locals go.

I shook my head, still playing her along. 'Ah, but you've forgotten already, haven't you?' I crooked a thumb back towards the '*Se Vende*' notice on the gate. 'I'm a potentially failed orange farmer, so such extravagances will have to cease forthwith.'

Ellie wagged a finger at me, pointed into her basket, then pulled out a wad of notes from her shirt pocket. 'Otto, the German jelly-maker from Port d'Andratx, just bought the last of the quinces, so…?'

'So, that buys a nice dinner of chargrilled rabbit for two at the Celler Ca'n Renou?' I smiled expectantly.

'Right first time,' she smiled back. 'Except you're paying!' She stuffed the money back into her pocket. '*I* picked the quinces for Otto, so his quince dosh gets stashed away safely towards the cost of that nice emerald ring, OK?'

'Like I said, Ellie, you're worth it. Yes, and without waiting any longer for it, either.'

Ellie's face lit up. 'You mean the emerald ring?'

'No,' I replied, 'a bit of chargrilled rabbit!'

– THREE –

THE UPS AND DOWNS OF LIFE

Ellie's suggestion of going to the Celler Ca'n Renou that evening turned out not to be entirely generated by her appetite for rabbit. Not actually a *cellar* per se, Ca'n Renou is a street-level eatery which, like many in Mallorca, is a replication of some of the genuine old wine cellars in the inland town of Inca, some of which were converted into unintentionally trend-setting restaurants after the area's vineyards were decimated by the dreaded phylloxera grape plague over a century ago. Ca'n Renou was typical of many of the reproductions – mellow, terracotta floor tiles; whitewashed walls, complete with protruding 'wine kegs'; chunky wooden tables and chairs; soft 'lantern' light; and a big log-burning *brasero* on which to grill meat.

As an indication of how the number of foreign visitors to Andratx was increasing, Ca'n Renou had only recently re-opened after years of gathering dust and cobwebs, despite being centrally located on the town's main thoroughfare, the Calle Juan Carlos I. We knew young Gabriel, the tall and affable new proprietor, fairly well. Until recently, he had been a tanker driver for Pujol Serra, one of the companies supplying bulk drinking water to many of the area's country properties, including our own.

Gabriel had been given occupancy of the destitute little restaurant as a wedding present by his father, a local businessman, who also owned the adjacent cinema, the *Cine Argentina*, as well as the busy *Bar Nacional* next door to that. It was said that Gabriel's father and uncle had bought this valuable block of property with money earned and saved during years of working in Latin America, which had been a magnet for fortune-seeking young Andratx men for generations.

Gabriel's father hadn't come by his prosperity easily, and he had been determined that his son would learn the value of money the hard way as well. He wasn't going to be afforded the soft option of just falling into a job in the family business. Hence Gabriel's early 'career' as a tanker driver. Now, with the help of his new wife, María-José, Gabriel was busy building a reputation for the refurbished Celler Ca'n Renou – he waiting tables, tending the bar and grilling the meats, she working behind the scenes preparing salads, tortillas, sweets and other non-*brasero* fare. The business was doing well.

Grilled rabbit is one of Ellie's favourite dishes, particularly in rural Mallorca, where many households still keep one or two of the little thumpers in readiness for the table. Such home-reared rabbits are noted for their plumpness and tenderness, and Ellie soon discovered that Gabriel's were up there among the best, simply because, unlike most busy restaurateurs, he managed to find time to raise a steady supply of his own. He had a tiny *finca* just outside town, on which he also kept a few leggy Mallorcan sheep, which he tended in the same careful way.

Gabriel, you see, was a farmer at heart. Although a Mallorcan through and through, he dreamed that one day he would be able to raise a whole herd of pedigree *English* sheep – specifically Suffolks, a breed noted for the distinctive quality of its meat. The fulfilment of his dream would depend, though, on where and when he could afford to buy sufficient land for the purpose.

This, then, was the denominator common to young Gabriel and myself. Gabriel had his dream of pure-bred Suffolk sheep, I had my vision of prime Aberdeen Angus cattle, and both of us hoped to create a niche market for our quality produce right here in Mallorca.

So infatuated with livestock was Gabriel that he even spent what little spare time he had doing the rounds of farms with the local vet, Dr Puigserver. In this way, he learned more about the welfare of animals and, equally importantly, he would hear first-hand of any land that was about to come on the market, and within a fairly wide area at that. He promised to keep me posted about any that might suit our particular requirements.

Ellie, then, when suggesting a visit to Celler Ca'n Renou, really had been thinking ahead, and not just about grilled rabbit either. And Gabriel proved to be as good as his word. Over the next few months, he told us about a couple of available farms that he'd heard about. We looked at them both.

One was actually a bit nearer Palma city and, therefore, closer to Charlie's school than Ca's Mayoral. At present, getting him there and back involved a thirty-five-mile round trip every day, so any reduction on that score would be welcome. The farm was located just off the main road leading inland to Calvià, an unassuming little town that is the administrative centre of one of the richest stretches of holiday-resort coastline in the whole of Spain. Set on a hillside looking over a wide valley, the farmhouse was a simple, though beautifully proportioned, two-storey building in the typical Mallorcan style. Its honeystone walls were glowing golden in the evening sunlight as we turned into the long approach.

Two tall palms stood sentry at the front of the house, with orange groves spreading out at either side. The pine-carpeted hillside provided a pleasing backdrop, and it was clear that it would also afford shelter from the cold Tramuntana winds of winter. We could already see that there was more than enough level land within the walled boundaries of the property on which cattle corrals could be set up, and, according to Señor Grimald, the 'owner' who met us at the farmhouse door, there was enough good water in the well to sink the Titanic. The asking price that Gabriel had mentioned seemed unbelievably reasonable for such a perfect spread as this. We were soon to find out why.

Señor Grimald, a stocky, cheery man in his sixties, had the classic appearance of a Mallorcan small farmer – corduroy flatcap on his head, seen-better-days jacket and trousers, dusty old boots on his feet, the skin of his face and hands tanned and toughened by a lifetime of working in the sun. He would show us the house first, he said, shepherding us inside.

Ellie took two steps, then stopped in her tracks. 'Oranges!' she gasped. 'Tons of them!'

I peered over her shoulder, and there, piled high and filling all of the wide entrance hallway, were… oranges! Tons of them! Access to the stairway and the two doors that flanked it was totally blocked.

There was a big inglenook fireplace over in one corner, Señor Grimald told us. Big enough for all the family to sit inside on chilly winter evenings. This was typical of Mallorcan farmhouses, he went on. A much sought after feature in houses of this authentic type. Such fine houses with such fine inglenook *chimeneas* did not come on the market very often, he was at pains to stress.

No doubt, I thought, but burying such a sought after feature under a mountain of oranges was hardly the most obvious way of backing up such a persuasive sales pitch.

Señor Grimald must have read my thoughts, or, more likely, my stunned expression. The storage shed, he casually informed us, was on a part of the farmstead that belonged to one his five brothers. The significance of this bit of information wasn't immediately apparent, nor was the reason for storing so many oranges *any*where, as even I knew that oranges keep a lot longer on the tree than when picked.

I gestured in the direction of the heap. 'A cancelled order?' I asked.

Señor Grimald shrugged in a couldn't-care-less sort of way and said that was his brother Tomeu's problem. He then guided us back out of the house. Leading us round the back, he said that he would now show us the piece of land that he was selling.

This confused me. 'The *piece* of land?' I queried. 'But I was led to believe that the *entire* farm was for sale.'

Oh yes, it was indeed all for sale, he replied with a reassuring smile. It was just that I would have to deal with his five brothers for their parts of it. The farm, he explained matter-of-factly, had been divided up between them in their late father's will.

I had heard of this Spanish practice, which could result in one farm being split into several properties, each belonging to different members of the same family, and each with its own individual title deeds. This confusing state of legalities could carry on from generation to generation, with each consecutive inheritance creating an even more fragmented farm, even though it might still *look* intact.

Señor Grimald led us to a little dirt enclosure behind the farmhouse. Within its rickety, chicken-wire fence were five goats and a scattering of hens, which was about all there was room for. This, he said, was part of his property. The rest of it comprised four rows of trees in one of the orange groves, a section of the woods on the hillside, and a narrow strip of land bordering the entrance track from the main road. Exactly which parts of the house were owned by whom was a little more complicated, he said blandly, but it was nothing that a good lawyer wouldn't be able to sort out.

Suddenly, the asking price that Gabriel had mentioned didn't seem like a bargain any more.

Noticing our faces fall, Señor Grimald swiftly added that it probably wouldn't be too difficult to get the agreement of his brothers to sell their sections of the farm as well... now.

'Now?' I asked, curious as to why he had hesitated before saying it.

'*Sí, sí*,' Señor Grimald replied, nodding confidently. He had been trying to persuade his brothers to sell up for the past twenty years, so he was sure they would all fall into line soon. Certainly within a year – or *maybe* two at most. *Sí, sí*, he insisted, he was very sure about that. 'Ah, *sí, claro!*'

Even if we had been prepared to plunge into the legal quagmire that attempting to purchase this property would create, we didn't have two years to spare – maybe not even one. I didn't have to explain this to Señor Grimald. As I'm sure he had done many times when previous prospective buyers had visited, he could tell by our faces that we weren't about to do business.

'Would the *señora* like to buy a few kilos of oranges?' he asked Ellie as he escorted us back round to the front of the house. 'Wholesale price – *naturalmente.*'

Ellie politely declined, saying that we had more than enough oranges of our own to sell at present, *muchas gracias* all the same.

'Well, you can't fault him for his optimism,' I told her on the way home.

'No, you certainly can't fault him for that,' Ellie agreed with a sigh.

Neither could we fault Gabriel for not warning us about the complications surrounding the ownership of this *finca*. In all probability, he hadn't even known about them himself. He was a sincere and honest lad, so I'm sure he hadn't been aware either of the web of potential legal wrangles that enmeshed the other *finca* he'd told us about.

It was located about twenty kilometres east of Palma, in elevated, gently undulating country out towards the little market town of Algaida. We knew the area quite well, as the road linking Algaida with the city is dotted with wayside restaurants on which extended Palmesano families routinely converge for Sunday lunch. This uninhibited occasion is regarded by many to be as much an essential of Spain's culture as football and paella, and we had developed a habit of joining in the clamorous junketing whenever we could.

The *finca* we had come to look over was tucked away along a brush-enclosed lane behind Ses Maioles, one of the biggest of these eating places. As we drove along the track, clumps of pine trees rose up here and there from the *monte bajo*, the evergreen maquis that is prolific in this part of the island and is made up of scrubby myrtles, mastics, holm oaks, junipers and various other wild shrubs and herbs. The resinous air wafting in through the car's open windows was both refreshing and soothing, as was the sound of birdsong.

Though the landscape was markedly less manicured than the orchard-quilted cosiness of the Sa Coma valley, it had a good feeling about it. We felt at home here. Whether or not it was its relative wildness and visual resemblance to certain parts of our native Scotland that made us feel that way, I don't know, but we did take to it instantly.

As we passed through a gateway at the end of the lane, there was an unfenced dirt track leading through what appeared to be the one field that comprised the whole farm. Nevertheless, it was flat, and looked amply big enough to suit our purposes. The house sat right in the centre of the field, and even from a distance of a hundred metres or so we could see that it didn't amount to much – just a small, rectangular construction that could easily have passed for an implement shed, if it hadn't been for its curtained windows and a vine-draped pergola made from galvanised conduit pipes spanning the front door. Unfortunately, though, it wasn't a traditional, stone-built *casita de aperos*, but a much more recent construction, with a definite utility look about it. There was no garden, not even a garden fence, and no farm buildings – only the house, a bare field surrounded by *monte bajo*, and a copse of pines tucked away in the far corner, where the land appeared to fall sharply away.

There was no sign of life, save for a dozen or so skinny sheep lying disinterestedly chewing the cud under the shade of the pine branches. I parked the car and wandered off to take a look around the field, while Ellie busied herself surveying the outside of the house and peering through its windows.

The land had been grazed almost completely bare, the only surviving greenery being a smattering of asphodels, those lily-related weeds with single stems sticking up like thin pokers. Greek mythology tells us that asphodels used to cover the fields of Elysium, but I'd learned since coming to Mallorca that the local farmers have a much less poetic view of the plant. Its presence, instead of having connotations of the afterlife, merely indicates that the land is impoverished. It has been over-grazed and starved of fertility-replenishing nutrition for a very long time. Still, I thought, any such land that ended up as the floor of a feedlot for Aberdeen Angus cattle wouldn't need to be productive, and the rest would have its fertility restored in due course with the application of dung produced by the feedlot's occupants. No long-term problem there, then.

Feeling positive, I strolled over to the edge of the field. Sure enough, the land did fall away beyond its fringe of *monte bajo*, and the views down over *Es Pla*, the vast, windmill-bristling central plain of the island, were stunning. I could even catch a glimpse of the Bay of Palma, glinting blue and inviting in the far distance. Yes, this place had a good feeling about it, and I liked it fine.

Just then, the rattly sound of a two-stroke engine drew my attention to the entrance of the field. An elderly man riding a moped was making a beeline for the house, leaving a trail of blue smoke in his wake. This was obviously the owner of the *finca*, arriving late and in some haste. He was already showing Ellie round the inside of the house by the time I joined them.

Small, smiling and surprisingly smartly dressed for a working farmer, he introduced himself as Sebastià and apologised for not being on time for our appointment. He explained that he had come here en route from his house in Algaida to his granddaughter's wedding reception at Ses Maioles, but had been held up by a friend he'd met on the way. 'Time goes by so quickly when you are in a hurry,' he shrugged. 'Modern life. You know how it is, *señores*.'

What I did know was that the very notion of being in a hurry was one that seldom, if ever, entered the minds of old *campesinos* like this. I didn't hold that against him, though. It was all part of the art of being *tranquilo*, and I'd learned to accept and adapt to that a long time ago. There's nothing else for it in rural Spain, and once you get used to the routine, there isn't much wrong with it.

'You say you came from your house in Algaida,' I said by way of openers, trying not to sound too nosey. 'You, uh – you don't actually live here on the farm, then?'

He shrugged again. Sometimes they lived here in the *finca* house, and sometimes they lived in their town house in Algaida. '*Depende*,' he smiled. 'It depends.'

Clearly, he wasn't about to be probed further on that topic, so I drew him back outside and moved the conversation on to matters relating to the farm, while Ellie got on with inspecting the house.

I thought I'd adopt the old horse-trading ploy of picking out faults with what was for sale before even discussing price. Old Sebastià, after all, had already revealed a hint of his caginess, so best to play him at his own game.

'The, ehm, asphodels…?' I said, leaving the question hanging in mid-air.

'*Sí*…?' That one-word response and the innocent way he delivered it provided ample evidence that this old fellow wouldn't be a pushover. He instinctively knew that I didn't want to be *off*ensive, and had cleverly put me on the *def*ensive.

'Yes, well, it's just that, I mean, there seems to be a –'

'A lot of them?'

'Yes, and I'm told that this means the land is –'

'*Aubons*, we call asphodels in *mallorquín*. A very valuable plant. We use their long, woody stems to make the frames on which we dry our figs and apricots, you know. We sometimes interweave the *aubons* with the fronds of the wild *palmito*, the dwarf fan palm, to make a sort of basketwork, you see. Ah, *sí*, lucky is the farmer with many *aubons* on his land.'

Considering that there were neither apricot nor fig trees nor even *palmitos* on his farm, I sensed that it would be a waste of time to pursue the subject of asphodels further – for the moment, anyway.

'*Agua?*' I asked, moving matters along. 'Plenty of water here, is there?'

He pointed up to the roof, on which was perched a cylindrical, asbestos *cisterna*. It looked about the size of a standard, forty-gallon oil drum. 'Plenty water in there for a small house like this, *amigo*,' he assured me. 'We get it delivered when we need it. *No problema*.'

'So, there's no well on the farm? What about water for the livestock, for irrigating the crops, things like that?'

Old Sebastià shot me a puzzled look. 'Livestock? Crops?' He swept a hand in a wide arc. '*Hombre*, see for yourself. There are no crops, and a dozen sheep need little water. And anyway, that is for their owner to worry about. I only rent him the grazing here.' He quickly anticipated my next question. 'Mallorca is like a giant turtle shell placed over a vast puddle. If you want more water, you can drill a borehole and pump it up. *No problema*.'

Which begged my next question. 'Electricity?'

'*Perdón?*'

'A pump needs electricity to drive it. The house needs electricity for light and everything, no?'

'*Sí, sí* – this is also *no problema*.'

It was now my turn to sweep a hand in a wide arc. 'But I don't see any electricity poles, cables or anything.'

Señor Sebastià gave a little chuckle and beckoned me to follow him to the side of the house. He opened the door of a little, brick-built hutch and pointed to a tiny petrol-driven generator tucked away inside. 'Here we have enough power for a little house like this, no?' True to form, he then anticipated my next question. 'But if you need more power,' he smiled, 'GESA, the electricity company, will run the poles and cables from the mains supply out there on the Palma road for you.' He chuckled again and gave me a reassuring pat on the shoulder. 'Hey, *no problema*, eh!'

'The Palma road?' I frowned. 'But – but that must be nearly a mile away!'

Another reassuring pat. 'You are right, *amigo*. It is not far, so it will not cost much.' Seeing my sceptical look, he promptly added, 'But they say that very soon GESA will provide power to all *fincas* like this for free.' He pulled a no-big-deal shrug. '*Coño*, you will have *problemas* with nothing.'

I didn't even bother to ask about a telephone line, as doubtless that would have elicited an identical answer. The horse-trading never having left the starting gate, I decided to come right out with it and ask him how much he wanted for this place.

The price he quoted, although seeming fairly high for what was on offer, might still have been within our budget, provided we got what we hoped for Ca's Mayoral. But then there was the unknown cost of converting this bare field into a viable business to consider. Difficult one. I scratched my head.

Old Sebastià was quick to head off the negative reaction that he assumed was about to be forthcoming. '*Naturalmente*,' he shrugged, 'the price can be negotiated, depending on whether or not you will require *facilidades*.'

I'd heard about *facilidades*, or, to give them their full title, *facilidades de pago* – easy-payment terms. This is a long-established 'facility' that is sometimes offered by private vendors of property in Spain, whereby the purchaser is given the option of paying a percentage of the asking price up front, with the balance payable 'by mutual agreement'. Nothing unusual about that, you may think, except that here, such *facilidades* are created without a bank or mortgage company being involved. It's an arrangement that obviously requires a fair amount of trust on behalf of the seller, and I was pleasantly surprised that, as an *extranjero*, I was being given access to it. Debt of any kind was something that we'd vowed to avoid at all costs since coming to Mallorca, however, so I thanked Señor Sebastià sincerely for his offer, while assuring him that *facilidades* would not be required.

'In that case, *amigo*,' he beamed, 'a very *interesante* price can be negotiated. *No problema*.'

As generous as his gesture seemed, it left me with a lot to think about. Promising to do just that, I bade him *adiós* for the present, and headed for the car, where Ellie was already waiting. Her inspection of the house had been decidedly short-lived.

'I need a coffee,' she muttered as I drove out of the field. 'Take me to the nearest one!'

The Ses Maioles car park was full to overflowing, and the sound of the wedding reception taking place inside indicated that a good time was being had by all. We sat at a table under the arched *porche* that runs the length of the front of the building. Ellie had already explained to me that I'd missed nothing by not doing the full tour of the interior of old Sebastià's house. It had been on the frugal side of spartan, she said. 'A bit like a breeze block caravan,' was how she described it. All the essentials were in there – a kitchen, a loo, a living room, a couple of bedrooms – but all tiny and equipped with the most basic of stuff. It would take a lot of money to do the extensions and improvements required just to bring the house up to scratch, and to make it anything even remotely as well appointed as we'd made Ca's Mayoral would cost fortunes.

'Still, it's a beautiful spot, with a load of potential,' I said, mustering up as positive an attitude as I could. 'And we needn't do everything at once. I mean, we could do it *poco a poco*, like they say here – little by little, as the cattle business develops and starts to earn money.'

Ellie gave me one of her old-fashioned looks. 'You know well enough that that'll take several years, with money going out all the time and nothing coming in.'

'Hmm, admittedly we'd have to do our sums carefully.'

'Yes, including the cost of laying on basics like mains electricity and a supply of water before anything else. Let's face it, we'd need to buy the place for next to nothing to make it a viable proposition.'

I felt my positive attitude rapidly melting in the warm spring sunshine.

'Hey, *auf wiener schnitzel*, good buddies! Yeah, and don't forget – keep yer little ol' asses clear of them thar water jets!'

It was the unmistakable voice of Jock Burns, an old friend of ours from the same home town in Scotland. Jock had lived in Mallorca for many years, following his main profession as a schoolteacher in the international school that Charlie now attended. But Jock had more strings to his bow than all the merry men in Sherwood Forest, as his flamboyant wife Meg was wont to say. He was a musician, too, playing keyboards and singing for the nightly entertainment of holidaymakers in one of the island's most popular hotels. Somehow, he also found time to live the life of a *bon viveur* and to dabble in various sorts of wheelings and dealings into the bargain. 'Anything for a wee earner, son,' was how he'd once put it to me in his native Scots accent. 'Oh, aye, get yer fingers intae all the pies. That's the only way tae survive on this island, by the way.'

But the accent that Jock was speaking in now was the mid-Atlantic one he liked to employ when schoolteaching, performing or 'doing a wee earner'. Jock reckoned it gave him more 'panache' on such occasions, and it probably did. I wondered why a touch of phoney German had been added to his normal affectation today, however.

His voice rang out again. '*Jawohl*, and *hasta la* Visa card, *mein* herrings, right? Yeah, you betcha!'

I turned my head to see Jock's ample frame filling the restaurant doorway. A melon-slice grin was spread over his chubby face as he waved goodbye to a well-heeled couple getting into a large Mercedes. Jock was obviously in fine form. I gave him a shout.

'Wow!' he grinned back. 'Sure is a surprise to catch you two guys way out here in the boondocks – high-rollin' dudes-about-town that ya are!'

'I could say the same to you, Jock,' I smiled. 'Playing for the dancing at the reception here, are you?'

Jock ambled over and sat down at our table. He checked to make sure no one was within earshot before reverting to his natural Scots way of speaking. 'Nah, the regular evenin' gig's enough for me.' He shook his head. 'Nah, nah, son, there's easier ways o' makin' some coin durin' the day than bustin' ma guts churnin' out ancient tunes for a bunch o' pissed and bubblin' weddin' guests.'

Jock then proceeded to tell us that the 'good buddies' he'd been seeing off were a German couple he'd met briefly at a party the previous week. He'd arranged to meet them again at Ses Maioles today to finalise selling them the latest in top-of-the-range jacuzzis for a luxury villa they'd just bought nearby.

I couldn't resist a smile of admiration. Good old Jock. He never missed a trick.

'Goes without sayin' that they're well pleased wi' the deal I got them,' he winked, patently chuffed with my reaction. 'Trade price, tax free and no questions asked. Nice one, eh?' In addition to buying the jacuzzi, the 'good buddies' had bought him lunch as well, he grinned. He patted his ample midriff and burped discreetly behind his fist. 'Yeah, get the freebie grub intae ye whenever ye can, son. Aye, that's the only way tae survive on this island. Hey, and you better believe it, by the way.'

'So,' Ellie put in, coming straight to the point, 'how do you reckon we'd survive out in these parts without mains electricity and a good water supply?'

'Just tell me more, darlin', just tell me more.'

Jock liked nothing better than to have his advice asked on island matters, and his wide knowledge of them had been of enormous help to us on many occasions. He listened carefully while we explained our ideas of breeding quality beef cattle in Mallorca, and the essentials needed to undertake that on any farm we might buy. He nodded his approval of everything we said, until we started to describe the farm we'd just viewed. A knowing smile began to tug at his cheeks.

'That'll be the wee *finca* belongin' to that old bugger Sebastià, eh?' he chuckled.

I was momentarily taken aback by Jock's sharpness of perception. 'But how the hell did you know that?' I said. 'Are you dabbling in estate agency these days as well?'

Jock tapped the side of his nose. 'Aha, ye never know, son. Ye never know.'

But no, he went on, he didn't have anything to do with the sale of this particular property. It was just that he knew the owner and his family well. Old Sebastià's eldest son Miquel was actually the manager of one of the banks that Jock used for his various financial 'transactions', as well as being a good personal friend. Moreover, Miquel was also father of the bride here at Ses Maioles today.

'So, I'm here as a weddin' guest first and foremost, so tae speak. But ye know how it is – I thought I might as well slip in the wee bit o' jacuzzi-floggin' business while I was in the area. Saves makin' a special trip, like.' Jock patted his stomach again. 'And it turns out I'll get two free feeds in one day, because o' that wee bit o' forward thinkin'. Big weddin' banquet laid on for later, ye see.'

But Ellie was more interested in Jock's inside knowledge of Sebastià's farm than she was in hearing about his eating schemes. 'He told us we could drill for water,' she said, getting matters back down to essentials.

'And he also said the electricity company would lay on mains cables to the farm soon,' I offered, then added hopefully, 'and for free at that.'

Jock took a deep breath. 'Hmm,' he exhaled, 'well, he's no' actually been tellin' ye fibs, but…'

Jock could be the master of the dramatic pause when it suited him, and, annoyingly, this seemed to be one such occasion. Or was he just being careful about not giving us too much bad news too suddenly?

Either way, we needed to know, and the sooner the better.

'But?' we urged in unison.

'But it depends on what "soon" means when ye're talkin' about gettin' the electricity supply laid on. *Mañana*'s been known tae mean years in such matters out in the sticks here, ye know. Yeah, and don't bet on not havin' tae pay for it when it does eventually happen.' Jock gave a little chuckle. 'He's a crafty one, that old Sebastià. Like I say, he's no' tellin' fibs – just repeatin' hopeful rumours.'

Jock's advice on the water situation was no more encouraging. We certainly *could* drill for water, as the old fellow had said, but the chances of finding it were almost certainly non-existent. It had been tried on that land before, but without success.

His information about the house was even more depressing. It had been built as a *casita fin de semana*, a weekend cottage, intended only for sleeping in after family barbecues, Sunday paella feasts, partridge-shooting expeditions and the like. Jock had been invited to such events by Miquel many times, so he knew the property well.

He saved his most damning piece of information until last, though. The house, like many similar weekend *casita*s, had been built not only on the cheap (like a breeze block caravan, to quote Ellie's description), but also without planning permission. The local authorities had turned a blind eye to many of these breaches of regulations forty or fifty years ago, and still might – until the property changed hands. The new owners would then have to enter into lengthy legal proceedings which could result in the building having to be demolished, with nothing being allowed to take its place. Jock hastily added that old Sebastià may not have given such 'official trivialities' much thought. He was one of the old school, brought up in a rural environment at a time when a man could do what he liked, within reason, on his own property. Also, having owned a bar-restaurant in the area, he had done well in life and, in addition to having a comfortable home in Algaida, he owned several little unoccupied *fincas* like the one we had just viewed. He was a businessman as opposed to a hands-on small farmer, so all of these properties were permanently for sale.

Jock crossed his forearms in front of his face. 'Avoid like Dracula's teeth,' he warned, before going back inside to join the wedding revellers.

★ ★ ★ ★ ★

If you're locked into the roller-coaster type of life that we were in, you have to hold onto the belief that every time you appear to be heading into a dip, things will take an upward turn again – sooner or later. True to this conviction, any sense of despondency that we were beginning to feel about our chances of finding the right farm were quickly dispelled by Jock a couple of days later.

'I've found the very place for ye, son,' he told me on the phone. 'Good farm – belongs tae a rich Mallorcan contact o' a good Mallorcan friend o' mine. Got all the stuff ye need for raisin' yer beef cattle.' Jock didn't even wait for a reaction from me. 'Meet me in the car park at the Mercadona Supermercado outside Palma Nova in half an hour and ye can follow me out tae see it.' Then, without giving me a chance to say whether or not I had other

80

commitments, he added before hanging up, 'Hit while the iron's hot, son. That's the only way tae get ahead on this island.'

Jock's phone call couldn't have come at a better time. We had just received the latest analysis of the financial state of our orange-growing business from our accountant in Palma, who confirmed what we had already worked out for ourselves over the year. We'd had bigger yields of oranges than previously – a tribute to the skilled surgery done to our neglected trees by the local tree doctor after we bought the place. And we flattered ourselves to think that our own hard work in tending the orchards since then may have contributed a bit towards the improvement in the farm's output, too. But such self-flattery got us nowhere. The bottom line in the accounts showed that, despite having sold more oranges, our already meagre profits were down to danger level. As the prophets of doom had predicted, Spain's entry into the European Union had created an oversupply of citrus fruit, resulting in reduced prices for the growers. Meanwhile, the cost of every essential we'd *bought* in the same financial year appeared to have gone up. Another correct prediction for the anti-EU brigade to claim? That's certainly the way it struck us at the time.

While our accountant's corroboration of our own calculations seemed to vindicate our decision to sell up and move on, the lack of progress we'd made in achieving that goal was becoming a real worry. There had been very little interest shown in Ca's Mayoral since the '*Se Vende*' sign had been hung on the gate and 'For Sale' ads placed in the press, yet until it was sold, we couldn't buy another place. For all that, we couldn't turn down the opportunity to look over the farm that Jock had found out about either. After all, maybe this would turn out to trigger the upturn in our fortunes that we were looking for. And maybe, now that summer was on its way, we'd have prospective buyers coming to Ca's Mayoral by the planeload. Well, if you're going to be an optimist, you may as well be a super one!

The village of Consell straddles the old road that runs north-east from Palma to the historic Roman settlement of Pollentia, now the busy resort port of Alcúdia. A monument to strip development, Consell's elongated main street used to rumble to the thunder of endless convoys of trucks and coaches plying their respective trades between the two centres. Since the completion of a much-needed bypass, however, the village has now won back the sleepy atmosphere it enjoyed in days of old. A little farther up the road is the wine-producing town of Binissalem, with its associated vineyards occupying more and more of the surrounding countryside. The property that Jock led us to bordered this broad and beguiling landscape.

First impressions as we approached the farm from Consell were of a mini-prairie – flat, but with views of the twin bluffs of the Alaró and Alcaldena mountains in the west, and beyond to the peaks of the Tramuntana chain towering rugged and blue on the horizon. Even farther away in the other direction, the table-top summit of the Holy Mount of Randa floated mysteriously above a garland of cloud against the distant backdrop of the Serres de Llevant, the long ridge of hills that rises above the eastern seaboard of the island. We had driven through this part of the island on many occasions, but it was only now, when we got out of the car at the farm, that we were able to appreciate just how tranquil and beautiful an area it is. Understated, compared to the more spectacular mountain and coastal scenery for which Mallorca is famed, but equally captivating in its own way.

Jock leaned out of his car window. 'What do ye think? No bad, eh?' Before I could answer, he selected first gear and said, 'Right, I've got a wee bit o' urgent business tae attend tae up at Binissalem. A wine-supply deal I'm puttin' together for a few Brit bars round the south coast.' He nodded towards the farmhouse. 'There'll be somebody in there that'll show ye around. See ye later for a few Frank Zappas in the Los Pinos grub joint back in the village square.' With that, he was off in a spray of flying gravel.

The outward appearance of the farmhouse wasn't unlike the one near Calvià that had been chock-full of oranges, except that this house had a balustraded balcony along the front, from which it was obvious that the whole of the farm's land could be seen, not to speak of the panoramic views. Though unpretentious in the typical Mallorcan style, it was a handsome house, even if it did look more workaday than pretty. Still, Ellie said, all it needed were some flowers to brighten it up. A couple of bougainvillea climbers and a few hanging baskets with trailing geraniums would work wonders for a start. Ellie is a natural and incorrigible homemaker, and I knew when she started talking like this about a house that she had only just clapped eyes on that she was favourably impressed.

There were fifty acres of land, according to Andreu, the young chap who answered the door – all of it irrigated via a standpipe sprinkler system. The land was in excellent heart, too, he said, and capable of producing high yields of cereal and fodder crops. Behind the house was the ubiquitous Mallorcan orange grove, and beyond it a raised 'swimming pool' that doubled as a *deposito* into which the irrigation water was pumped from an adjacent borehole. The water was pure, sweet and abundant, the young fellow said. He then showed us the cattle accommodation – covered feedlots (at present empty) with accompanying silos, machinery sheds and even a range of calf pens. All of this was in flawless condition.

We were at one and the same time impressed and dispirited. This farm was exactly as Jock had said. It had everything we needed for raising beef cattle. Better than that, we wouldn't have to do a thing except move the livestock in. That was the upside. The downside was that such a model spread would surely cost the earth. And we hadn't even seen inside the house yet. Trying not to appear too keen, I asked young Andreu what his asking price was.

His reply was preceeded by a little laugh. I would have to ask the owner, *el senyor*, as he himself was only *el labrador*. He explained that, as was common in such cases, *el senyor* – by necessity a man of independent means – lived elsewhere; usually in the city, or perhaps even on the mainland. Meanwhile, *el labrador*, literally the owner's farm labourer-cum-manager, lived at the *finca*. Andreu then informed us that, being this farm's *labrador*, he lived with his wife and two young children in the farmhouse, just as his parents had done before him. He had been born in that house, had lived in it ever since, and could only hope that the new *senyor*, whoever he might turn out to be, would allow the arrangement to continue. There was a pleading look in his eyes as he told us that it would break his heart to leave this place. It meant the world to him. Assuring us that he was a hardworking and trustworthy employee, he said he would leave us to look over the farm at our leisure now, but we shouldn't hesitate to come and find him if there was anything at all we wanted to ask about.

His failure to invite us to see round the inside of the house was prompted, we realised, not by any lack of manners, but by his assumption that we were potential absentee *senyors*, like the present owner, and not merely *labradores*, like himself. But *labradores* we were, and even as *senyors*, we'd still be *labradores*, running the place by ourselves. And that meant we would have to live in the house.

We'd been confronted by yet another unforeseen quirk of the Spanish system, and our roller coaster took yet another downward plunge. There was no way we could ever bring ourselves to turn that young man and his family out of their home, yet neither was there any way that we could afford to continue the present arrangement. It was a dilemma, and we related it to Jock when we met up with him in the Bar-Restaurante Los Pinos back in Consell village. We had been there with Jock once before – car-buying as opposed to *finca*-buying – so we knew that their *tapas*, or Frank Zappas as Jock referred to them in his individual brand of rhyming slang, were excellent.

'Aye, well, I always say ye've got tae be hard tae survive on this island,' he told us over a dish of his favourite Carnegie Halls (meatballs) at a table under one of the pine trees from which the bar takes its name, 'but turfin' a young family into the street is a bit severe. Hmm, ye'd have a problem on yer hands there, right enough.'

'The problem won't even arise if we can't afford to buy the place,' Ellie said, having swiftly shifted from predicament to practicality. 'How can we find out about the asking price?'

Jock popped another meatball into his mouth, then stood up. 'No sooner said than done, darlin'. I'll go and phone ma contact right away.'

The information that Jock returned with didn't surprise us merely because the asking price was high. We had assumed that it would be. It was just *how* high it was that took our breath away.

'But that's over four times more than we got for our farm back in Scotland,' I wailed, 'and both places are exactly the same size!'

Jock raised his shoulders. 'Aye, well, this is a holiday island, remember, and ye can't blame a landowner for tryin' tae get top dollar for his property – especially if he's filthy rich, like the guy that owns the farm ye've been lookin' at. He can afford tae wait until another filthy rich bloke comes up wi' the askin' price – and one will some day, never fear.'

'And that bloke won't be a small farmer,' Ellie muttered, 'that's for sure.'

'Well,' I sighed, 'we'll just have to keep looking, because all we have to spend is the price we got for our place in Scotland –'

'*If*,' Ellie cut in, '*if* we get it all back when we eventually sell Ca's Mayoral.'

The roller coaster had taken another downwards plunge, and even mega-resourceful Jock was stuck for a way to set it back on an upwards trajectory.

'Maybe it's time for ye tae start thinkin' o' another way tae make a livin',' he suggested with an uncharacteristic note of resignation in his voice. He hunched his shoulders again. 'Maybe it's time for ye tae admit that the days o' the small farmer are over.'

– FOUR –

IF YOU DON'T HAVE A DREAM…

Maybe Jock was right on both counts, but we had come too far and tried too hard in our efforts to continue farming to give up now. And although we had never contemplated totally changing our way of life (because that's what farming is, rather than just a business), we hadn't closed our eyes to the possibility of diversifying since coming to Mallorca as rookie orange-growers. In fact, just a week or so before Sandy made his decision to return to Scotland, he had suggested to us that running the farm in conjunction with a restaurant would be worth considering. Serving our own produce on a plate would make good commercial sense, and if we utilised all the space between our fruit trees, the quantity of vegetables we could grow would probably be enough to supply much of the restaurant's needs.

The idea had been put into Sandy's mind when he stopped off for a coffee in the King's Restaurant in the town of Peguera on his way home from driving Charlie to school one day. The King's was located in a prominent position just back from the main street in the thriving though somewhat sedate resort just a few kilometres along the coast from Andratx. Catering mainly for Peguera's predominantly German clientele, the King's served unpretentious, value-for-money food in bright and sunny premises that also boasted a pavement terrace, a small dance floor and a popular bar. It was a friendly little establishment that welcomed families and, according to Sandy, the sort of enterprise he'd enjoy running – in conjunction with farming *and*, of course, us. The current proprietor had mentioned to Sandy that he was thinking of moving on and was looking for someone to take over the tenancy. The price he was asking for the transfer of the lease was within our means, and the annual turnover he quoted made the King's look a really attractive business proposition. In addition, it was no more than a fifteen-minute drive from Ca's Mayoral.

But, when push came to shove, the pull of the big East Lothian fields and the modern methods of farming that he was used to proved irresistible for Sandy. He reverted to his original plan of going to agricultural college in Scotland. Although Ellie and I had promised to give him all the backing we could in the King's venture, we knew deep down that he had made the right decision. We realised that, after the novelty of running a restaurant had worn off, he would have longed for the open-air life, part of which at least he would have forfeited on little more than a whim. We also realised that, under those circumstances, the onus of managing the restaurant would gradually shift more and more onto our shoulders. Did we really want to attempt to keep two full-time businesses going on our own? Well, we did give it serious consideration for a while, but then the old Mallorcan adage that you work to live, not vice versa, persuaded us that the best way forward would be to persevere with trying to carry on the way of life that our hearts were in.

Notwithstanding Jock's pragmatic observations, then, we continued our quest for another farm throughout the ensuing summer months. And, as we had somewhat hopefully predicted, the incidence of prospective buyers for Ca's Mayoral did start to increase with the rising temperatures. Most of them had seen the ads we'd placed in the British press and had then arranged to view the property while spending their next holiday on the island. A few of them even made return trips, raising our hopes that a sale was in the offing. But it never came to anything. As much as all of them said they loved the house, its facilities and dramatic location, the feature that put them off was, perhaps naturally, the very one that had prompted us to put the farm on the market in the first place. Namely, the land – or the insufficient quantity of it in our case, but, in the eyes of our urban viewers, the fact that there was so *much* of it.

How would they cope with maintaining all of it, they gasped, and what on earth would they do with all that fruit? Our assurance that there would be no lack of assistance offered by some of the old boys in nearby Sa Coma hamlet didn't cut any ice, not even when we said they would ask for nothing in return for their work but a small share of the orchards' produce to sell themselves. No, our prospective purchasers didn't fancy the idea of having their privacy invaded by 'locals'. Some of them came right out and said so, while others merely gave the clear impression of the same with a shake of the head or a wrinkling of the nose when we ventured the suggestion of such willing help.

What, I pondered, would old Pep and Maria make of such insular and aloof folk coming to live in their welcoming little community? Fortunately, it was a question that never required answering, because not one of these people ever got round to making an offer for the *finca*. The other side of the coin, however, was that time was passing and we were getting nowhere nearer that elusive goal of both selling Ca's Mayoral and finding a bigger farm. And all the while we had the accountant's prediction of hard financial times to come hanging over our heads.

In a less *tranquilo* place than Mallorca, panic may well have been starting to set in by now. But it was summertime, the living was hot if not always easy, and the pace of life in the valley was descending as the mercury in the thermometer climbed. Now, my initial concerns about the cost of having the swimming pool built evaporated as I saw just how great an asset it had turned out to be.

During the long school holidays, Charlie and his chums had the time of their lives flitting between it and the snooker table in the games room, before lending a hand with cooking (and eating!) alfresco evening meals under the softly lit pine trees in the barbecue area. And then, on the most muggy of hot August nights, even a devout non-swimmer like me could cool off by sitting up to my neck in the water at the shallow end of the pool, while admiring the stars shining in velvet skies above the silhouetted ridges of the mountains. An ice-cold beer brought by Charlie from the fridge in the games room bar never failed to complete the feeling of unaccustomed and (almost) unashamed luxury I was wallowing in.

These were good times – the most relaxed and satisfying we'd enjoyed since coming to Mallorca, and we savoured every moment, knowing that it would be a long time, if ever, before we'd have the good fortune of being able to repeat them.

But, soaring temperatures or not, there was still work to be done on the farm every day. The summer-maturing fruits had to be picked, sorted and transported to Señor Jeronimo's wholesale warehouse in Peguera, and the evening routine of irrigating the trees had to be adhered to religiously. This latter chore had always fallen to me. Firstly because lugging about a wide-bore hosepipe filled with water is fairly heavy work – too much for my conscience to allow either Ellie or young Charlie to attempt. Secondly, although Sandy was big enough and strong enough, he had always skilfully managed to avoid doing this particular job when he was still at Ca's Mayoral. In his opinion, it was about as boring as watching paint dry.

And so it could be, if you let yourself think about it too much. But I'd quickly learned that the secret was just to let the passing time wash over you like the water gushing into the irrigation channels round the trees. The sound of flowing water is always therapeutic, and never more so than in a Mediterranean orange grove on a sultry summer evening. I grew to enjoy lugging that hose about, and I enjoyed watching the movement of the water as much as Bonny loved playing in it. She never tired of leaping into the channels and worrying the gurgling outflow of the pipe as if it were a liquid rag.

Yes, those were happy and memorable times, when even a 'boring' task like irrigating trees became a simple pleasure, rounded off with a leisurely stroll home through the orchards at dusk, with Bonny nibbling playfully at my finger tips, and all around the pine-fringed *sierras* looking serenely down. Often, when I rounded the corner of the terrace, I'd be greeted by the sight of a brightly-coloured dragonfly or two flitting over the surface of the swimming pool, while hawk moths hovered like tiny hummingbirds among the blooms cascading from Ellie's flower baskets on the house wall. Then, as the sun finally set, the aroma of orange-wood logs smouldering on the barbecue fire added that final touch of Mallorcan allure to a charming though unexceptional old house that we had lovingly transformed into a home to be proud of. And we were. More than that, we could hardly have felt more content or, indeed, lucky with our lot. A dream had come true for us – at least at priceless moments like those.

However, we could never allow ourselves to lose sight of reality either, and the stark truth of that became more apparent with every passing week. The net that we had cast originally between nearby Andratx and its port had been flung wider and wider in hopes of finding that elusive larger farm that would give us scope to embark on the next phase of our 'ongoing Mallorcan adventure'. We had scanned the property-for-sale pages of *Ultima Hora*, one of the island's Spanish-language newspapers, every day for months and had made a point of going to view any farm whose description looked promising. But the snags we'd encountered when looking at the first three *fincas* that young Gabriel and Jock told us about had recurred with disturbing regularity. There would either be an ownership complication in the title deeds, an unresolved problem with the original planning permission of the dwelling, or the place was just too expensive for practical farming purposes – particularly if it had an old stone farmhouse ripe for renovation. Occasionally, we were presented with all three cans of worms at the same time. Nevertheless, we searched on and on – all the while casting that net farther and farther across the island. And Mallorca *is* a big one.

By the time summer began to drift towards autumn, the initial enthusiasm we'd had for seeking out and exploring possible farms was on the wane, though despondency was being kept determinedly at bay. Even so, viewing properties that fall a long way short of matching up to the way they're described in newspaper ads does eventually become both tiring and depressing.

The crunch came one early September morning. Charlie and Bonny were with us in the car as we set out in a mood of dogged optimism. Our lawyer in Palma had just phoned to say that he had received a formal offer for Ca's Mayoral from a British couple who had viewed it just a few days previously. They were prepared to pay our asking price, but only on condition that we would allow them an early entry date. So, it was now or never. The *finca* we were going to see today would *have* to fit the bill.

You won't find Llubí featured in many guide books, simply because it's essentially a no-frills working agricultural town, lying a bit off the beaten tourist track away towards the north of the island's fertile central plain. But its relative prettiness – or even lack of it – didn't bother us. Llubí is surrounded by some of the most productive land in Mallorca, the majority of it perfectly flat as well. Just what the doctor ordered. The ad in *Ultima Hora* had defined it as a 'retired' pig farm within a block of level land, with a compact house, mains electricity, a reliable water supply and a range of useful farm buildings. Our hopes were high as we took the *autopista* highway north-east from Palma and on past Consell, the village near which Jock had led us to look over the one farm that had been perfect in every respect, except its price. We were heading towards the town of Inca, renowned for its leather goods, its much-copied old 'wine *celler*' restaurants, an excellent range of shops, a daily covered market, an open-air weekly market and Mallorca's biggest agricultural fair, Dijous Bò, which attracts thousands of visitors every November. Since Llubí is only nine kilometres from Inca, we felt heartened in the knowledge that all the benefits of a large, bustling town would be within easy travelling distance of what might well become our new Mallorcan home.

'Never in a month of Sundays!' was Ellie's muttered reaction when we walked through the farm gate into a jungle of weeds that looked as if they had been allowed to grow and re-seed unchecked for years.

The land was certainly level, so the ad had been correct in that respect. But that was the only one. The 'house' was just a brick-built, one-room shack big enough for the pigman to have a siesta in, and the 'useful' farm buildings were no more than a collection of semi-derelict pig pens. They were fit, like the 'house', for nothing but demolition. We didn't bother to ask the estate agent who was showing us around about the electricity and water supplies. To add to the *finca*'s other shortcomings, the extent of its land was not only tiny, but totally surrounded by houses. It was easy to guess why the former piggery had closed, and the smell from a cattle feedlot on their doorsteps would elicit an equally damning response from those same neighbours.

'A prime development site, *señores*,' said the estate agent, with an estate-agently smile lifting the corners of his droopy black moustache like a vulture's wings. He surveyed the field and nodded his head. '*Sí*, with the requisite *permisos* from the planning department at the town hall, you could build four, maybe six, fine houses in here.' He rubbed his thumb and index finger together, then grinned, 'Potential profits *estupendos, sí?*'

I was tempted to explain to him that our ideas for the farm didn't quite tally with his, but what would have been the point? He'd only have thought me a totally *loco extranjero*, and at that moment I felt like one. Eventually, a property developer would come along and pay the asking price, which, now that I'd seen the place, was many times more than it was worth to small farmers like ourselves. I glanced at Ellie. As game as she had been to tackle any challenge that she'd been confronted with in our life together, and there had been many over the years, I could tell that this was the final straw.

'Never in a month of Sundays,' she muttered again.

Charlie looked up at me, his face a picture of confusion mixed with sympathy. 'I know what you had in mind, Dad,' he said, then cast a critical eye round the *finca*, 'but, in the words of the great John McEnroe, you can-*not* be effin' ser-i-ous, man!'

A clip on the ear would have been his usual reward for such a lippy quip, yet all I could do on this occasion was heave a shuddering sigh. The kid had spoken the truth.

But at least Bonny was impressed by the place, rummaging about in the undergrowth and rubble, her nose to the ground, sniffing up a multitude of pigshit pongs of rare vintage. Unfortunately, though, our needs were a tad more sophisticated than hers. I called her back, thanked the estate agent for his time, told him we'd think about it, and made my dejected way back to the car. Ellie and Charlie were already inside.

Shaking her head slowly, Ellie cast me a candid look as I slumped in behind the wheel. 'I think it's time to face the facts, don't you?' she said.

'Yeah, Ellie,' I conceded with another sigh, 'I'm afraid it is.'

She patted my hand and gave me a consoling smile. 'Come on then, cowboy, let's find somewhere nice to sit down and have a good old chat about what we're going to do next.'

★ ★ ★ ★ ★

Just outside Inca, a minor road winds its way up the steep slopes of the *puig* (mountain) that takes its name from the town. On the summit is situated one of the many *santuaris* that occupy similar prominent locations all over the island. This one is the Santuari de Santa Magdalena, and in common with a few other such former monasteries, the Santa Magdalena, while continuing to welcome spiritual 'pilgrims' to its chapel, now also caters for the corporeal needs of visitors via its own café-bar. This tranquil place seemed an apt venue for the meditative mood we were in. Ellie and I went inside to find a table in the café, while Charlie took Bonny for a walk round the old monastery grounds.

Hardly a word had been spoken during the drive from Llubí, but each of us was pretty sure that we were all thinking the same thing; our quest to find another farm had come to an end. Now, looking out of the windows of the restaurant, we noticed Charlie standing with Bonny, gazing at the panoramic views spread out beneath the Puig d'Inca. He could see all the way from the heights of the mighty Tramuntanas in the west, around over the sweeping bays of Pollença and Alcúdia to the north, and beyond to the far summits of the Serra de Calicant and the medieval hilltop town of Artà in the east.

'For all the potato fields of Sa Pobla,' I murmured reflectively.

'Potato fields?' Ellie queried.

'Yes. Old Maria's saying – the one she quoted to me on the evening of her lost duck, so-called.' I chuckled quietly at the memory. 'She said it was better to own a little that is dear to you than have all the potato fields of Sa Pobla.'

Geography has never been Ellie's strongest suit, so her mystified expression didn't come as much of a surprise.

'The town of Sa Pobla is what Charlie's looking down on now,' I explained. 'And all around it are its wide, fertile, profitable fields – the ones in Maria's proverb, the ones that supply many of the early potatoes for the London market, for instance.'

'Mmm, I see what you mean now. Ironic, isn't it? We've come farther and farther away from Maria's valley and we still haven't found what we're looking for.'

'Yeah, but the twist is that the little place that's dear to us, the little place that we own back in the valley, is still going to become less and less viable as time passes. So...'

Ellie said nothing at first, but sat looking out of the window, deep in thought. 'The sea,' she said at last.

'The sea?'

'Well, I admit my sense of direction isn't that great, but even I know that the sea I'm looking at now is at the opposite end of the island from the sea at Palma, and Charlie's school is at the opposite side of Palma from here, so the daily journey there and back every day would have been a nightmare anyway – even if that last farm *had* been what we were looking for.'

I could have reasoned that there would have been the option of sending him to the local state school in Inca, but I knew that at his age, just turned thirteen, having to make his way for the first time in a Spanish-language school would have been difficult, unsettling and, therefore, potentially detrimental to his education. Enrolling him as a boarder at his present school would have been a less disruptive alternative, but we couldn't have afforded that, even if we'd wanted to. The fact was that, in our determination to cast our net wider and wider, we had relegated to the back of our minds the aim that should have been foremost – the retention of the reasonably simple, country lifestyle that we already enjoyed. Maria's proverb had been correct, at least in that respect.

'We've been on a wild goose chase all along,' I said, unable to disguise the sense of disappointment I felt. 'We've been on a hiding to nothing from the very first day I mentioned the idea of raising Aberdeen Angus cattle on a holiday island where land's at a premium. We'd have to have been stinking rich, even to do it on a small scale.' I shook my head wearily. 'It was just a daft dream.'

Ellie gave me another consoling pat on the hand. 'You should think yourself lucky.'

'*Lucky? Me?*' Self-pity was beginning to set in. 'How the blazes do you make that out?'

'Well, as the song in that old musical about American sailors in the North Atlantic goes, "If you don't have a dream, how you gonna make a dream come true?"'

From down-in-the-mouth dejection, my mood was instantly changed to laugh-out-loud elation. And Ellie's clanger of mistaking North Atlantic for *South Pacific* was only part of the reason. As intentional as her geographical gaffe may have been (and I suspect it was entirely *un*intentional), her philosophy was, nevertheless, spot-on. I *was* lucky, not just to have had a dream, albeit a daft one, but even more so, to have a wife who'd been daft enough to go along with it. I told Ellie so.

'Well,' she giggled, 'why change the habit of a lifetime now?'

Suddenly, the frustrations and tensions of spending a year scouring the island for a will-o'-the-wisp property were relieved. Much to the bewilderment of the occupants of adjacent tables, we both began to laugh out loud now. It looked as though the roller coaster was coming to an abrupt stop, and if it turned out to be against a brick wall, then all we could do at this stage was hope that it would be a padded one.

'So, what *are* we going to do next?' Ellie eventually asked.

I wagged a cautionary finger at her. 'Don't you go worrying your pretty little head about *any*thing,' I smiled. 'I have another dream.'

'Yes,' Ellie replied, 'and that's precisely what I *am* worrying about.'

'So, *padres*, when are we going home?' asked a surprisingly cheerful-looking Charlie as he strolled in and sat down beside us.

'Not until your dad buys us lunch,' Ellie replied. 'I'm not having us travel all the way home to Ca's Mayoral on empty stomachs.'

'No, I didn't mean home to Ca's Mayoral,' grinned Charlie. 'I meant our *real* home. Scotland.'

Ellie and I exchanged confused glances. Even if we'd said we were thinking of returning to Scotland, which we hadn't, why on earth would Charlie look so pleased at the prospect of leaving Mallorca and all the delights of luxury living that he'd grown accustomed to indulging in at the homes of some of his richer school friends?

He answered the question without it being asked. He'd been thinking about everything as he was walking around outside with Bonny, he revealed, and he'd come to the conclusion that going back home would be what Ellie and I would decide to do now. The farming thing was never going to be a proper earner for us in Mallorca, and as farming was all we wanted to do, there would be no point in starting some other sort of business, just for the sake of staying on the island. We'd given it our best shots, we'd all had a great time, but he for one wouldn't mind calling it a day. Charlie had always missed his grandparents, as we knew, but now he even admitted that he missed his big brother as well.

'Yeah, *padres*, you won't hear me complaining about going home. OK, for sure it'll be tough saying goodbye to all my pals here, but I can always come back and see them for holidays occasionally.' Charlie's expression then changed from confident to cautious. 'I mean, you *have* decided to go back to Scotland, haven't you?'

Ellie and I shook our heads. No, we hadn't even discussed the prospect, Ellie told him.

Charlie's face fell.

But, yes, now that he mentioned it, Ellie went on, and in the light of how things hadn't developed on the farm-finding front, she supposed it *could* be the logical thing to do, right enough. She looked at me for confirmation.

I raised a shoulder. 'Could well be,' I said in a tentative sort of way.

Charlie's face lit up. 'Phew! I was crappin' myself in case you guys had been planning on heading over to mainland Spain – somewhere in the middle of nowhere, where the farmland's cheaper. Don Quixote windmill country or somewhere. Honest, having to cut the mustard in *another* new school would have been a real bummer – 'specially if I was the only non-Spanish guy there.'

I gave him a pat on the back. 'Congratulations, Charlie,' I joked. 'You had me fooled into thinking you were being unselfish when you said you wouldn't mind going back to Scotland.'

'We-e-e-ll, *padre*,' he drawled, 'that's the benefit of having a schoolteacher like Jock Burns.' Charlie pulled a Jock-type face, laid a paternal hand on my shoulder and said in an exaggerated Scottish accent, 'Always think ahead, son. Aye, aye, that's the only way tae survive on this island, by the way.'

So, in an atmosphere of surprising conviviality – considering the uncertain future that we now faced (again) – Ellie suggested that we have lunch and let *mañana* take care of itself.

The art of Mallorcan *tranquilo*ness, I told her, had taken a grip of her at long last, thank goodness – though perhaps, I thought, a mite too late.

Charlie rubbed his stomach, opened the menu, then came out with another example of Jock's classroom influence. 'Wow, I'm really Lee Marvin!' he muttered.

Ellie gave an exasperated shake of her head. 'For goodness sake, why don't you just talk in plain English that everyone can understand? I mean, all that Frank Zappas, Carnegie Halls and Lee Marvin nonsense. Honestly,' she scoffed, 'what a load of Brad Pitt!'

Impressed by the unexpected rudeness of his mother's improvisation, Charlie dissolved into fits of laughter that, once again, must have had the occupants of neighbouring tables wondering if they were sitting next to a family on day-release from a lunatic asylum.

Offering them smiles of apology, I concentrated on the menu. 'OK,' I said after a cursory glance, 'it's all fairly basic stuff, so I reckon we should just follow the old when-in-Rome rule.'

'I don't see any spaghetti listed,' Ellie objected.

'No pizzas either,' Charlie added.

'That's because this isn't Rome – or even bloody Naples! It's a mountaintop overlooking the lush fields of Sa Pobla in Mallorca. The source of the best vegetables on the island – probably in the entire Mediterranean – *and* they're all in season right now.

'Oh no,' Charlie groaned, 'don't tell me it's gonna be the healthy alternative.'

'Don't knock it 'til you've tried it,' I told him. Then, with a nod of approval from Ellie, I ordered a communal dish of *Tumbet*, a wholesome Mallorcan stew of aubergines, red peppers, potatoes, tomatoes and garlic, with, on the side, a refreshing *Trempó* salad of sweet onions, mild green peppers, tomatoes, apples and capers, all drizzled with olive oil and purslane vinegar. We may not have been destined to farm any of the fertile fields of Sa Pobla, but one small consolation was the privilege of enjoying their produce, simply but honestly prepared for us in a way that probably pre-dated the old monastery itself.

'Nine out of ten,' doubting Charlie enthused as he mopped up the last of the *Tumbet* juices with a chunk of crusty bread. 'Yeah, but some good, unhealthy fries would have added that final point.'

'Don't worry,' Ellie said drily, 'if your prediction about us going back to Scotland proves right, you'll soon be able to shoot your cholesterol levels sky-high with some local delicacies like pie soup followed by a deep-fried Mars Bar or two.'

'Right on, *madre*,' Charlie winked. 'I can hardly wait.'

For all his bravado, Ellie and I sensed that Charlie was only trying to lighten the way towards what he knew was about to become an uncertain and worrying time for us. Like his big brother, he was showing that he had an old head on young shoulders. What's more, it was becoming obvious that his exposure to the hedonistic aspect of some of the richer expats' lifestyles on the island hadn't turned his head, as Ellie and I had always been concerned that it might. It looked as if his feet had remained firmly on the ground after all.

We fell silent for a few moments, each of us thinking our own thoughts again.

It was Ellie who eventually spoke first. She threw me a wary glance. 'You, uhm – you said you had *another* dream…'

'Certainly have.'

She narrowed her eyes. 'And, uh, I don't suppose this one would have anything to do with some other *unusual* niche of farming, would it?'

'Certainly would.'

Charlie shot me a tell-us-more look.

'It's one that I was looking into even before we left Scotland. One that we could start off on a reasonably small farm, then expand as the demand for the produce increases.'

Ellie raised her eyes heavenward. 'What's the hearing equivalent of *déjà vu*?'

'No, don't pooh-pooh it,' I said. 'It's not as daft as dreaming about breeding Aberdeen Angus cattle in Mallorca.' I rolled my shoulders, feeling a bit embarrassed by the way Ellie and Charlie were staring at me – as if they were waiting for me to claim that I'd just returned to Earth after being abducted by aliens. 'No, the livestock I'm talking about now wouldn't be at all out of place… in Scotland.'

'So, we *are* going back,' Charlie quickly concluded.

Ellie fixed me with a knowing look. 'And this is a dream with antlers, right?'

'Certainly is.'

'Ah well,' she stoically sighed, 'herding deer on a rain-lashed Scottish hillside will make a pleasant change from picking oranges in a sun-soaked Mallorcan valley.'

I managed a weak smile. 'Well, as you said yourself once, at least you can't accuse me of making you lead a dull life.'

'Hmm, but I think you'll find that I've said that a *lot* more than once, dear.'

★ ★ ★ ★ ★

The next day, the contract for the sale of Ca's Mayoral was signed and the deposit from the buyers lodged in our bank account. We now had just over a month to wind up our affairs in Mallorca and make preparations for our return to Scotland.

'Changed your mind, *tío*?' old Pep asked when he saw me removing the '*Se Vende*' sign from the gate. Of course, he knew very well that I hadn't. This was just his way of finding out, without asking in so many words, what we were planning to do next and who would be taking over at Ca's Mayoral. He greeted my answers to both with the same poker-faced reply of, '*Va bé* – that's fine.' If our plan of returning to Scotland to farm deer interested him, he didn't show it. Neither did he react in any perceptible way to my positive news that the non-farming, retired couple who were to be the new owners of Ca's Mayoral had assured us that they would invite some old *vecinos* from the village to maintain the orchards for them.

However, I had learned enough about Pep's character to realise that he wasn't being in any way disdainful or dismissive about what I'd told him. Beneath his veneer of indifference, he would have been *extremely* interested, but to have made this obvious would have risked appearing nosey – an affront to his old-fashioned code of country politeness.

Old Maria also displayed this typically Mallorcan trait when I broke the news to her during one of her fallen-fig-gathering visits a couple of days later. Doubtless, Pep would already have told her everything I had to say anyway, but Maria didn't let on. Instead, she quoted one of her precious old sayings… 'Only bad neighbours are never missed.'

I waited for her to follow that with something else – some kind of pithy punchline, perhaps. But none was forthcoming. She merely glanced up, flashed me an uncharacteristically shy little smile, then continued to pick up figs for her pig.

Jordi, however, was much more voluble in his response when I met up with him at his favourite pavement table outside the Bar Nuevo in Andratx on the morning of the next Wednesday market.

'Bloody 'ell, man,' he guffawed, 'you be tell Jordi you be being go back to damn-bugger *Scotch*land?'

I nodded sheepishly.

'Stone the baster crows!' He slapped his thigh, released a breeze of wheezy laughter, then turned to a quartet of bewildered British tourists at the next table. 'You all be coming Mayorky for the sunshines, right?' He paused to hook a thumb in my direction. 'Yes, and he being live here the many year, and now being go back to the baster bollock freezings! Is ridickliss!'

But behind all the bluster, Jordi was a sensitive fellow, and after he had put on his extrovert show at my expense, he leaned towards me and said quietly, 'Jordi be knowing the problems, man. Jordi been being work in far countries the many year ago also as well.' He nodded sagely. 'Jordi being know the forking problems, oh yes.' That was all he had to say on the subject, except to add a moment later that I would come back to live in Andtratx again one day, *if* I being have any forking brains in my baster Scotch head. And, I suppose, that was about as close to a compliment as I was ever likely to get from Jordi.

Jock, conversely, was far from complimentary when he learned of the decision which, more or less, had made itself for us. I'd parked in the yard in front of the school to pick up Charlie one afternoon when Jock emerged through the door, simultaneously hailing waiting parents and shouting mid-Atlantic farewells to their offspring. Jock's Mr Affable performance in public never ended, but the look on his face as he strode across the yard towards me was unaffectedly severe.

'The headmaster just told me that Charlie's gonna be leaving us,' he said. 'Says Charlie told him you're goin' back to Scotland.' He didn't wait for me to reply. 'Well, I think you're makin' a big mistake, son.'

I sensed a schoolteacher-style ticking-off coming on, and I got one. Why were we chucking in the towel now? he wanted to know. We'd come through all the hard times, he reminded me, we had integrated well, had settled perfectly into the Mallorcan pace and way of life, so why turn our backs on it now?

My explanation about not being able to afford to continue farming on the island didn't wash with Jock, however. The way he saw it, a change of career was what I should be thinking about, instead of chasing rainbows – especially all the way back to Scotland. If I *really* wanted to live in Mallorca, he reasoned, I should be prepared to do anything for an earner that would allow me to do so.

'Look at me, for instance,' he said. 'Nobody loves Scotland more than me, and at times I miss it like crazy. But I've made ma home here, and I work bloody hard at anything and everything tae make enough dosh tae enjoy it tae the full. Aye, and there's nothing tae stop you doin' the same.'

I expected him to add that that's the only way to survive on this island, by the way, but he didn't. And I didn't try to convince him that my outlook on life was more focused on trying to keep doing what I *wanted* to do in order to earn a living, as opposed to surrendering that goal just for the sake of staying in Mallorca, no matter how much I enjoyed it. Young Charlie had grasped that and accepted it, but not so Jock.

'I'm disappointed,' he stated bluntly as he got into his car. 'I thought ye'd stay the course.' At that, he drove off, clearly miffed and doing nothing to disguise the fact.

I was left feeling really bad about having disappointed Jock. More than that, I had hurt his feelings, and that was the last thing I wanted to do. He had proved himself to be a good friend by going out of his way to help us however he could since we'd first told him of our intention to come and live in Mallorca. Jock had smoothed the way for us on many a tricky occasion that, without the support of such a well-connected and willing ally, might well have seen our Mallorcan adventure stumble and fall. Jock had never sought any recompense for his kindness, except the satisfaction of knowing that our continued presence on the island brought him a tangible contact with the 'home' that he admitted to still missing. The news of our intention to leave had cut deep, therefore, and knowing that made our impending departure even more difficult for us to face. That said, we knew that Jock would eventually come round to understanding and accepting that our decision had been made for what we genuinely believed was for the best, even if he didn't agree with it.

We didn't have the consolation of that knowledge where Bonny was concerned, however. She was only a dog, after all, and a big softie at that. The country's strict anti-rabies laws dictated that she would have to spend six months in quarantine before being allowed into Britain. She had only been in kennels once before, and that had been for just seven days when we'd gone to visit friends on the mainland of Spain. But that one week of 'imprisonment' (as she would have regarded it) confused and distressed her so much that we swore we'd never subject her to such an ordeal again – even for just one week. In my view, the difficulty for a dog is that, once deposited in a strange enclosure in alien surroundings, no matter how 'humane' the conditions, the dog has no way of knowing when, if ever, its family are going to return to take it home. We couldn't bring ourselves to even think about sentencing Bonny to such mental torture for six months – a length of time that would surely break her heart. Much as it would break *our* hearts to part with her, we realised that we'd have to leave her behind in Mallorca, which meant finding a new and loving family for her to look after, in her own little way.

Robbie and Lulu Gordon lived in an old stone house with a big walled garden on the outskirts of Es Capdellà village, on the opposite side of the Garrafa and Grua ridges from the Sa Coma valley. Robbie, a fellow Scotsman, was a freelance yacht captain, and we had met him and his young wife when their four-year-old daughter Kate started at the same school as Charlie. We fell into an arrangement of sharing the 'school run' with them occasionally and had become close friends. We didn't have to ask them twice if they would consider being

Bonny's new family. Like us, they were boxer fans, and they had established a great rapport with Bonny from the first moment they'd met her. What's more, the timing of her joining their household couldn't have been better as far as they were concerned. A new baby had just arrived on the scene, so the addition of a much-loved four-legged friend like Bonny would complete their picture of family bliss.

Although we were delighted that Bonny was going to a good and caring home, it was with lumps in our throats that we drove over to Capdellà with her on our last but one evening on the island. The next day would be taken up with doing the last of the packing and then seeing our personal effects loaded into a removal van for shipping to Scotland. It would have been both bewildering and upsetting for Bonny to have been exposed to the apparent dismantling of her home prior to being parted from us, so we thought it best to take her to her new abode before all the commotion began.

Sandy had flown over to join us for our last few days at Ca's Mayoral. Naturally, both he and Charlie insisted on coming along to say their personal farewells to Bonny. A light rain had started to fall as we drove down the steep driveway to Robbie's and Lulu's house. Grey clouds descending over the mountains with the approaching night added a further touch of gloominess to the melancholy mood we were already in.

Bonny, though, was in fine fettle, electing to go for a solo jaunt round the scattering of almond trees in the garden instead of heading directly for the front door with us. Having visited the Gordons on many occasions, she was perfectly familiar with all the sniffing places and exploring corners in the grounds. She wasn't going to be allowed to indulge herself for long this time, however. As soon as little Kate heard us at the door, she ran out and called Bonny's name.

'Is she *really* going to be my dog?' she asked Ellie, her smile of Christmas-like anticipation not quite disguising the trace of doubt in her voice.

Bonny came bounding over, and if the thorough licking she gave Kate's face wasn't enough to answer that question, the enthusiasm of her tail-wagging – so unbridled that it made her entire body wiggle – should have.

'We only told Kate about it an hour or so ago,' Lulu told us as she ushered us inside. 'Didn't want to get her too excited. As it is, it's past her bedtime, but there would've been no point in tucking her in until Bonny got here. She'd never have gone to sleep.'

Robbie, ever the genial host, made us welcome with drinks round the big, open hearth in the living room, and we chatted about anything and everything, except dogs, while Kate and Bonny cuddled up together on a sheepskin rug in front of the fire. A few minutes later, Kate was sound asleep, only to wake up with a start when her mother lifted her to take her off to bed.

Kate rubbed her eyes. 'Where's Bonny?' she asked. 'Is Bonny still here?'

'Yes, yes,' Lulu assured her, 'Bonny's still here.'

That was all Kate wanted to hear. With a contented smile, she snuggled her head against her mother's neck and was carried upstairs to bed.

'And don't worry,' we heard Lulu tell her as they disappeared from sight, 'Bonny will still be here when you come back down in the morning.'

But Bonny had other ideas. She had been here on a few previous occasions when Kate had gone off to bed, but now, for the first time ever, she decided to follow her. I began to apologise to Robbie and was about to call Bonny back, but Robbie held up a hand, smiled and told me it was all right. Bonny was welcome to go anywhere in the house that she wanted to. It was her home now, after all.

'I usually have to tell Kate a bedtime story,' Lulu said when she came back into the room, 'but tonight she told me not to bother. *She* would tell Bonny one instead.'

I thought that that would be Bonny settled on Kate's bed for the night, just as it had become her habit to be on Charlie's. But not many more minutes passed before Bonny reappeared, wagging her tail, and with what looked very like a self-satisfied grin on her face.

Lulu went over and listened at the bottom of the stairs. 'Kate's fast asleep,' she whispered. 'I can hear her snoring.'

So, Bonny had adopted the role of little mother already. She had started a nightly routine that would be repeated every bedtime – trotting upstairs with Kate, staying cuddled up to the little girl until she fell asleep, then, mission accomplished, trotting back downstairs to keep Robbie and Lulu company until they themselves went to bed.

But that was all in the future. For tonight, Bonny spent the remainder of the hour or so that our visit lasted by lying at each of our feet in turn – first Charlie's, then Sandy's, Ellie's, and finally mine. It was as if she knew that this was to be our last little while together, and she wanted to savour each farewell moment in her own quiet way. Even when we finally said our goodbyes to Robbie and Lulu, instead of following us to the car as she normally would have, Bonny stood between them at the front door, a wistful look in those expressive brown eyes of hers, but a little wag of her stubby tail telling us that all was going to be well. It was a touching moment that none of us will ever forget.

Not a single word was exchanged during our drive back over the mountains to Ca's Mayoral that night. The sound of sniffles and nose-blowing said it all.

We received two phone calls at breakfast the following morning. Ellie answered the first one. She smiled when she recognised Lulu's voice, then a worried frown furrowed her brow.

'Bonny,' she said anxiously. 'Oh dear – what's happened?'

The boys and I caught our breaths.

Ellie listened intently, her frown easing into a smile again as Lulu described the problem. 'Injured her foot?' Ellie asked. 'Sitting outside the front door with her front foot raised?' She gave a little chuckle. 'And she refuses to move?'

Recognising the scenario, we all released sighs of relief. The drizzle that had greeted us when we arrived at Capdellà the previous evening had developed into steady rain overnight, with the result that any bare ground had turned to mud. The land at Ca's Mayoral was predominantly heavy clay, which became a sticky quagmire after a downpour, so Ellie had trained Bonny to wait at the door until she'd had her feet wiped clean after being out in such conditions. We'd neglected to tell Lulu about this, so Bonny's raised paw, following her morning sojourn round the garden, was her own way of trying to get the message across to her new 'lady-in-waiting'. Ellie was still smiling, but with her chin starting to quiver, while she explained this to Lulu. A solitary tear dripped from the end of her nose as she put the phone down.

'Bless her,' she murmured, the words catching in her throat. 'She's a little angel, that dog.'

The boys and I joined in an impromptu chorus of contrived splutters and coughs in a futile attempt to disguise that we had gone all dewy-eyed ourselves.

'Ah well,' I said after a while, 'at least we know that the future for Robbie, Lulu and family will be fine. Bonny will see to that.'

That raised smiles and nods of assent all round and, no matter how forced those smiles may have been, we welcomed the consolation of knowing that Bonny's future would be fine as well. Robbie, Lulu and their children would see to that.

The second telephone call came in shortly after the removal van arrived, so chaos reigned as I lifted the phone. It was Jock, the first time I'd heard from him since he'd given me that sharp rebuke about deciding to leave the island a few weeks earlier. As I'd hoped, he had now reverted to his usual breezy manner…

'Fancy an *adiós* feed tonight, son?'

I was taken off-guard, being preoccupied with trying to keep out of the removal men's way while they lugged boxes and crates this way and that. Eating had been the last thing on my mind.

'Well, yes… I mean, I suppose that would be –'

'Just as well,' Jock butted in. 'I've booked a table at that Celler Ca'n Renou place in Andtratx ye told me about. Thought ye might fancy the idea under the circumstances.'

'Ehm, right… I'll, eh, I'll just check with Ellie first and –'

'Ca'n Renou. Half-past nine. See the four o' ye then.'

The phone went dead.

That's one thing about Jock, I thought – once he makes his mind up, there's no arguing with him; particularly if there's food involved. But, on this occasion, he obviously had been thinking about us more than his own epicurean urges. Under the circumstances, as he had implied, we would neither want to prepare our last Mallorcan supper in what, by then, would be a forlorn and empty kitchen, nor would we want to travel too far to eat out. I guessed that, by checking the flight departure times, Jock would already have found out that we'd be leaving for the airport early the next morning.

We had already made up our minds to delay saying our final farewells to our immediate neighbours in the valley until then. At one stage, we'd wondered if throwing a party and inviting them along, together with Jock, his wife Meg and some of the expats we'd got to know through them, would have been the right thing to do. But we had come down against the idea. For one thing, we suspected that we wouldn't be feeling in much of a celebratory mood, and for another, we feared that the wrong impression might be given to the likes of old Pep and Maria. We might be seen by them as the one-time, mud-on-our-boots small farmers who had turned all swanky, showing off our tarted-up-and-sold *finca* to other *extranjeros*, most of whom they had little or nothing in common with. No, we'd decided, keeping our departure a low-profile affair would be the best way to go.

With all the recent traumas and upheavals of preparing to leave, we had forgotten that today was the Fiesta of Santa Catalina Tomàs, Mallorca's only native saint. Throngs of people from all over the island would have converged on Palma to see the colourful, costumed processions in the saint's honour. Even in outlying towns like Andratx, many local folk celebrated the occasion by taking to the streets to create an informal festive atmosphere of their own, before ending the day with their extended families in a favourite eatery. That's the wonderfully paradoxical thing about Spain. Few let the piety of a saint's day get in the way of having a good time.

The Celler Ca'n Renou was already filled to capacity when we walked in.

'Hey-y-y-y, Don Pedro!' rang out the mid-Atlantic holler from the back of the restaurant. 'Over here, ya gringo son of a bitch!'

Being jocularly abusive is a sure sign that Jock's in a good mood, so it seemed my apprehensions that he might be intending to give me a hard time about giving up on Mallorca had been unfounded. I was thankful for that. My emotions were in enough turmoil as it was.

The volume of the cheer that rose up in approval of Jock's affectionate insult indicated that he and Meg weren't alone, and as we eased our way towards them through the obstacle course of crowded tables, it became increasingly apparent that he had assembled a fair cross-section of our mutual friends. Jock likes nothing better than to arrange such gastronomic gatherings, and they invariably turn out to be fairly festive occasions in their own right – even on non-*fiesta* days.

The first thing Jock told me, after he had directed us to our designated places at the table, was that he had talked young Gabriel and María-José into making enough paella to feed all of the twenty people in his party – no mean feat at any time, but especially obliging on such a busy night as this. Making a paella properly requires the cook's close attention, and the time-honoured process of cooking the rice, meat, seafood and vegetables in a shallow, flat-bottomed *paellera* pan over a wood fire can't be rushed. Well aware of this, Jock had made sure that he and his fellow diners wouldn't go hungry – or thirsty – in the meantime. The full extent of the long table was amply decked with a selection of favourite Mallorcan 'picks', like *pa amb oli* (literally bread drizzled with olive oil), stewed snails, pickled olives, raw carrot and celery strips with a garlicky *all-i-oli* dip, and enough wine of the three hues to set alarm bells ringing at the local headquarters of Alcoholics Anonymous.

True to their standing as the king and queen of hospitality within their wide social circle, Jock and Meg (whom I'd once described, justifiably, as a one-woman Rio Carnival) made sure that the cross-table banter never flagged for a moment. The conversational content of their dinner parties had never been noted for a surfeit of genteel small talk, though. Having fun was the name of their game, and they were obviously intent on ensuring that our last night on the island would be as full of that as they could make it – even if everyone's ability to be the butt of derogatory wisecracks was tested to the limit in the process.

Jock's long experience of supervising school dinners stood him in good stead on such get-togethers as this, when the judicious placing of guests at the table can make all the difference between a successful social mix and an awkward friction of unkindred spirits. He'd come up trumps again this time, even ensuring that Sandy and Charlie were sitting among the younger members of the group, with whom they could empathise more easily than with Jock's inner circle of veteran party animals.

By the time the paella arrived in a procession of four large *paellera*s, borne aloft by Gabriel and three young assistants who had been drafted in for the night, the atmosphere was well and truly set in carnival mode. The sound of high spirits emanating from Jock, Meg and their guests was competing favourably with the conversational clamour of the local folk occupying the rest of the Ca'n Renou tables. For that's the wonderful thing about eating out in Spain. It isn't just a matter of eating, but more a social occasion involving the whole family. It's an uninhibited celebration of good company, lively talk, wine *and* food, carried on in a relaxed, *mañana* way that's both good for the digestion and the promotion of bonhomie. And, wholesome as it is, Mallorcan country food is essentially very simple, so there's nothing snobbishly 'foody' about any of this. The mealtime communion has been part of Spanish culture since time immemorial, and its pleasures are enjoyed just as much by a few farm hands sharing some bread, olives and wine during a break from working in the fields as they are by people crowding into restaurants to be served hand and foot by willing waiters.

This was one important aspect of the lifestyle we had become accustomed to in Mallorca that I knew we'd find hard to replicate on our return to Britain, and it was to Jock's credit that he had arranged such an excellent example of it for our last night on the island. By the time we were saying our goodbyes out in the street, the amount of wine-fuelled hugging, back-slapping and hand-shaking going on would have out-bonhomied even the most convivial of Hogmanays in Scotland, where everyone (the most disliked of neighbours included) becomes a bosom buddy for those fleeting, bell-chiming moments that ring in the birth of every new year.

'Well, son,' Jock said to me before we finally went our separate ways, 'it's been paella for ye tonight, but it'll be porridge tomorrow, eh?'

With a resigned sigh, I nodded my head, which by now was singing with wine and filled with self-doubt about the decision we'd made to give up all the good things that living in Mallorca had come to mean to us. Maybe I should have followed Jock's advice by doing something, *anything*, else for a living that would have allowed us to stay.

But Jock then came out with a statement that set me back on my heels. He leaned in close and said *sotto voce*, 'To tell ye the truth, I wish I was comin' with ye.' Then, noticing that Meg had an inquisitive ear cocked and a threatening eyebrow raised, he swiftly added out loud, 'Aye, but only for a wee holiday, like.'

★ ★ ★ ★ ★

Old Maria 'just happened' to be knocking a few weeds out of the ground with her trusty mattock hoe when Ellie and I took one final stroll through the orange groves before the taxi came to take us to the airport. Maria was standing on her side of the crumbling gap in the wall that she usually came through on her fig-gathering visits. When she saw us approaching, she carefully picked her way through the fallen stones, then, as was her wont, she spoke directly to Ellie, apparently regarding me as a third party to be addressed only if absolutely necessary.

'As I told *him*,' she said, with but the slightest of sideways jerks of her head in my direction, 'we have a saying that only bad neighbours are never missed.' She stepped up to Ellie, pulled her head down to her own height, kissed her on the cheek, then whispered, 'I will miss you, *señora de Escocia. Sí*, I will miss you.' While Ellie warbled her thanks and dabbed a tear from her eye, Maria turned to me and, with that elf-like grin of hers seeming to brighten the overcast skies that were hanging over the valley, she chuckled, 'And I will also miss you, *muchacho* – as will at least one of my ducks.'

With that, Maria was gone, shuffling her way between her lemon trees back towards her little farmstead for another day to follow the ninety-plus years of near-identical days that she had already lived through in the valley. We envied her and the old way of life that now rested so fragilely on her stooped shoulders. She had been a good neighbour, and we would miss her as well.

Our final meeting with Pep was no less 'coincidental', though considerably more dramatic. We were loading our suitcases into the taxi out in the back yard when we heard the crunch of metal wheel rims on tarmac and a yell that might have come straight from the soundtrack of a vintage cowboy movie…

'*ARRIBA! ADELANTE, CABALLO! AY-Y-Y-Y, ARRIBA-A-A-A-A!*'

Pep's gravelly voice was urging on his *caballo*, his horse. Well, he always referred to it as a *caballo*, although it was without doubt one hundred per cent *un mulo*. I'd always suspected that this distortion of the truth had less to do with Pep's wish to flatter his mule than with his desire to classify himself as a *caballero* – literally and originally a horseman, but in the noble form of a knight and, in more recent times, simply a gentleman of the highest order. To Pep, being referred to as a *caballero* would have a much more desirable ring to it than being dubbed a mere *mulero*. Thus, his lowly *mulo* had been elevated to the rank of *caballo*.

The four of us walked out to the lane to see Pep emerging from his gateway, standing Ben Hur-style in his cart behind his distinctly peeved-looking mule. Pep may have seen himself as a latter-day Charlton Heston, but his mule was under no such delusions about its own identity. Acting the make-believe movie star's *caballo* clearly didn't feature very high on its list of priorities, particularly at this early hour.

With a hoarse shout of 'WHOAH!', Pep reined in his barely-moving steed. He then produced something from his trouser pocket and lobbed it to me. It was a duck's egg.

'It is hard-boiled, *tío*,' he laughed as I gingerly caught it in cupped hands, 'and it will remind you of me whenever you look at it.'

Just as Maria had done earlier, Pep was having one last laugh about the lost-duck episode, but I was left no more enlightened as to what the truth of it had really been. Only Pep and Maria knew that.

Still laughing, Pep goaded his mule into reluctant motion with a flick of the reins. Then, doffing his beret, he called out theatrically, '*Adéu, amigos! Hasta que no hay mas uvas en el mundo!* Until there are no more grapes in the world!'

As his 'chariot' gathered speed along the lane, he shouted one last puckish proverb over his shoulder...

'And always remember, *compañeros*... Life is like a sewer. What you get out of it depends on what you put in! *ARRIBA, CABALLO! ARRIBA-A-A!*' With a final John Wayne salute, the valley's self-styled gentleman of the highest order galloped off into an imaginary sunset.

Sandy shook his head slowly, a grin of admiration on his face. 'We'll never meet another one like him,' he said.

The rest of us smiled our sad acknowledgement of that.

★ ★ ★ ★ ★

There was something melancholy about the valley as we left Ca's Mayoral for the last time that October morning. Doubtless, the way we were feeling was responsible for much of this, since we were leaving a place in which we had spent three of the most memorable and enjoyable years of our lives. Yet there was more to it than that. The normally benign mountains had a moody look to them, looming dark and dismal in the shadow of gathering thunder clouds. This signified nothing more sinister, of course, than the approach of autumn. Back in Britain, this time of mists and mellow fruitfulness would already have become established, while here in Mallorca, those clouds darkening the mountains were but the harbingers of the spectacular storms that soon would mark both the Mediterranean change of seasons and old Pep's six-monthly change of underwear.

The sea, too, had an ominous look to it as we passed along the coast-hugging Paseo Marítimo boulevard en route to the airport. Yachts and fishing boats tugged at their moorings around the curve of Palma Bay, their masts like upturned metronome pendulums set rocking to and fro by little breakers already beating against the quay. Lightning flickered on the horizon, followed by a peal of thunder that rumbled towards us over the grey expanse of water.

Ellie, a self-confessed wimp in the presence of electrical storms, was a nervous wreck by the time we arrived at the check-in desk for the Edinburgh flight. She's never the happiest of flyers at the best of times, but the thought of being in a mid-air rendezvous with a lightning bolt renders her numb. Every cloud has a silver lining, though, and the normally depressing news that our flight was to be delayed by over an hour brought the cheering word from the check-in girl that, come our revised take-off time, the threatening storm was expected to have moved off in the opposite direction from the one we'd be flying in.

In the meantime, however, our long wait in International Departures turned out to be as boring as expected, though with a surreal factor *un*expectedly thrown in. It seemed, strangely, as though we were returning from a holiday, yet the combined buzzes of having had a good time for a couple of weeks and the prospect of returning home were missing. It was as if we were in limbo. I think that even Sandy felt this, despite the fact that he had already started to re-establish his life back in Scotland. The truth was that, as a *family*, we were facing just as uncertain a future in our native country as the one we were giving up in our adopted one. This feeling persisted when our Edinburgh-bound flight eventually took off.

As the plane rose from the runway, we were presented with a stunning panorama of Palma. We could see all the way round the bay, from the Gothic grandeur of Sa Seu Cathedral to the circular mass of Bellver Castle, sitting stately and staunch on the green-carpeted slopes of the Serra de Na Burguesa Mountains to the west of the city. But awe-inspiring as these views were, we knew that they amounted to but a tantalising foretaste of the spectacle that was about to unfold. Moments later, though, we entered a solid mass of cloud, and it seemed that our hoped-for parting view of the summits, cliffs and gorges of the mighty Tramuntanas had gone. But then something happened that was to stamp an even more indelible vision of Mallorca on our memories.

The pilot banked the plane steeply to the right, setting a course northwards. It was Charlie who noticed it first. He was sitting in a window seat next to his mother and in front of Sandy and me. Suddenly, there was a break in the clouds.

'Down there!' he exclaimed. 'It's Port d'Andratx! See – there's the jetty along from the Bar Central, where we used to sit sipping drinks under the palm trees on Sundays. Yeah, that's it all right. You can even see the fishing boats tied up in front.'

He was absolutely right, and as we climbed higher, we were soon passing over Andratx town itself.

'Look now!' Charlie gasped. 'It's the valley! And along there… yeah, that's got to be…' His voice trailed away as he hesitantly added, 'that's got to be… home.'

I peered out of the window and, sure enough, there was the ribbon of road winding north from Andratx towards the mountains, with the lane meandering off to the left through the Sa Coma Valley. And along there, just as Charlie had said, was 'home' – the house at Ca's Mayoral. From this height, the swimming pool in front was a mere fleck of blue amid postage-stamp orange groves, old Pep's and Maria's higgledy-piggledy farmsteads no more than little clusters of Lego bricks discarded in a toytown Mallorcan landscape.

'Before long, it'll seem as if it was all just a dream,' I heard an oddly meditative Charlie tell his mother, while they both continued to stare downwards through the window.

'Hmm, well, maybe,' Ellie replied with a sigh. 'But it was one dream that really *did* come true… for a while, anyway.'

Sandy and I glanced at each another, shrugged our shoulders and said our own silent amens to that.

– FIVE –

CHASING ANOTHER RAINBOW

Broken cloud also welcomed us to Scotland, but the views intermittently revealed during the plane's descent could hardly have been more at odds with those we had somewhat longingly looked down upon just a couple of hours earlier. Instead of the majestic, saw-toothed summits of the Tramuntanas, we were passing over the Southern Uplands, age-worn folds of land whose undulations make up much of the Border country between England and Scotland. Grazing sheep seemed like speckles of white scattered on rolling expanses of turf and bracken already touched by the muted shades of autumn. This is an unassuming landscape, contriving to conceal its beauty behind the bleakness of its moors and in deep glens carved by streams rising profuse and pure from hidden sources in the higher slopes of the hills. What, I wondered, would a water-coveting Mallorcan farmer give for access to one of those unfailing springs for just an hour or two each day? He'd give as much, I fancied, as many a Borders farmer would for an equivalent share of his Mallorcan counterpart's sunshine.

But, then, neither of these lands or their people would be what they are without the influence of their respective climates. And I suspected that, ultimately, each farmer would prefer to stick with what is already his, no matter how attractive certain elements of the other's might initially appear. Having now sampled both alternatives, I would soon discover whether or not this theory held good for me, however.

First, though, Scotland had other visual charms to seduce us with before we even set foot on the ground. Preparing to make his final approach to Edinburgh Airport, the pilot flew the plane out over the watery expanse of the Firth of Forth, then turned slowly through 180 degrees above what is regarded as one of the engineering wonders of the modern world. The cantilevered, steel tracery of the Forth Rail Bridge has been a universally recognised icon for well over a century. In more recent times, the construction nearby of a magnificent suspension bridge to carry road traffic over that same mile-wide stretch of the mouth of the River Forth has created a worthy companion for this monument to human ingenuity. These twin bridges make a spectacular aerial gateway to Scotland's capital.

It occurred to me that even Palma de Mallorca would be hard pushed to present an initial impression more pleasing to the eye than the one offered by Edinburgh to passengers of an aircraft descending westward over the Forth. Beyond the now fashionable docklands of the Port of Leith, Edinburgh ascends gracefully towards a spire-pierced skyline dominated by one of the most instantly recognisable buildings in the world, Edinburgh Castle. Its ramparts rise from a rocky throne against a backdrop of the scarped heights of Arthur's Seat, and above a city steeped in history.

Scottish émigrés have always waxed lyrical in song about the longed-for joy of returning to their native land, of coming 'back tae bonnie Scotland where yer ain folk bide'. And while this could be scoffed at as being little more than bubbling-into-your-whisky schmaltz, dished up by exile-pandering music hall performers at a time when the world was a bigger place, it would have taken a very insensitive Scotsman indeed not to be moved, even just a wee bit, by the welcome mat his capital city laid beneath our inbound plane on that October day. Although I hadn't been away all that long, I admit to having felt a big tug at the heart strings as I looked out towards the well-kent outline and dependable presence of Edinburgh Castle – even though, on this occasion, its silhouette was framed (perhaps ominously) by one of those very rainbows that Jock had warned me against chasing.

But such practical thoughts were far from my mind just then, because, despite the pangs of sadness that I'd had on leaving Mallorca, I now felt genuinely happy to be back in Scotland. After all, we hadn't left here to escape any kind of rat race or to find a more satisfying way of making a living. On the contrary, we'd been perfectly happy raising cattle and growing barley on the little farm of Cuddy Neuk, and would never have moved from there had we been on the right side of the 'size matters' farming equation. And anyway, given that you're fond of where you come from in the first place, there's nothing more heart-warming than going back there. You're returning to your roots, to all things familiar and to the bosom of your family and friends.

Yet not everything was familiar. Not surprisingly, some changes *had* happened in the time we'd been away. The most immediately noticeable was the new dual carriageway that bypasses the city of Edinburgh and cuts by more than half the time required to make the twenty-mile journey from the airport to our destination. The route taken by the new road has also opened up some interesting views of the landscape previously denied the car-bound traveller. In a wide arc, it skirts the flanks of the Pentland Hills, Edinburgh's landward sentinels and the most northerly of the conjoining ranges that comprise the Southern Uplands, before finally entering the lush farmlands that fan out beneath the big skies of East Lothian.

Bowling along parallel to the coast, you're now treated, on one side, to views over the wide waters of the Firth of Forth as far as and beyond the shores of the 'Kingdom' of Fife and, on the other, to a glorious panorama of field and woodland stepping gently upward to the soft, heather-cloaked shoulders of the Lammermuir Hills. Then, as the road sweeps down in the direction of the dome-topped outcrop of Traprain Law – a local landmark that is the ancient, eroded 'plug' of an extinct volcano – a solitary steeple peeping over the treetops in a valley just ahead tells you that you are approaching a town. It's the old 'Hidden Toon' of Haddington, the historical hub and county town of East Lothian – and, for us, home.

However, for us to call it 'home' was, in truth, a reference to the past, because for the present it could be little more than a spiritual notion, an inherent state of mind. For this part of Scotland to be our home again, we would first need to find a house to turn into a home, and that house would have to be part of a new farming enterprise which, in itself, was still also no more than a notion, and a fairly vague one at that.

My parents' house stood in a row on the brow of a hillside overlooking the town. In the middle distance, the River Tyne winds its way through grassy 'haughs' (riverside meadows), past St Mary's old parish church, the biggest in Scotland, and on under the 'Auld Brig', a stone bridge that's said to date back to Roman times. As the song goes, you sometimes don't know what you've got 'til it's gone, and I confess to having taken for granted the mellow, timeless beauty of Haddington as seen from the windows of my folks' house when I lived there during my youth. The surrounding stubble fields ready for the plough, the trees along the riverbank wearing the red and gold mantle of autumn, the roofs and chimneys of the old town, the modest but reassuring slopes of the Garleton Hills rising up on the far side of the valley.

But the best sight of all was the look of pleasure in my parents' eyes when they met us at the door. We were a small, close family and, although they had paid us a few visits at Ca's Mayoral, I knew that my mother and father had missed the daily contact with us that had been the order of things before we went away. For all that, being typically undemonstrative Scots, our reunion on home soil wasn't marked with any great show of emotion – just a plethora of broad smiles and discreet, almost shy, little touches of hands and pats on arms and shoulders. It was a greeting at the other extreme from the effusive, kisses-and-hugs custom of the Latin country we had just left, though none the less heartfelt for that.

My mother had prepared a meal which, thankfully, didn't include the porridge that Jock had symbolically predicted. It comprised such good, old-fashioned, no-nonsense Caledonian favourites as Scotch broth, mince and tatties and, for pudding, big slabs of home-made, fruity 'Clootie' dumpling smothered under lava flows of custard. As magnificent as it had been, Gabriel's paella of the previous evening was suddenly facing stiff competition.

'I was speaking to an estate agent yesterday,' my father told me once all the welcome-home pleasantries were over, 'and he just laughed when I told him you wanted to buy twenty or thirty acres with a house on it.'

'What's funny about that?' I asked.

'Said he hoped you were feeling flush.'

I was a bit miffed by this. Who the hell did this smart-arsed estate agent think he was, and what business of his was it whether I was flush or otherwise? 'Well,' I said, preparing to mount my high horse, 'we've come back here without losing a penny of the money we got when we sold Cuddy Neuk, so I reckon we can afford to buy a place that's smaller than that and still have enough capital left to set up the deer-farming business.'

'That's just the point, though. Property values have increased since you sold Cuddy Neuk.'

'Fair enough, but surely not by *that* much. I mean, we've only been away three bloody years.'

My father, never one to do anything but encourage me to go wholeheartedly for any goal I set myself, gave me a cautioning look. 'It's the house element,' he said. 'Since they opened that new road you came along today, East Lothian has become a property hot spot. Beautiful countryside, beaches, golf courses, *quaint* towns and villages, good local schools and shops, and fast, easy access to Edinburgh. A rainbow's end for commuters.'

That damned rainbow analogy again. I groaned inwardly as the reality of what my father had said began to sink in.

He speeded it on its way…

'The estate agent bloke said that farmhouses, sold separately, are fetching almost as much as the entire farm, including the house, went for not that long ago. So, what he said about hoping you were feeling flush wasn't intended to do anything but mark your card.'

Slightly built but wiry with it, my father always prided himself in cutting a natty sartorial dash – at least in respect of what was visible to the public, as my mother was wont to cynically qualify. Sporting a slim, David Niven moustache on his cheery, well-lived-in face, and a jauntily-tilted porkpie hat on his head, he was a popular local character, a gregarious little chap who noted his keen perceptions of people and places in on-the-spot cartoon drawings and spontaneously composed verse. He was also a keen amateur pianist in what might loosely be described as the 'honky-tonk' mould, and could be relied upon to contribute a generous helping of foot-tapping ivory-tinkling at any gathering where there happened to be a jangle box handy. The products of his creative talents, devoutly dismissed by my mother as absolute rubbish, hadn't been honed by serious study, but had remained steadfastly freeform and impromptu, and that was the way he liked it.

He had only recently retired from spending much of his working life supplying fuel oil to the local farms, so he knew the agricultural community and what was happening in it very well.

'Now that everything's getting more and more mechanised,' he went on, 'farmers don't need many of their workers' cottages any more, so... Well, you get the picture.' Just in case I hadn't got it, he added, 'I mean, right now, even your wee house at Cuddy Neuk would probably fetch about twice what it was worth when you sold the place three years ago.'

I got the picture now all right, and it didn't look too attractive.

Always one to see the bright side of things, my father's optimistic nature was accompanied by a sense of fun that the Scots describe as 'pawky'. Typical of many examples in the Scottish vernacular, there isn't one individual word in English that is the equivalent of 'pawky', which denotes, in essence, a laconic and impishly droll way of expressing humour. It can be tinged with wry observation and maybe even a touch of mischievously disguised criticism or advice, but it's never malicious. Pawkiness is an intrinsic feature of the Scottish character, and, if you can recognise its subtleties, you'll find it in much of the country's music, writing, art and, of course, in the barbed banter of bar-room wits.

Noticing the desponding effect that his revelation about the potential difficulty of being able to buy a suitable property had had on me, my father then told me to cheer up. If the worst came to worst, he said, I could always pitch a tent in his back garden.

'Thanks,' I replied drily. 'Very pawky!'

'Aye, well, in the meantime,' he said with a sly wink, 'why don't we go out to the garage with the boys and have a game of darts?'

There was nothing Dad liked better than a wee tipple. Mother, on the other hand, was strictly teetotal; a result, perhaps, of her own mother's influence during a childhood in Orkney, where Highland Park, the local whisky, didn't develop into one of the highest-regarded single malts in the world because of the total abstinence of the islands' male population. So, in her own home, the presence of alcohol in anything beyond medicinal quantities was only reluctantly condoned by my mother.

Hence my father's occasional visits to the garage 'for a game of darts'. Of course, she was well aware that he had a small stash of booze in a cupboard inside the back door, which, to his credit, he never partook of alone, but was quick to draw from whenever non-abstemious male 'company' dropped by. That was usually when a sojourn in the garage was suggested, and as long as he didn't come back into the house and 'pollute the place with his breath reeking like a brewery horse's backside', as she delicately put it, his 'darts games' were tacitly tolerated by my mother. Despite her dismissive attitude towards my father's creative attributes and happy-go-lucky nature, my mother wasn't without a sense of humour herself. She'd always claimed that, living with him, she needed one, and I've no doubt there was truth in what she said.

Devoted as our parents must have been to each other, during our childhood, my sister Minnie and I had become accustomed to the unique way they showed it – or, rather, didn't. It was just the way things were at home…

Father was the incurable social animal, who thrived on and was inspired by lively companionship. He was also very conscious of his image and of how the local community might regard his standing within it. This concern was manifested, rather perversely, in his becoming a staunch member of the Haddington Conservative Club, although I'm convinced he was actually a closet Socialist.

Mother, in contrast, was a self-effacing homebody, dedicated to bringing up her two children in a secure, happy household and, subsequently, to relishing the company of her grandchildren, on whom she would shower her affections while managing never to appear in any way gushing. That Scottish reserve again; an intrinsic quality of hers, though anathema to my father – except when displaying affection, that is.

Yet, retiring and basically shy though she was, my mother, in the company of people she felt comfortable with, could be the most fun-loving of characters, dissolving into fits of girlish giggling whenever something tickled her. Even in her maturing years, her face, when she laughed, still exuded ample evidence of the carefree, young-at-heart side of her nature, an unspoilt inner beauty born of a happy childhood spent with her sisters and brother on their parents' farm on the remote but equally unspoilt Orkney island of Sanday.

That inner beauty was reflected in her outward appearance in an old group photograph taken when, at the age of twenty, she joined the civil service in London. My father was a civil servant then as well, and, although neither of them had been known to admit it since, the buds of mutual attraction must have popped and blossomed among HM Government's filing cabinets and teacups of the time. According, once again, to a contemporary photograph, it's easy to see what the physical side of that attraction may have been. The young country girl, slim, sunny of disposition and elegantly demure, as befitted the Norse heritage of her native islands. The young man a dashing David Niven lookalike (even if the resemblance was carefully cultivated), his pale blue eyes sparkling with humour, his easy, outgoing demeanour emitting a self-confidence that sprung from a big-city upbringing in Edinburgh, where his father was a well-known and much-admired professional football player.

Such surmised physical attractions apart, however, my folks were something of an enigmatic couple as far as their individual personalities, priorities and outlooks on life were concerned. But their marriage had survived intact for well nigh on half a century, so they must have had *some*thing in common, no matter how difficult for the onlooker to identify. Perhaps, as that much-quoted law of physics states, it was simply that unlike poles attract.

Be that as it may, we all loved them dearly and equally – although none of us ever got round to actually *telling* them so. I suppose we felt we didn't need to, believing that all it took to express our feelings was a look, a smile, a gesture. Here, typically, was the kind of emotional restraint, the 'subtlety' of communication, that goes hand-in-glove with 'pawkiness' in the Scottish psyche. Also, I think that my sister and I had always regarded our mother and father as our best friends as much as our parents, and that perspective had been passed on to our own children, whose affection for them in both regards couldn't have been greater. But it was a relationship that thrived on fun as well as respect, and laughter was never in short supply when we all met up as an extended family.

On such occasions, the freedom of spirit that had motivated my father to rebel against returning to the constraining security of a career in the civil service on demob from the RAF at the end of the Second World War surfaced in the form of boyish high spirits that, much to my mother's irritation, would sometimes verge on hooliganism. The boys loved it. Even when well into his sixties, he'd out-dared them on a family holiday in Menorca by repeatedly climbing onto the roof of the house, letting out Tarzan calls and doing what he called 'star dives' (belly flops with arms and legs splayed) into the swimming pool some four metres below. Not the type of behaviour normally expected of a senior citizen, perhaps, but guaranteed to earn him street cred in the eyes of the younger generation. And he loved that.

On the evening of our homecoming, he was in his element. Well lubricated with darts-playing juice and buoyed up even more by the arrival of my sister and her family, he gave the piano a real going-over for hours on end. My mother's obvious disapproval was more than compensated for, in his eyes, by the equally obvious delight his over-the-top keyboard antics were eliciting from Sandy, Charlie and their two similarly-aged cousins. In Mallorca, I'd always likened old Maria's infectious, gap-toothed smile to a visual tickle, and I suppose the sound of my father's laughter could fairly be described as the aural equivalent – though notably more manic than elfin. Once his fun batteries were fully charged, he would laugh until his eyes were streaming, his face was crimson, the veins were standing out on his brow, and until there was nothing coming out of his mouth but hoarse, breathless croaks and wheezes. It wasn't just infectious, it was a side-splitting epidemic with no antidote. I've even known my mother to succumb to a surreptitious titter when he was in the grip of a full-blown fun convulsion, and such was the way of things that evening.

Yes, it was good to be home.

★ ★ ★ ★ ★

The euphoria that came from re-establishing family bonds was bound to be tempered, sooner or later, by the need to get on with the business of reorganising our lives, and it didn't take long for that to happen. Charlie was the first one obliged to bite the bullet. As we'd arrived back in Scotland during the half-term school holidays, he had a few days' grace before having to face the discomfort of being the classroom 'new boy' once again. And the fact that he was returning to the same school that he had left three years ago didn't make it any easier.

We had rented a furnished cottage on a farm in the hamlet of Bolton, a couple of miles or so outside Haddington. The farmer, a genial big bear of a man in his late thirties and referred to by his friends simply as 'The Fermer', was a good friends of ours. He and his wife Rona were also the most hospitable of couples, their large farmhouse having been the scene of many a memorable party for their wide circle of pals and playmates. Their two sons and two daughters had inherited their parents' gift of conviviality. Being all much younger than Charlie, they seemed to regard him as something of an exotic 'freak', who had suddenly arrived in their little community from a strange, far-off land – if not actually from outer space. His mid-Atlantic accent fascinated them, as did the golden glow of his skin, still showing the evidence of having lived an outdoor life in the sun for the best part of three years. They held Charlie in the friendliest kind of innocent awe, and the warmness of their attentions did much to ease his getting used to the sudden drop in air temperature that we'd all been acutely aware of since the moment we stepped out of the plane at Edinburgh.

A chill even more biting than that was about to blow through Charlie's first day back at school, however. Although he knew the kids who'd been in his class before he went away, that had been in primary school, and he was now enrolling at its secondary counterpart, a much larger, more impersonal place that also had on its student roll youngsters who had previously attended junior schools in the various surrounding villages. There were many new faces and names for Charlie to get to know – yet again. But this utilitarian and, in some ways, impersonal local authority seat of learning was a world away (in more senses than one) from the cosy exclusivity of the small, fee-paying school he'd attended in sunny Mallorca. 'Poncy' mid-Atlantic accents were anything but the norm here, and anyone speaking in one – especially through lips surrounded by a healthy suntan – could expect short shrift from the bully element so sadly present in many such schools these days.

'Fuck off back tae where ye came from, ya Spanish bastard!' was typical of the salutations grunted at Charlie by members of the corridor-shuffling Neanderthal tribe. And that particular 'welcome back' speech came from a girl! This made it impossible for Charlie to react in the only way such kids understand. His response to the male insult-hurlers didn't have to be restrained by such unappreciated chivalries, however, and he was soon left to pick up the threads of his old school life in peace, while the little packs of cave-dwellers turned their browbeating attentions on others less capable of looking after themselves.

Fortunately, as it had now turned out, Charlie's initiation into the juvenile society of Mallorca had taught him a valuable lesson in self-preservation. The first time he rode his bike up the lane from Ca's Mayoral and into the village of Sa Coma, a couple of local boys had called the virtue of his mother into question. 'Hijo de puta', meaning 'son of a whore', is a favourite insult in Spain. Charlie was by no means a pugnacious kid, but his normally easy-going nature had an assertive side to it that came as a sharp surprise to those taking him for a soft mark. Apart from being stung by the derogatory remark about his mother, he realised that his own standing among local youngsters in his adopted homeland would hit rock bottom if he didn't show that he could stand up for himself. His stock was suitably and permanently elevated, then, after he'd shown those two lads that he was very capable of doing just that. So, in one respect, being taunted by the Haddington school bullies amounted to no big deal. He knew well enough that these 'hard cases' would probably have peed their pants if they'd had to handle his own Sa Coma experience – alone and far away from the big-fish delusions of their own tiny puddle.

As is usually the case everywhere, though, such antisocial misfits in the Haddington secondary school were far outnumbered by decent, well-brought-up young people, who, even if some of them (like Charlie) didn't particularly like school, all accepted that they were there for purposes essential to their own future progress in life. Being able to get along well with fellow members of the human race is a prerequisite of that, and, to his credit, Charlie was good at making friends, albeit that making academic progress didn't come quite so easily. Although he was capable of excelling at things that came naturally to him, he needed a bit of goading in respect of subjects that didn't. And this is one example of how a small school with a high staff-to-pupil ratio, like the one he'd attended in Mallorca, differs from big state schools – perhaps everywhere, but certainly in Britain. In many cases, there just aren't the resources in the latter to allow teachers to spend extra time with pupils who might benefit from additional tuition. Charlie would have to get used to this, and Ellie and I would have to get used to ensuring that he did.

★ ★ ★ ★ ★

The Scottish climate was something all three of us would have to get used to. So far, the weather had been unusually mild for the time of year, but as October drew to a close, the first of the frosts that signal the approach of winter had begun to blanch the dawn landscape with a dust as fine as icing sugar. We would gaze at it through the cottage windows at breakfast time and marvel at the Christmas card scenery that, perhaps rather callously, we had come to dismiss as a run-of-the-mill aspect of our past during the time we lived among the sun-kissed orange groves of Mallorca. But the East Lothian countryside was beginning to flaunt its beauty in the most delicately seductive of ways, and we'd soon become captivated by other aspects of it that we had once taken too easily for granted as well.

Initially, however, the first-thing-in-the morning need to venture out into the cold to chop kindling and fetch logs for the fire had me thinking back to what I'd been doing so recently at a similar hour. Invigorating though the frosty Scottish air was, and as much as I was intrigued by the novelty of *seeing* my own breath again, I couldn't help comparing this routine with the essential maintenance 'work' to our swimming pool that I'd become accustomed to doing at Ca's Mayoral at the start of each day…

You could feel the warmth of the first rays of the sun as it peeped over the crest of the mountains and sent long fingers of light creeping through the waking orchards on the valley floor. While I skimmed the night's scattering of insects off the surface of the pool with a long-handled net, a passing swallow might swoop down and lend a hand by scooping up a fly or two, or a fan-crested hoopoe bird might alight like a giant butterfly on a nearby pomegranate tree and hoot me its 'Poo-poop!' compliments of the new day. Then, across the lane, I'd hear old Pep shout a hoarse 'Weh-*ep*!' greeting to a fellow *campesino* passing by en route from the village to work on his *finca* farther up the valley. Next, I'd connect the bendy tubes of the underwater suction cleaner to the filtration system and make my leisurely way round the edge of the pool, 'hoovering' up any grit that had settled on the bottom overnight. By the time I'd finished the entire unhurried process by testing and adjusting the chemical balance of the water, then emptying and back-washing the main filters in the pump house beneath the terrace, the sun would have risen into a cloudless sky above Sa Grua Ridge. Now, the valley would be bathed in golden light, the scent of opening blossoms and the musty smell of warming soil would be wafting in from the orchards, old Maria's cockerel would be winding down his dawn reveille for another day, and the 'chug-chug' of little tractors, the tinkling of sheep bells, the distant barking of a dog, and all the sounds typical of a tranquil Mallorcan morning would be echoing round the mountainsides.

Here in Scotland on a frosty October morning, the sun was also rising into a clear sky, though its progress through the heavens would follow a trajectory much closer to the horizon than it would in Mallorca, and the resultant shadows cast across the countryside would remain long throughout the shortening autumn days. Instead of wiping beads of sweat from my brow as I'd often had to do while doing the daily swimming pool chores, I was now blowing my cupped hands every few minutes in a futile effort to warm fingers numbed by the frost clinging to the bark of the logs I was gathering. That swimming pool and those orange groves seemed a long, long way off now.

There were certainly no strikingly plumed hoopoe birds around to add a splash of colour to the wintry scene. Even in the height of the British summer, none of those exotic softies had been known to venture this far north. Yet, right on cue, my southerly-drifting thoughts were cheered by a sound that brings to the autumn countryside in this part of the world a touch of magic that, until that moment, our time in Mallorca had all but banished from my memory. The plaintive call of the wild goose is synonymous with the end of summer in this corner of south-east Scotland, when huge flocks of these handsome, pink-footed birds fly in from their breeding grounds in the Arctic Circle to overwinter in what are (for them) our more hospitable climatic conditions.

Hearing the strident, yelping cry of the geese took me back to times in my childhood when we spent weekends with my grandparents at Cuddy Neuk, just four miles north of here and only a couple of miles from the sea as the goose flies. On autumn mornings such as this, I would gaze out of my bedroom window and watch flights of the great birds rise from their nocturnal resting places down at Aberlady Bay on the Firth of Forth and fly inland to graze our stubble fields during the daylight hours. I was no less enthralled as I watched them again now, appearing high over the horizon in two huge V-formations, then breaking ranks to circle down towards some unseen feeding ground beyond the woods above the farm.

'Must be some rough weather coming,' said The Fermer, squinting skyward while ambling towards me from the direction of the farmhouse. 'It's not often we see the buggers flying this far in from the coast.' He shook his head and added despairingly, 'Ah well, that'll likely be one of *our* fields of young wheat they're going to fill their bellies on today.'

Despite his disgruntled tone, The Fermer knew well enough that the freeloading eating habits of these wild geese would probably do little harm to crops like his autumn-sown wheat, especially if it had grown a bit too vigorously during a mild spell like the recent one. In fact, in times when there was more livestock kept on local farms, it was common practice to allow herds of sheep to nibble down excessively 'proud' growths of young winter wheat to save the tender leaves from the lasting ravages of frosts, such as the one blanketing the landscape this morning. So, come the spring, the crops would recover from these goosey attentions and would grow all the more vigorously for it. Their unwitting feathered benefactors, therefore, could graze the fields without too much risk of becoming targets for the farmer's gun. And just as well, too, as the annual return of the geese to East Lothian is the county's most spectacular wildlife event.

'I was thinking of taking the wife and kids for a walk,' The Fermer said right out of the blue, 'so I just wondered if you and Ellie fancied coming along. Charlie can come as well, if he can put up with being pestered by my brood of young sprogs.'

'A *walk*? Did you say a… *walk*?'

The Fermer nodded his head. 'Yeah, a walk. Good to stretch the legs occasionally, I always reckon.' Then, as an afterthought, he swiftly added, 'Eh, not right now, though. Yeah, a bit later in the morning would suit me better. Say, round about midday, maybe?'

I could hardly believe my ears. Here was a man whose only known source of non-workaday exercise was limited to the occasional game of rugby and lifting post-rugby-game pints of beer.

'A *walk*?' I repeated. 'But this is Sunday, and you always go to the pub at lunchtime on a Sunday to get rid of the morning-after-the-Saturday-night-before cobwebs.'

'Well, ehm, that's right enough, I suppose, but I just, you know, kinda thought you'd like to see bits of the county you've never seen before – I mean, after just coming back from Spain and everything. A wee walk through the woods here would make a change from all those bloody palm trees you've been loafing about under.'

This proposition had taken me completely by surprise. As hard a worker and as excellent and dedicated a farmer as he was, The Fermer was a devout Sunday lunchtime pub-goer, never failing to meet up with his cronies in the village of Gifford, a couple of miles up the road – except, of course, when pressing farm work like autumn ploughing got in the way. Yet, although the ground was too hard-frozen for any ploughing to be possible today, his invitation to go for a walk with wives and kids, in preference to heading for the pub on his own, seemed genuine enough, so I readily accepted.

★ ★ ★ ★ ★

It was one of those days when the frost never lifted, and when, as The Fermer remarked to Charlie as we set out, the air was so still that a carefully released fart would lurk as motionless as an invisible statue until someone inadvertently wandered too close and breathed in. This observation had the expected effect on our younger son, who, like most schoolboys, entertained a healthy infatuation with all things flatulent, especially if a cheap laugh could be derived therefrom. It's a form of humour that's lost on members of the opposite sex, all of whom, as they'd have us males believe, never break wind anyway – apart from the occasional cough-camouflaged, self-propelled one, perhaps. It goes without saying, of course, that such genteel ladies' farts don't smell either. It's always the dog's fault. How many unjustly maligned pooches, I wonder, have been whipped off their mistresses' laps and hurled out of the room, confused and disillusioned, during gentlewomen's soirées down the ages? If only they could talk, indeed.

Apparently, Charlie was just as fascinated as I'd been by a reintroduction to our exhaled breath assuming a visible form in the frosty air. This once familiar phenomenon, combined with The Fermer's static-fart observation, had fired his imagination. The result, as already mentioned, was entirely predictable.

'Check this out,' I heard him whisper to The Fermer's two young sons, who were aged about six and seven respectively, and were, therefore, ripe for the appreciation of any novel type of vulgarity. With that, I could have sworn a puff of white vapour shot silently from the seat of Charlie's jeans, hung suspended like a lonely little cloud for a second, then, as The Fermer had predicted, made itself lethally invisible.

The two young boys bellowed guffaws of delight, before, also predictably, trying to emulate the trick themselves. Their sisters, whose ages were about a year on either side of the boys', giggled coyly behind their hands, while their mother and Ellie strolled nonchalantly ahead, remaining suitably aloof from such puerile behaviour. At the rear of the procession, The Fermer and I exchanged smirks of approval.

We had crossed a little bridge spanning a burn, the Colstoun Water, that meanders through the farm just below our rented cottage, and we were now making our way up a gentle rise along the headland of a field bound on three sides by woods.

Without saying anything, The Fermer stopped and turned to look back the way we had come. I paused beside him and followed his gaze. There, nestling in the glen below, was the hamlet of Bolton, looking as idyllic as the subject of a Constable painting. The big, stone farmhouse stood four-square and elegant on the other side of the burn, with the farm's numerous cottages and old smithy strung out beyond the little church and graveyard in which are buried the mother and brother of Robert Burns, Scotland's national bard. Behind the church, the old farm steading and its attached *doocot*, or dovecote, are a reminder of times when all of those cottages would have been occupied by families who worked on the farm and whose characters were integral parts of it. Although those days were long gone, The Fermer's love of the place was understandably undiminished, though tinged with regret that the social side of the little village had become more diluted as commuting newcomers had gradually replaced the worthies who once had been not just the life, but the very soul of the place.

'It's always been my home,' he said with an unusually reflective note to his voice, 'and I can't even imagine ever living anywhere else.'

I couldn't blame him. It really was a very enviable place in which to have been born and brought up. It was also, in a more practical sense, the hub of the large farm that The Fermer's family had tended assiduously for three generations. The Fermer was a fortunate fellow, but he didn't take that good fortune for granted. Like his forebears, he worked long and hard to maintain his farm's justifiable reputation as one of the best in the area. He also liked to play hard, and he now told me that he planned to revive the sadly departed social buzz of the village by organising the first ever 'Bolton Festival'. I could hardly wait, although the mind boggled as to what form this extravaganza would take. I had a hunch, though, that the world-famous Edinburgh International Festival wouldn't be facing too much competition from it on the arts front.

Resuming our walk, we now entered a large wood, made up of a wonderful blend of mature deciduous trees – oak, beech, chestnut, sycamore, elm and ash, interspersed with the occasional conifer, like larch and Scots pine. This is one of the surviving remnants of the ancient mixed forests that once covered much of the Scottish landscape, but which are now limited to areas like this, where the terrain had been deemed unsuitable for agricultural purposes, or where the 'lairds', the landowning gentry of old, had purposely preserved them for their own amenity and sporting purposes. East Lothian is generously blessed with such fine areas of woodland, which not only enhance the appearance of the landscape, but also act as shelter belts for the rich farmlands that surround them.

Although the New England states of America are rightly famed for the stunning beauty of their countryside in the fall, it struck me that it would be hard to imagine an autumn scene more breathtaking anywhere than the one we were wandering through now. The unseasonably mild weather of late had encouraged the trees to retain for longer than usual much of their foliage, now ranging in colour from muted shades of green to rich golds, russets and reds. Yet the ground was already covered by a blanket of fallen leaves that the night's frost had turned so brittle that they crunched under our feet like spilt potato crisps on a bar-room floor. Well, that was The Fermer's description of an effect that doubtless deserved a more poetic interpretation, although I couldn't think of one myself.

'Clacherdean Wood, we call this place,' he informed me, while producing a couple of cans of beer from inside his coat. He handed me one and returned my smile of appreciation with one of self-congratulation. 'Be prepared, as the boy scouts say. We're a long way from the nearest pub here, you know.' Then, reverting to his theme, he pointed northward through the trees. 'A bit farther over there there's Weirds Wood, then further on this way we've got Crown Wood, and away over there to the right a bit there's Fawn Wood. All places where you'll seldom see a soul, except maybe for the odd poacher.' Then, nodding towards a gap in the trees up ahead, he said under his breath, 'In fact, you've more chance of seeing a few of *them*.'

A little roe deer was pawing the ground with a front hoof in an attempt to rid the grass of its hoary coating of leaves. On hearing us approach, it lifted its head, looked towards us, sniffed the air, then turned and took off, white tail high, into the safety of the undergrowth. The farther into the woods we ventured, the more wildlife we saw – rabbits, pheasants, pigeons, a rare red squirrel as cute as it was busy, even a covey of grey partridge rising startled from behind a hedge with a whirring of their wings, before flying away fast and low over the clearing they'd been feeding in. Their panicky, jarring cry echoed in their wake through the silent trees. Then, once more, all that could be heard was the crumpled-paper sound of our feet trudging through dead leaves, the murmur of our adult conversation and the occasional jingle of children's laughter as Charlie cracked another rude joke to his pair of young disciples.

I couldn't help but try to compare this sharp, still, autumn morning to the balmy quality of the Mallorcan days of 'winter spring', as the island's elderly country folk call this selfsame season of the year. Here in Scotland, the falling leaves and the busy, nut-gathering squirrel were signs that the things of nature were preparing for their long winter slumber, whereas back in Mallorca, seeds were still being sown in the warm soil, and migrating thrushes would be arriving in their millions from the cold expanses of central Europe to start their annual 'vacation' beneath the comforting caress of the Mediterranean's winter sun. But what, I soon decided, was the point in trying to compare the two places? Each had its own individual charm and beauty, and even a preference for one's climate over the other's was entirely subjective and, to a large extent, relative. After all, those flocks of geese arriving here from the Arctic Circle were just as pleased with the change in temperature *they* were experiencing as were all those thrushes simultaneously winging their way to Mallorca.

Some would say, however, that both sets of birds had more brains than I had, due to the fact that I'd flown my little flock of three in the wrong direction. No doubt the time would come when I'd be obliged to agree that they had a point. But, for the moment, I was too enthralled with all the sights, sounds and scents of our immediate surroundings to allow such negative thoughts to cross my mind. When The Fermer had suggested going on this walk earlier, he'd said it would let me see parts of the county that I hadn't seen before, and, although I'd spent much of my youth living less than a couple of miles from here, he spoke the truth. From the upstairs windows of my parents' house, I had looked out towards the treetops of these very woods every day of my youth, yet this was the first time I'd actually set foot in them, and the experience was proving to be well worth the wait.

As we made our way through gates and over stiles, down banks and up braes as bonny as any I'd seen in places celebrated in song, The Fermer casually took over the lead of our little procession from Rona and Ellie. We were now a long way from Bolton, and I for one was beginning to feel like Hansel of Gretel fame – but without the benefit of a trail of shiny pebbles to lead us back out of this particular forest.

The Fermer's wife must have been thinking along the same lines. 'Are you sure you know where you're going?' she eventually called out to him.

'Yeah, yeah, yeah,' he called back with a dismissive swipe of his hand. He then flashed me a conspiratorial wink. 'Did Pooh fuckin' Bear know where the honey pot was stashed?' he muttered out of the corner of his mouth.

I'd wondered all along why he had suggested this uncharacteristic form of exercise slap-bang in the middle of the time he made his habitual Sabbath pilgrimage to the pub. The reason was now beginning to dawn on me, and, sure enough, a few minutes later we emerged from the woods and found ourselves on the outskirts of Gifford, the village in which The Fermer's 'local' was located.

'I've booked us a table at the Goblin,' he told me with a smug grin. 'You see, it was actually the wife who suggested that we should all go for a *nice* walk today, so I had to do a bit of fast thinking – know what I mean?' He checked his watch. 'Yeah, and my timing was just about spot-on as well. They should start serving high tea not long after we get there, so that'll keep the women happy.'

The 'Goblin' he referred to was the local abbreviation of 'Goblin Ha'' (or Hall), one of two historic Gifford inns – the other being the Tweeddale Arms – that are the focal points of socialising for the surrounding rural area. Moreover, on beautiful weekend days like this, people would drive from far and wide through East Lothian's sylvan hillfoots to savour Gifford's visual charms and to refresh and refuel themselves at one of these two old hostelries. The village, unarguably one of the prettiest in the county, takes its name from Hugo de Gifford, the first laird of the surrounding lands and, according to legend, a powerful wizard. In 1250, with the aid of a troop of attendant hobgoblins, he built a castle with a subterranean vault (the actual Goblin Ha'), set deep in the woods outside the present-day village. The ruins of that castle are still there, though little evidence remains of the amazing craftsmanship that its goblin builders are said to have lavished on their 'Ha''.

The Goblin Ha' Hotel is located on the corner of the old market square at the bottom of Gifford's main street. At the top of the village, and looking down the entire length of that same street, stands a little whitewashed church, so timelessly pretty that it has been featured as a backdrop in several period films over the years. But Gifford's scenic attributes aren't confined to its main street, attractive though it is with so many of its shop fronts and houses echoing the pristine white of the church. Just opposite the market square is the start of 'The Avenue', a wide colonnade of majestic lime trees leading to the gates of Yester House. This magnificent mansion was built three centuries ago and sits in formal gardens surrounded by manicured woodland not far from the ruins of Goblin Ha' Castle. It replaced a series of ever larger and grander dwellings that existed on the same site over the ages. Until comparatively recently, when it was bought by the world-famous classical composer Gian-Carlo Menotti, Yester House was the seat of Hugo de Gifford's eventual successors, a long line of the Marquises of Tweeddale.

The Tweeddale family's warmly remembered connection with the village is preserved in the name of the Tweeddale Arms Hotel. This chintzy old inn, complete with its stepped 'louping-on' stone, conveniently placed opposite the entrance to assist ladies of olden days to access their horse-drawn carriages, overlooks The Avenue, which, in turn, is flanked by the village's former bleaching field. A reminder of the days when cloth mills were dotted along the leafy banks of the adjacent Gifford Burn, this broad meadow is now a public recreation park, and it would be difficult to find a more idyllic location for one anywhere.

It was a bit too chilly to stand about admiring the enchanting scenery of Gifford today, however, so The Fermer, not surprisingly, strode purposefully towards his habitual Sunday haunt, the Goblin Ha' Hotel.

'Where do you think *you're* going?' an irked Rona called after him. 'Come on – you *prom*ised you wouldn't go to the pub today!'

Although, like her husband, Rona was a fun-loving soul, she was, unlike him, essentially a quiet, retiring person who was happier spending a Sunday afternoon at home with her children than accompanying him to the pub for a cobweb-clearing session with his pals. But scold The Fermer as she might about his weekend carousing, he only had to turn on his boyish charm and her objections would usually dissolve into nothing more threatening than a cascade of giggles. He didn't even have to resort to that well-tried ploy on this occasion, though. As he had anticipated, his deviously planned trek through the woods was forgiven the moment he mentioned that he'd booked us all in for high tea.

Max Muir, the kilted owner of the Goblin Ha', was the epitome of a jovial, welcoming, village inn landlord. His greeting when we trooped into his lounge bar was as warm as the log fire blazing away at the far end of the room. Although, more recently, this part of the Goblin Ha' Hotel has undergone extensive refurbishment, at that time it still retained most of the cosy, olde-worlde qualities much cherished by its faithful regulars.

Max, never failing to assume the duties of the courteous mine host, was quick to ensure that the ladies and kids were seated comfortably round the fire before he personally brought them their chosen refreshments. The Fermer and I, in the meantime, had seated ourselves comfortably at the bar.

'The usual freshly squeezed orange juice for you?' Max laughed as he dispensed The Fermer a double whisky from one of a long row of optics on the gantry.

'Aye, that's right,' The Fermer replied, then made a sideways jerk of his head in my direction. 'And make sure you give

Don Pedro here the best in the house. As you know, he's a big expert on oranges these days, so better make his juice of the single malt variety.'

And so began what was always guaranteed to be a thoroughly enjoyable interlude in the company of Max and a collection of The Fermer's cronies, who arrived in a fairly steady stream, all looking ruddy-faced from the combined effects of the frosty air and the previous night's liquor intake. I knew most of them of old, and it really was great to be surrounded by a bunch of good-humoured lads who spoke the same language as I did and were interested in talking about the same things as well. I never realised until then how much I'd missed this simple pleasure while away. Scotland and 'home' were seducing me with yet another of their easily-taken-for-granted charms. And there was another waiting in the wings – or, rather, in the Goblin Ha's snug little dining room.

'High tea' is a singularly British institution, an eating-out tradition evocative of a more decorous era that had all but disappeared, except in establishments like the Goblin Ha', where such social niceties were lovingly upheld. Why it was dubbed 'high' is unclear. It's an adjective that, in this context, has a slightly snobbish ring to it. Yet high tea used to be available in many a humble chip shop with only a few simple tables and chairs, as well as in starchy 'Palm Court' tea rooms with string quartets scraping out medleys of Viennese waltzes for their well-heeled clientele. Perhaps the lofty-sounding prefix was just to differentiate between 'tea' – the basic, one-course, early-evening meal that was, and still is, the equivalent of 'dinner' in many British households – and the fancier fare on offer when the 'high' tag was attached.

For, in its universally accepted form, high tea consists of that same unpretentious cooked course, but followed by a selection of dainties, and always accompanied by pots of tea, to be drunk – in the more exclusive places at any rate – from fine china cups.

As might be expected of such a quintessentially Scottish tradition, the most popular main dish on the high tea menu, no matter how swanky the establishment, was good old fish and chips. The Goblin Ha's version consisted of Scotland's favourite white fish, the incomparable haddock, golden-fried in breadcrumbs, with a selection of boiled vegetables to accompany the mandatory chips. Then, of course, there were wedges of lemon, matching glass shakers of salt and malt vinegar, little bowls of tomato ketchup and brown 'nippy' sauce, with plenty of buttered, sliced bread on the side. If there's a better recipe than this for keeping adults and children equally happy at the table, then I've yet to see it – given that the vegetables are normally discarded by the younger fry in order to leave room for the treats to follow.

And this is where any modern notion of 'healthy options' goes the same way as the kids' vegetables. We were now about to scale the dizzy heights (at least as far as cholesterol levels are concerned) of the time-honoured high tea ritual.

As soon as the debris of the fish and chips course was cleared from the table, it was replaced with cake racks tiered with plates of oven-warm scones, all begging to be spread with layers of butter, whipped cream and strawberry jam. Then more cake racks appeared. These contained a selection of such mouth-watering delights as chocolate éclairs, iced biscuits (each with a glazed cherry on top), cream-filled fairy cakes, slices of marzipan-coated Battenburg, custard tarts, cream doughnuts, shortbread petticoat tails, and 'flies' cemeteries', which is the appetising Scottish name for a slab of compressed currants wedged between two 'tombstones' of sugared pastry.

The Fermer inclined his head towards mine and muttered, 'I dare say that, like me, you haven't got much of a sweet tooth, eh?'

I gave the scones and cakes a disapproving glance. 'Nah, never touch 'em,' I assured him.

That was all the encouragement he needed. Standing up, he excused us in the politest of ways to Rona and Ellie, and explained that, while they and the kids enjoyed the rest of their high tea, he and I would, with their permission, repair to the public bar to discuss a bit of important business with a certain (non-existent but aptly-named) Angus MacFlannel.

Under normal circumstances, such a blatantly implausible excuse would have been rejected without ceremony by our spouses. But The Fermer, when plotting this outing, had been shrewd enough to anticipate that giving them the opportunity to scoff our share of the high tea's 'main attractions' would be more than enough to make them turn a blind eye to this great escape. His version of my father's 'game of darts' ruse worked, and we were to spend the next half hour or so chewing the fat with the lads in what was, by then, the rumbustious atmosphere of the bar. Saturday night's cobwebs, under Max Muir's skilful direction, had already been washed cleanly away.

Meanwhile, our wives and children were content to do their own sweet-toothed thing in the more sedate environment of the dining room, with nobody more obstreperous around than a pair of blue-rinsed ladies swapping hushed appraisals of proceedings at a nearby doily-decked table.

When I say the wives and *children*, I do Charlie an injustice, however.

'Just told Mum I was going for a hose,' he announced, appearing all-smiles by my side at the bar. 'Yeah, the cups-of-tea thing isn't really my scene either, *padre*,' he added with an us-guys-are-all-in-this-together shrug.

Here, I immediately thought, was an obvious hangover from his time living in Mallorca, where minors are not regarded as *personae no gratae* in licensed premises. It's part and parcel of the way of life in Spain, and the value of it is manifested in the civilised attitude that its young people have towards alcohol as they grow up. We had always followed the Spanish principle in that regard, and we could only hope that our two boys would benefit from it. Time, as ever, would tell, however. In any case, Charlie was a young social animal who liked nothing better than to be 'in the body o' the kirk' when people were gathered together for the sake of having a good time. So he had been drawn from the staid politesse of the dining room to the raucous hubbub of the bar in the way that a marooned sailor swims towards a passing sail.

Never one to miss a trick, the ever-smiling Max leaned over the bar and murmured to him, 'Coke on the rocks for the young *señorito* as before, I take it?' He then handed Charlie a glass of his preferred refreshment, declaring aloud that, 'This one's on the house, m'boy!'

'Aye, and never fear, son,' a wag called out from a bit farther along the crowded bar, 'he'll charge ye for it wi' interest as soon as ye're old enough tae buy yer first round!'

Charlie joined in the ensuing laughter and clearly felt delighted to be included as one of the boys in the ongoing banter. Again, his time spent with a few of Mallorca's 'filthy rich' expat families had honed his natural ability to mix in all sorts of company ('all sorts' being the operative words in relation to some of the members of that colourful clique of Brit exiles!), and he was obviously in his element here, back on home soil with the Gifford worthies – down-to-earth country chaps all.

It pleased me to see it, and to hear that his adopted mid-Atlantic accent of the past few years was rapidly morphing back into his native brogue as he exchanged wisecracks with the stalwarts of the Goblin Ha's public bar.

★ ★ ★ ★ ★

We returned to Bolton by taxi, The Fermer having sensibly deemed it 'fuckin' daft' to even think about traipsing all the way back through the woods on foot. No matter how self-interested his motives for engineering what had turned out to be a thoroughly pleasant family afternoon, The Fermer had opened my eyes to a few of East Lothian's untrumpeted attributes, both natural and human, the true value of which the recent allure of Mallorca had been in danger of making me forget.

As we walked down the path to the cottage, the smell of smoke from pinewood logs hung in the still evening air, while away to the west, a delicate fretwork of treetops was etched against the glow of the setting sun. In that twilight sky, flocks of cawing rooks were whirling and tumbling like scraps of burnt paper above Clacherdean Wood, where they would soon settle down to roost until dawn.

Despite myself, I couldn't stop my thoughts drifting back to Mallorca again – to Maria and Pep and, of course, to our fellow son of East Lothian, Jock Burns. I wondered what our two old neighbours in the valley would have thought of the scene we were part of now. I was sure they would have loved it, and I knew that Jock certainly did.

– SIX –

THE GYPSY IN MY SOUL

The first thing Ellie did after the transfer of our funds from Mallorca to Scotland had been completed was to take me to a little jeweller's shop called Ness's in the west end of Edinburgh. Her mission was to purchase the reward she had promised herself for all the hard work she'd done in adding value to our Mallorcan *finca*. I had no problem with that. As I'd told her many times, she thoroughly deserved the emerald ring she had set her heart on. She was worth it.

'*That* one?' I gasped when she pointed out the reward of her choice in Ness's window. 'You have *got* to be bloody joking! Tell me you're only pulling my leg, *please!*'

Ellie merely smiled demurely at me, batted her eyelashes and shook her head.

'But – but,' I spluttered, 'just look at the price! I – I mean, hell's bells, woman, that's nearly as much as I got for the tractor *and* all the farm implements when we sold up back in Mallorca!'

'Oh,' she coyly returned, 'so you think I'm worth less than that old plough and stuff now, do you?'

'Well, yes – I mean, no – that is, well, I just didn't think that, you know, it would cost –'

Ellie put her forefinger to my lips. 'Just think of it as an investment, dear.'

'An in*vest*ment? How the blazes do you make that out?'

'Emeralds are for ever.'

'I don't get it. And anyway, I think you'll find that should be *diamonds* are forever.'

'Same difference,' she shrugged. 'In any case, there are a few diamonds set between the emeralds in that ring as well. That's why I like it.' Her eyes sparkling like gems themselves now, she took another admiring look at the ring through the window, nodded her head and purred, 'Hmm-mm-mm, nice.'

'Sorry, Ellie, but as much as I appreciate all the hard work you did at Ca's Mayoral –'

'*And*,' Ellie cut in, 'at Cuddy Neuk, in those grubby flats and bedsits in London, in the run-down cottage we rented when we came back from there, and that's not to mention –'

I held up a silencing hand. 'OK, OK, you don't have to rub it in. I remember all the details. But, while I'll be eternally grateful for everything you mucked in with in the past, we have to act responsibly here. We've got to safeguard our capital for starting that deer farm. So, much as I regret having to put my foot down, I'm afraid we simply can*not* afford to splash out on a ring as expensive as that one. And that's final!'

'You've got to admit it's a real stunner,' Ellie grinned as she flashed me the glittering, diamond-studded emerald ring, now firmly installed on her finger. 'Hmm-mm-mm, *very* nice indeed!'

We were sitting at a table in the Bar Roma, one of Edinburgh's most popular Italian eateries, which is tucked away just round the corner from Ness the jeweller's in Queensferry Street. Ellie had shepherded me in there in the hope that 'treating' me to lunch would help me recover from the state of shock I was now in.

'Ah, *si, signora*! Very nice-a ring indeed,' grinned Bruno our waiter, crooking a thumb in my direction. 'You a very lucky woman to 'ave-a thees *milionario* for a 'usband, *si*?' He gave me one of those typical Italian winks that are both innocent and suggestive. 'And a nice-a geeft you been make for the bee-*oo*-ti-ful-a lydee, *signor. Si, si*, she gonna be *molto* thank you very much please for-a you tonight, no?'

I forced a smile.

'*Allora*,' he breezed, then flipped open his order pad, 'let-a me guess, eh! OK, so is gonna be nice beeg-a fillet steak for *la signora* and a glass of the tap water for *il milionario*, correct?'

'If I was paying, it would be two glasses of water,' I replied, 'but as *la signora*'s on the bell, I'll throw financial caution to the wind and have a pizza margarita, please.'

'Yes, Bruno,' Ellie smiled, 'and don't spare the basil.' She gave my hand a cursory pat. 'He's worth it.'

My ordering the cheapest pizza on the menu reflected my awareness that the cost of Ellie's so-called treat would be debited to our joint bank account anyway, so financial prudence was still my priority. However, to Ellie's credit, once the skylarking with the waiter was over, she did temper her spending frenzy by rejecting his suggestion of a fillet steak and ordering a modest spaghetti carbonara instead.

Ellie knew that, as ever, my reaction to her buying something that I thought overly extravagant was being exaggerated in the hope (usually forlorn) of making her feel guilty about the damage done to my wallet. What she didn't know, though, was just how little exaggeration was involved on this occasion. But, then, as she'd been quick to point out, I knew nothing about the value of the finer things in life, like, for example, her *nice* new ring. Also, in fairness to her, she'd had all of her original jewellery stolen when the house at Ca's Mayoral was broken into a couple of years earlier, and, as the insurance company had coughed up for its value, the money for this one replacement item wasn't really coming out of my pocket anyway. As soon as she reminded me of that, I felt a whole lot better.

'Hey, Bruno,' I called after the waiter, 'make that two fillet steaks instead, please. One medium rare, the other blue.'

'Blue, *signor*?'

'Yeah, the missus likes it *really* rare.'

'*Va bene*!' Bruno acknowledged. 'I tell the chef just-a leave the hoofs on.'

Ellie looked at me with an eyebrow raised. 'What's got into you? You hardly ever order anything as pricey as fillet steak when we're eating out.'

'Yeah, well, it's just the thought that the Commercial Union are actually paying for this in a round-about sort of way. I kid you not, after all the trouble I had getting the money out of them after the house-breaking, I'd order a whole roast swan if it was on the menu.'

Ellie shook her head. 'I suppose there must be some kind of logic in there somewhere, but it escapes me. To be honest, I'd sooner we had a pizza and a pasta instead of the steaks, and then I could put the difference in price towards saving up for another ring.'

'Uh-huh, and to quote your good self, there must be some kind of logic in *there* somewhere as well, but it escapes *me*! So, we'd better just agree to differ and sit back and enjoy lunch.'

There had been more to Ellie's reason for ushering me into the Bar Roma than just its proximity to Ness the jeweller's, however. We had been there on several occasions before going to Mallorca, and we liked its free-and-easy atmosphere, which attracted a wonderfully eclectic clientele. Kids' birthday parties and office girls' hen nights comprised just as much of the Bar Roma's trade as did businessmen's lunches and romantic dinners for two. Now, however, like the Goblin Ha', it had undergone extensive refurbishment and had even expanded into the premises next door. Here was a restaurant that had been growing in popularity for years, and Mario Cugini, the astute and affable owner, knew that it wasn't good business to be turning customers away because demand exceeded available space. Although it now had more of a 'swish' ambience than before, one distinguishing feature of the original little restaurant had been retained. It was a huge mural depicting an olden-days Italian piazza, in which a show-a-leg lady in a crinoline dress was alighting from a gilded coach, while all around so many characters were going about their various daily routines that you could sit staring at the scene for ages and still keep noticing little details that you'd missed before.

Such aesthetic considerations aside, however, it was the good-natured exuberance of the waiters that had always been a hallmark of the place, and, as Ellie had correctly anticipated, Bruno and his colleagues would provide just the atmosphere needed to cheer me up today. Italian waiters, given the right audience, can be a great source of entertainment. They are vociferous, exhibitionist and even occasionally swaggering, but invariably full of the joys – outwardly at least. In the Bar Roma, I liked their noisy exchanges of patter, all laid on for the benefit of whoever was listening, particularly if it happened to be a table occupied by some of those unattached office girls. Anyway, there's something about the Italian waiter's approach to his job that is refreshingly sunny and enthusiastic, and I always feel better for being in their company. Which, as already mentioned, was why Ellie had steered me into the Bar Roma today.

It wasn't just a matter of chasing away my emerald-and-diamond-ring blues either. The weeks had been slipping away with what seemed like ever-increasing speed since we returned from Mallorca, and, much as we were enjoying life in the rented cottage at Bolton, we were feeling increasingly frustrated by our lack of success in finding a suitable property for our planned deer farm. We were running into the same kind of brick walls as we had during the previous year of searching for more land in Mallorca. The difference now, of course, was that we didn't have a crop of oranges to sell while we searched. Something would have to be done about generating income – and soon.

The advice that my father had passed on to me from his estate agent contact had proved to be depressingly accurate. Suitably-sized blocks of land with an existing house were now priced well beyond what we could afford to pay. I eventually came to the conclusion that there was only one way round this problem. It was common knowledge that it was cheaper to build than buy, so we would just have to buy an empty field and build a house on it. But even that simple solution had hidden problems. Firstly, all the approaches I'd made to farmers so far had met with a negative response. They may have been farming areas of land dozens or even hundreds of times bigger than the *campesinos* did back in Mallorca, but the same set of circumstances applied. Profit margins were getting slimmer, with the result that they would rather buy more land to compensate than sell even a square metre of what they already had. Secondly, I'd been told by the planning authorities that even if I could find an empty field that fitted our deer-farming bill, getting permission to erect a house and associated farm buildings on it would be fraught with difficulties. The regulations were weighed heavily against sanctioning such 'developments' in rural areas, and it was made very clear to me that no straightforward way of circumventing them existed.

Our future depended on being able to do just that, however, and my view was that I hadn't dragged the family through all the trials and tribulations of the past few years just to be defeated now by what I saw as unreasonably restrictive red tape. Indeed, the obstacles that officialdom had presented me with only made me all the more determined to achieve what I'd set out to do. Nevertheless, I did realise that we'd have a real struggle on our hands to surmount the two major hurdles we were now faced with. What's more, there was the worry about how to earn a living in the interim. The combined dilemmas had been preoccupying me more and more recently. Ellie, perceptive as ever, had noticed, and that's why I now found myself sitting opposite her within the cheery, positive atmosphere of the Bar Roma.

'No point in getting your knickers in a twist about it all,' she chirped as soon as she saw the tension fade from my face on taking a relaxing slurp of wine.

I gave her what I hoped would pass as a reassuring smile. 'Knickers in a twist? Me? Nah, it's just a matter of getting to grips with everything. Yeah, you'll see – it'll all work out fine, never fear.'

'That's what the ostrich said before it got a hippo's horn rammed up its backside.'

'Excuse me,' I objected with as much umbrage as I could feign, 'but if you're suggesting that I'm burying my head in the sand, you're very much mistaken, my dear.'

'OK, so what are we going to do for an earner while you get to grips with everything? It could take you years.'

I did my best to appear nonchalant. 'Oh ye of little faith,' I droned ecclesiastically. '*And*, by the way, I think you'll find it was a rhino that goosed the ostrich.' I tapped the end of my nose. 'I've yet to see a horn on a hippo.'

Ellie couldn't have cared less about that. 'Yeah, yeah, hippos, rhinos – same difference. The important thing is that we can't keep taking money out of the bank without paying anything in. We've got to stop the rot, and I think I know how we can do it.'

I resisted the temptation to remind her that she had just made the biggest non-essential hole in our bank account that I could remember. Instead, I casually asked her how she had managed to work out how to 'stop the rot', as she put it.

She poured me another glass of wine. 'Just call it the gypsy in my soul,' she said with a toss of her hair and a flick of a jewel-spangled hand.

'You're not suggesting we buy a horse-drawn caravan and go about flogging clothes pegs, are you?'

'Don't discount the possibility, but there *are* other, less romantic ways we can try first. However,' she swiftly added, 'finding somewhere to live without forking out rent *does* have to be our number one priority right now.'

Echoes of my father's quip about our eventually having to pitch a tent in his back garden came to mind. But we hadn't reached that stage yet – not by a long chalk. All the same, I knew what Ellie was getting at. I'd been giving a lot of thought myself to the detrimental effect on our finances that continuing to rent a home would have. There was one obvious solution to the problem, but I had been wary of suggesting it to Ellie for fear that she'd balk at being cajoled into setting out on yet another roller-coaster ride. The arrival of two juicy fillet steaks in the uplifting atmosphere of the Bar Roma went some way to allaying my misgivings, however.

'Are, ehm – are you thinking what I'm thinking, Ellie?' I hesitantly enquired.

'Certainly am,' she drooled, ogling her plate. 'Yes, I'm glad you talked me out of having the spaghetti.'

'Yes, I know – but, well, what I really meant was – I mean, what I'm actually trying to find out is what you'd think of, uhm…'

'Buying an old house?' she prompted without taking her eyes off her steak.

I was flabbergasted. Maybe there was a touch of the gypsy about Ellie right enough. Second sight or something. 'Well, yes, sort of,' I faltered. 'It's just a thought I had, but I didn't want –'

'To risk asking me if I'd fancy helping you do up an old house, then sell it in the hope of making a few quid to cover living expenses while you try to find a way through all the problems of setting up a deer farm?'

There was only one way of answering a question put in such direct terms. 'Yes,' I said, then held my breath while I waited for the almost certain knock-back that, all things considered, I felt would have been perfectly justified.

Ellie allowed my apprehension to build while she slowly sliced her knife through the perfect pinkness of the oval of meat on her plate. Just before she finally popped the first succulent chunk into her mouth, she looked up, gave me a what's-your-problem? smile, then said casually, 'I've already found just the place. Nice old town house in Haddington. Needs a fair bit done to it. Loads of character, though. Bags of potential as well.'

'You – you mean you wouldn't mind rolling up your sleeves again to –'

'As I've said more than once before, why change the habit of a lifetime? Matter of fact, I looked over the house yesterday, *and* the owner has agreed a really good price for a quick sale. I just didn't want to tell you until you were in a less gloomy mood than you've been in recently. Thought you might feel I was asking you to take your eye off the ball, so to speak. You know – distracting your attention from your deer farm plans and all that stuff.'

I felt a weight lift from my shoulders. We'd both been thinking the same way all along, except that Ellie hadn't let the grass grow under her feet while she waited for the right moment to broach the subject.

'And that isn't the only house I've had a look at recently,' she piped up before I had a chance to fully take in what she'd just told me. 'But it's by far the best bet of the lot. Should fetch us a tidy profit once it's all done up.'

I was still reeling a bit from this sudden bolt out of the blue, but I trusted enough in Ellie's judgement *and* her eye for a bargain to accept what she was telling me. There was just one little point, however…

'But if the old house needs a lot done to it,' I said, 'that'll mean we'll have to keep renting The Fermer's cottage while all the dirty work is being done, right?'

'Wrong!' Ellie speared another chunk of fillet steak with her fork. 'We'll be doing most of the dirty work ourselves, so we may as well live amongst it as well. You know, sort of camp in one room after another until it's all done.' She left her forkful of steak suspended in mid-air while she looked me in the eye and asked, 'Why pay rent when we can live in our own house for free?'

As that cynical friend of ours had opined all those years ago, this wife of mine either deserved a medal or a certificate of insanity. But who was I to question which? If she was up for undertaking a big house-renovation challenge like this, then I'd be right in there hammering, sawing, scraping and painting alongside her. What she deserved now, in addition to that expensive emerald ring and the juicy fillet steak, was a word of encouragement.

'Ellie,' I said, 'I really do appreciate the fact that you're prepared to rough it just one more time.'

'Just *one* more time?'

I was slightly taken aback. 'Well… yes. I mean, *surely* I'll have all the deer farm stuff lined up and ready to roll in the time it takes us to do up this old house you've found.'

Ellie almost choked on her steak. 'Take my word for it, sweet dreamer – there could well be more than one old house to do up before *that* happens.'

I had a gut feeling that she probably wasn't far wrong. 'And you won't mind the upheavals?' I asked.

She shook her head emphatically. 'Nope. In fact, I can't wait to get upheaving. Yes,' she breezed, 'it'll be great fun, and roughing it in a house for a while has got to be a lot better than roaming the countryside in that gypsy caravan you were on about.'

'Yeah, well, I'm sure we'll never have to resort to that,' I chuckled, crossing my fingers under the table.

Ellie shot me one of her old-fashioned looks. 'Maybe so, but forgive me if I look out my hoop earrings and crystal ball just in case.'

★ ★ ★ ★ ★

A week later, the prospect of being reduced to heading off into the wide blue yonder in that gypsy caravan was becoming more attractive by the second. The elderly man from whom we'd agreed to buy the old house hadn't been able to bring himself to live in it since the death of his wife a couple of years earlier. It had been a happy home during their long lifetime together, but now all he wanted was to see it in the hands of people who, as he said, 'would be good to it'. So, having taken a shine to Ellie and her enthusiasm for the place, he'd been trusting enough to give us the keys even before legal formalities were properly concluded. For our part, we had been sufficiently trusting in his assurance that the house was in sound condition to have agreed to buy it without having a survey or valuation done. Besides, going through all that rigmarole would only have delayed closing the deal, thus giving the old chap time to have second thoughts about the price he had agreed for a quick sale. Adopting the maxim of letting our own eyes be our merchant had done us no harm when we'd bought the Mallorcan property after all, so why pay someone else to do the job here?

'I'll start stripping the wallpaper upstairs first,' Ellie said, standing next to me inside the front door, surrounded by a clutter of boxes, cases and the bare essentials needed to help us sustain ourselves during the forthcoming weeks. 'No point in redecorating downstairs until we get all the rising damp and messy stuff like that sorted.' Her hands were on her hips, her eyes were everywhere, and she had the air of a general preparing to deploy the troops. In this case, however, the size of the army amounted to just one. 'Right,' she said without even looking at me, 'you could start ripping out that terrible fireplace in the upstairs living room. Best to replace that before we even *think* about papering and painting in there.'

We'd sold the biggest of our household effects with the house in Mallorca, and The Fermer had kindly stored most of the rest of our goods and chattels for us in a redundant poultry house. So the only items of furniture we now had were two newly-delivered beds, an ironing board and a folding table and four chairs. Those, together with a couple of clothes racks that Ellie had borrowed from a friend who owned a local dress shop, would be all the home comforts we'd have until the redecoration of each upstairs room was complete. Fortunately, the previous owner had left a cooker, fridge and washing machine in the kitchen, and although they'd seen better days, they would serve our immediate purposes just fine. Ellie and I, meanwhile, would have to resign ourselves to living out of suitcases in the main bedroom, while Charlie would spend his nights dossed down in the attic. It would be putting it mildly to say that, compared to being able to stop over at the palatial homes of his millionaire friends in Mallorca whenever the fancy took him, he was now about to hit the opposite end of the lifestyle spectrum with a thump.

Yes, it was even going to be a far cry from the relative luxury we had all enjoyed latterly in the Ca's Mayoral farmhouse, especially with those added 'leisure facilities' of swimming pool, games room, snooker table, bar, and rustic barbecue area on the edge of a lantern-lit almond grove. I was also coming face-to-face with a way of *trying* to earn a coin that I'd never have dreamed of in my younger life as a professional jazz musician, whether playing in the cramped steaminess of

Liverpool's Cavern Club, in the stately grandeur of London's Royal Albert Hall, or rubbing unlikely shoulders with famous stars of the day in TV, film and recording studios. Anyway, there was much work of a different kind to be tackled in the here and now, and neither dwelling in the past nor toying with the idea of becoming an itinerant Romany with a basketful of clothes pegs would alter the fact.

'Old Weston', as our new home was called, did exude a pleasant and welcoming feeling, despite its obvious need for some tender loving care. Like Ellie, I'm a believer in the adage that a house either has a good 'feel' to it or not, and I understood the moment I walked through the door why she had been so keen on this one. Interestingly, I'd often admired the simple elegance of its exterior in passing. Built in the unfussy Scottish style of the mid-eighteenth century, Old Weston boasted no embellishment on its two-storey façade, other than a little, triangular portico above the front door. Yet it had an understated charm that was in no way eclipsed by any of the many grander buildings nearby.

Court Street is a wide, tree-fringed avenue extending out from the apex of the medieval triangle of streets that still comprises the town centre. It provides an impressive entrance to Haddington when approached from the direction of Edinburgh, seventeen miles to the west. As its name suggests, this street was once the location of a palace, the residence of two of Scotland's early kings; William the Lyon and his son Alexander II, who was born there in 1198. On the same site, and just a stone's throw from Old Weston, there now stands the ever-expanding seat of East Lothian's local government, the County Buildings. The original part was built in 1833 with a nod of deference in the direction of the Tudor style of architecture. This is something of a paradox when you consider how the most ruthless member of the Tudor dynasty, King Henry VIII of England, had attempted to raze to the ground every building in this part of Scotland during his abortive 'rough wooing', as it came to be called, of the young Mary Queen of Scots. But that's typical of the blood-stained relationships that existed between Scottish and English monarchs over the centuries, and it also hints at the troubled past of this much fought over old town, strategically placed as it is at the heart of the fertile 'Garden of Scotland' and only forty miles north of the border with the 'Auld Enemy'.

Directly across from the County Buildings and set back from the street in its own grounds is the Bank of Scotland, regarded as the finest of several of the town's Georgian 'mansions' that were once the private dwellings of well-to-do local families, but have long since been turned over to commercial use. Dominating the centre of Haddington is the tall steeple of the Adam-designed Town Hall, which commands an uninterrupted view along the entire length of Court Street, with its divergence of architecture ranging from the simple 'vernacular' of Old Weston through the dignified Georgian of the former 'mansions' to the classic Victorian of the Corn Exchange. In no small part because of this unlikely juxtaposition of building designs, Haddington's Court Street is as pleasing an avenue as you're likely to see in any Scottish country town.

Although I had spent all of my school days in Haddington, I had never actually lived *in* the town until now, and it took a bit of getting used to. Instead of the clarion call of old Maria's little Mallorcan cockerel to awaken us in the morning, there was now the 4.30 a.m. coming and going of a stream of vans and trucks at the post office just across the street from our bedroom window. And even if you could eventually rediscover sleep by the time they had all dispersed to deliver their cargoes of mail, the bells in the Town Hall would clang out their reveille at seven o'clock to ensure that *all* the townsfolk, except the hard of hearing, were finally up and about.

However, at the end of a busy and noisy day of commercial activity, Court Street would become almost completely deserted after the last of the army of council-employed office workers made their way home. For Old Weston was one of only a handful of properties still in domestic use in that part of town. There are three pubs in Court Street, though – two at one end and one at the other – and the exodus of revellers from those provided a lively show, particularly at weekends when late-night drinking is the norm. Many a midnight hour we'd spend at an upstairs window watching bonhomie-loaded groups of young folk setting off for home as the night's disco or karaoke activities drew to a close. There was invariably a look of confidence about their gait, until they'd ambled about a hundred yards from the pub door, that's to say. Then, as the intake of fresh air reacted with the surfeit of alcohol in their systems, legs would buckle, senses of balance would evaporate, and the august wall of the Bank of Scotland's front garden would be used as either an object to ricochet off or to disappear over in an ungainly flailing of arms and legs.

Occasionally, a fight would break out, most often between a couple of girls, one of whom had probably taken delayed-reaction displeasure to the other's dance-floor eyeing-up of her boyfriend, or maybe she had just decided that she didn't like her chum's karaoke performance of Abba's greatest hits after all. But these scuffles usually amounted to no more than a flurry of swear words and a posturing of handbags before all was forgiven and the two maidens continued arm-in-arm homeward on wobbly stilettos, perchance to pause en route for a chummy puke in a shop doorway or two. On nights like this, it was easy to imagine that Court Street may well have known courtlier times.

Flashbacks entered my mind of the socially polite *paseo* strolls that we'd watched young Spanish folk habitually take of an evening. But shows of high spirits like those seen from our window overlooking Haddington's Court Street occur in town centres all over Britain on weekend nights now, and we realised that such late-night shenanigans, together with early-morning post office noises and the chiming of the Town Hall clock, amounted to a minor price to pay for living in such a lovely old town house. That said, we had to accept that it would be quite some time before we'd be able to complete all the work necessary to allow us fully to enjoy its many charms. What's more, as can so easily happen when you buy an old property without having a full structural survey done, it soon became apparent that we were going to be faced with a few essential improvement tasks that we hadn't foreseen, and some of those would be well beyond our own DIY capabilities. So, there was nothing else for it – although it would involve financial outlays that hadn't been bargained for, we'd have to call in the experts.

★ ★ ★ ★ ★

Pixie and Dixie, as they were affectionately known to their fellow tradesmen in the area, were two builders whom I'd known to be friends since childhood. Now in their early forties, they not only spent their working days together, but also enjoyed each other's company while indulging their weekend hobbies of fishing and shooting. They were honest country lads, who took a pride in their work, gave value for money and somehow managed to keep an almost endless stream of wisecracks going throughout their working day. In addition to being a cheery pair to have around the place, they were also well connected with other local tradesmen who could be trusted to do as good a job as they did themselves. Indeed, Pixie and Dixie were just the fellows we needed to keep us on the right lines while getting the renovation of Old Weston under way.

'All o' them downstairs floors has got tae be lifted and replaced,' was Pixie's blunt announcement after appraising the general state of the building.

'Wet rot in the timber,' was Dixie's explanation.

'Ye're just lucky it hasnae spread upstairs,' was Pixie's reaction to seeing my jaw drop.

'But the nice old flagstones in the front hallway – there can't be any kind of rot in *them*,' Ellie objected hopefully.

'Nah, but they're part o' yer problem wi' the risin' damp,' Dixie countered. 'See, they'll just be sittin' on clay – actin' like a sponge for the wet underneath them, like. Oh aye, always the same in old hooses like this.'

Pixie shook his head and concurred sagely, 'Oh aye – just like a sponge, like.'

'Could've telt ye that afore ye bought the place,' Dixie advised po-faced. 'Hope ye didnae go an' pay that old codger too much for it, like.'

The same hope rose to immediate prominence in our own thoughts, only to be ratcheted up even farther by Pixie and Dixie then informing us that the stonework of the house's two large chimney stacks required urgent pointing. In their present state, they were a danger to the public, and they knew that for a fact because they had seen the crumbling masonry for themselves when working on the roof of a neighbouring house.

'Oh aye,' Dixie advised again, 'could've telt ye that afore ye bought the place, like.'

In a few short moments, any hopes we'd had of being able to make a profit out of doing up this old property by mainly cosmetic means had been shattered. Fairly serious amounts of money would now have to be spent on putting right defects that, as Pixie and Dixie rightly cautioned, would be essential if we were ever to sell the house to someone requiring a mortgage – which meant just about every potential buyer. No lender would part with money on the basis of a structural survey of the house as it stood, so we had absolutely no choice.

Ellie took a deep breath, held it for a second, then blurted out, 'Right, tell us the worst. What, in layman's terms, is all this extra work going to entail?'

Pixie didn't beat about the bush. 'For a start,' he said, 'ye can forget about tryin' tae cure the risin' damp wi' any o' that so-called damp-stoppin' paint ye slap on the walls. Nah, nah, that'll never work in thick, old, stone walls like them. Would just be like tryin' tae put out a volcano by peein' intae it, like.'

Aye, that would be right enough, Dixie agreed, before going on to explain that all the internal ground floor walls would need to have their plaster removed up to a height of a metre. This was to clear the way for holes being bored into the masonry at regular intervals. Into these, silicone would be injected under pressure, so that a permanent damp-proof barrier would be created from foundation level up. This job would have to be done by specialist contractors, Dixie pointed out.

While Ellie and I listened glassy-eyed and slack-jawed, Pixie then went on to inform us that, while all the work to the walls was being done, the flagstones in the hallway and the floorboards in the downstairs rooms would be lifted, all rotted timber joists would be removed and, where necessary, the clay sub-floor would be excavated to a depth sufficient for the spreading of a thick layer of tar throughout.

'Another weapon tae defeat the risin' damp, like,' he casually added. 'Aye, and ye'll get certificates tae prove a' this work has been done tae the required specifications, of course.'

'Of course,' my mouth muttered of its own volition, the words sounding to my stunned ears as if they'd been said by someone else.

'The certificates is for the benefit o' the money lenders when somebody comes tae buy the place off ye in future, ye see,' Dixie elucidated brightly.

'Of course,' my mouth said again.

Then there was the matter of the chimneys, Pixie continued.

I prepared my ears for another verbal bashing.

'Scaffolding,' Pixie said, delivering the word like a left hook to the head.

'Scaffolding?' Ellie queried.

'Aye, tae access the chimney stacks, like,' Dixie replied.

'But scaffolding – that'll cost a fortune,' Ellie objected. 'What's wrong with using ladders?'

Pixie and Dixie chuckled at Ellie's optimistic naivety. 'Health and safety regulations,' they chorused.

'Cannae work up high withoot the right scaffolds these days, ye see,' Pixie explained.

'Against the law, like,' Dixie added.

'See, these days, it's *you* that'd be liable if anything happened tae us up a ladder,' Pixie warned.

'Fortunes,' they said in unison. 'Aye, ye'd be stung for fortunes, like.'

As a final verbal uppercut, Pixie then pointed out that, in addition to paying for the hire of scaffolding, we would also have to provide skips and trucks to take away all the waste material that would accumulate during the course of operations.

'OK,' I sighed to our trusted twosome after their frank counselling session was over, 'just get us the best quotes you can from whatever specialists you suggest, and we'll take it from there.'

'Never mind,' Pixie smiled, patting my stooped shoulders as he left, 'it could've been worse.'

'Do you think so?' I groaned.

'Oh aye,' Dixie grinned before following his mate out of the front door and into the bustle of Court Street, 'we could've discovered dry rot an' all. Nearly always find that in old hooses like them, like.'

As soon as they'd left, I offered Ellie a sad smile. Then, without saying a word, I started rummaging in one of the cardboard boxes heaped in the hallway.

'What on *earth* are you looking for?' she asked, sounding distinctly irritated. 'There's nothing in there except cleaning materials, and we're hardly likely to need any of *those* for a while now, are we!'

I pulled a can of Brasso and a bottle of Windowlene out of the box and handed them to Ellie. 'If I were you,' I told her, 'I'd get those hoop earrings and that crystal ball of yours polished up – and pronto!'

– SEVEN –

DOWN MEMORY LANE

The *mañana* syndrome that I'd tried so hard to master in Mallorca had now been put rudely into reverse. Because of the extra work and resultant additional cost involved in the renovation of Old Weston, we were now battling against the clock *and* a rapidly shrinking bank balance. There was no time to be *tranquilo* any more, and under no circumstances could anything be put off until *mañana*. We were now well and truly back in Britain and irretrievably caught up in the rush to get things done, not just today, but yesterday, if at all possible. Not that this seemed to result in getting things done any more quickly than it had in Mallorca, mind you, but that lovely sense of *tranquilo*ness had gone, nonetheless. The dreaded British work ethic had seen to that.

Since the Industrial Revolution, we've been conditioned in these 'sceptred isles' to accept that we all live to work, not the opposite, as is still the belief in Spain – at least in the minds of the older generation of country folk. I missed the feeling of wellbeing that such an approach to the art of living induces, but I knew there was no point in trying to revive it now. The unpredictable climate, the long winter nights, the predictable food, the mad dash to get somewhere/anywhere/nowhere fast, the nose-to-the-grindstone mentality – all of those things and more contribute to the irreconcilable difference in attitude towards life that exists between those born and bred in the temperate climes of Britain and the people native to sunny Spain.

I knew that the onset of this way of thinking was an indication that, at last, withdrawal symptoms were setting in for things left behind in Mallorca that could never be replicated here. And it wasn't material things like the swimming pool, the games room or even the entire property at Ca's Mayoral that I was starting to pine for. It was little things like the sound of old Pep's 'Weh-*ep*' greeting to a friend across the lane; the sight of Jordi sitting waiting for a chat and a swearing session outside the Bar Nuevo in Andratx on market-day mornings; the smell of sardines grilling on a wood fire on the shore; the tinny tinkle of sheep bells on the mountainsides; even old Maria's ribbings for my rejection of the use of a donkey and the keeping of a pig, or my dreadful *ignorancia* of the merits of other relics of her cherished 'old days'. And then I thought of Bonny, remembering how she used to bound about the orange groves joyfully 'worrying' the water as I irrigated the trees. I recalled how she had lain at each of our feet in turn on the night we said goodbye to her, and I wondered if she missed us as much as I missed her.

I've no doubt that Ellie and the boys felt exactly the same way at times, yet none of us ever mentioned it. We all simply got on with what we had to do and kept our own thoughts about Mallorca to ourselves. Fresh memories had to be made now, and looking to the future would be the only way to create those – no matter how easier-said-than-done that might yet prove to be.

Sandy was still away at college during the week, so the only time we saw him was if we all happened to meet up at my parents' house on a Saturday evening. He was thoroughly enjoying his busy life, though, and it went without saying that he had no regrets about having followed his own star instead of staying in the shadow of ours. The first time he saw the conditions we had committed ourselves to live in at Old Weston, he just shook his head and muttered something about not all the loonies being locked up yet. And, to be frank, there were times when the loonies in question (namely Ellie and me) would have heartily agreed with that observation.

Charlie, for his part, probably doubted his parents' sanity even more than his big brother did. After all, he was sharing the domestic squalor with us – though only because he had no choice. Yet he never once complained about the squatter-like conditions he found himself living in. He knew that it was all a means towards the end that I had set my mind on, and he was mature enough to realise that the home-comfort sacrifices he was being obliged to make were no more than those we had imposed on ourselves. At least he could escape the 'danger-men-at-work' scenario that pervaded at Old

Weston during the day, and this, for the first time in his life, must have made going to school an experience he actually looked forward to.

Ironically, it was Jock Burns, the arch-critic of our returning to Scotland, who was finally to become responsible for snapping me out of my reveries about our past life in Mallorca.

'Braw!' was the first word he uttered when I drove him over the county line into East Lothian some eight months after our own arrival along that same new trunk road.

There had been not a trace of his contrived mid-Atlantic accent since I'd picked him up half an hour earlier at Edinburgh Airport at the start of a short trip he was making to visit his elderly parents in Haddington. 'Braw' is another of those Scots terms that don't exactly have a one-word equivalent in English. Essentially, it means 'nice', but can denote anything from 'good' (as in 'Ye're lookin' braw for yer age') to 'fine' (e.g. 'It's a braw day for the funeral') or 'bloody magnificent' (as per 'A braw pint o' beer, this'). It all depends on the context in which 'braw' is used and the manner in which it's expressed. Jock's inflection of the word in this instance left no doubt that the highest level of superlative was intended.

'Braw!' he repeated as we approached Haddington. 'Ye cannae find bonnier countryside than this anywhere, son.'

Significantly, Meg wasn't with him, so he had no hesitation in confiding then that, when they first went to live in Mallorca, his homesickness might well have drawn him rapidly back to Scotland, if it hadn't been for Meg's insistence that their new life had to be given a chance to survive such initial misgivings.

And, of course, they had become so established and happy in Mallorca over the years that there was now no likelihood of their ever leaving there.

'But when I see the old country here again now,' he wistfully continued, 'it reminds me o' the words o' that song about what you've been all over the place lookin' for in life bein' right here in yer own back yard all long. Ye know the one I mean?'

Indeed, I did know the one he meant and, spookily, some fitting lines from the same song came back to me then – something about trying to build castles in Spain, while, if you'd only looked, they'd always been there on the other side of your own window pane. Or words to that effect.

Anyway, what Jock was trying to say to me was what I'd always known in my heart of hearts – that I should be grateful for having had the opportunity of 'living the dream' in Spain, but that I should now be doubly thankful for having been able to return, when the dream was over, to such an enviable home as this.

'If only my Mallorcan *amigos* could see it,' he said, casting his eyes over the lush East Lothian landscape as we drove towards Haddington. 'The fields o' barley, the woods, the green hills, the village pubs, the wee stone houses wi' the red pantiled roofs, the big skies, the hawthorn hedgerows, the coast o' Fife shimmering away over the Firth o' Forth there. Aye, braw!'

Even if Jock, however understandably, was seeing his homeland through slightly rose-tinted spectacles, the sentiments he was expressing were no less profound for that, and if I'd had any doubts about the validity of them, they were soon to be dispelled. No sooner had he paid his respects to his parents than he turned up at Old Weston to ask if I would accompany him on a stroll down memory lane – or, rather, round a few of his childhood haunts in Haddington. As the house was in a particularly shambolic state that morning, with tradesmen of several persuasions literally falling over one another as they did their respective things with wood, bricks, plaster, pipes and wires, I didn't need to be asked twice. Ellie had already escaped to Edinburgh for the day to buy wallpaper, so I figured that my taking a few hours out from stripping the stuff that it was to replace wouldn't have too drastic an effect on our overall work schedule either.

A recent architectural study of the town stated that 'The High Street of Haddington has evolved as one of the most satisfying 'places' in Scotland. The relationship of heights of frontages to the width and length of the street, together with the scale of the elevations combine to form a space of exceptional quality. The continuity of the façades, the survival of the original shop fronts and the discipline of style without regimentation... all contribute to the unique quality of this street.'

Perhaps this is just a polite way of saying that the charming character of the street results from the lack of interference by planners when it was created. However, one aspect of the visual attraction of this particular street does have to be attributed to a member of that oft-maligned profession, Frank Tindall, the driving force behind the first coordinated urban painting scheme in Scotland. This project, in 1962, resulted in the hitherto drab fronts of many of the buildings in Haddington's town centre being brought to vibrant, colourful life. As Jock remarked as we wandered down the High Street, if you half-closed your eyes, the range of pastel shades filtering through made you think you were standing in the middle of a Monet painting. Well, maybe he was allowing his rose-tinted specs a *tad* too much artistic license there, but on a sunny summer morning like this, he could be forgiven for allowing his imagination to go a bit impressionist for a while.

Certainly, it takes people who have been away for a lengthy period of time to see once familiar home-town features in a different light from their stay-at-home contemporaries. It soon became apparent that Jock had been thinking of things in and around Haddington that he'd been longing to reacquaint himself with for quite some time, and he had a definite order in which he intended to visit them. After half an hour of soaking up the visually stimulating atmosphere of the town centre – including a 'pit stop' for a Scotch pie and a pint of the locally-brewed Belhaven Best in the bar of the George, an old coaching inn that occupies a prominent position at the bottom of the High Street – he strode off, refreshed, refuelled and with renewed purpose.

Like every ancient settlement built on the banks of a river, Haddington has a number of water mills dotted along the meandering course of the Tyne, which, incidentally, has no connection with its famous namesake that flows through Newcastle a hundred miles to the south. Jock's destination today was a spot just beyond a former woollen mill on the western edge of town. He led me to a place on the river that, being a non-swimmer, I'd never bothered to go near before, even though it was within fifty yards of the path along which

I used to walk home from school every day. Jock, however, like countless generations of Haddington boys down the ages, had regarded a deep pool called 'the Tubby' as a mecca for aquatic fun and games during the long, lazy days of summer, and it was to this beloved old swimming hole that he was drawn today.

'Even now, I wouldnae swap it for all the fancy swimmin' pools in Spain,' he murmured, while gazing longingly into what I considered to be the distinctly murky-looking water.

'All the same, it seems as if it could maybe do with a bucketful of chlorine,' I casually remarked, though a mite too flippantly for Jock.

He went immediately on the defensive. 'Nah, nah, nah, son, the Tubby always looks like that. It's just because o' where it's situated, see – here in a wee neuk in the river where the water swirls a bit under the surface. That's what made it so deep in the first place. Bottomless, they say it is.' Smiling to himself now, he said, 'Anyway, we never used tae even think about the colour o' the water, 'cos it would get a damned sight muddier than that when we were thrashin' about in it for hours on end. Aye,' he chuckled, as a detail from the past tickled his memory, 'and never mind yer chlorine. Everybody peed in it while they were swimmin', so no self-respectin' bugs ever hung about in the Tubby for long.' He sniggered at the thought. 'Yeah, and you better believe it, by the way!'

While Jock wallowed in his childhood memories, I paused to take in the surroundings. How, I asked myself after a couple of moments, could I have lived in this area for so long without ever having appreciated the presence of such an enchanting little spot as this? Looking upstream, the water seemed to be hardly flowing at all, its limpid surface disturbed only occasionally by a trout taking a fly, or by a moorhen plopping shyly into the gentle flow from the cover of a clump of hogweed. The entire picture-postcard scene was framed in the overhanging branches of trees already heavy with the fresh foliage of summer, and it struck me then that Jock's previous suggestion that his Mallorcan friends would have been enthralled by the visual attributes of his own little corner of Scotland hadn't been quite so rose-tint-influenced after all. Not just for agricultural purposes would the people of that sun-drenched Mediterranean island envy such a consequence of Mother Nature's much-disparaged 'gift' of a comparatively rainy climate. I knew only too well myself that I'd often dreamed of being magically transported to a shady riverside refuge like this when toiling away in our orange orchards on searingly hot days in the height of the Mallorcan summer. Yet it never occurred to me that such a perfect example existed back here in my own backyard.

Jock started to chuckle again, and I turned round to see him precariously perched on a branch of an ancient weeping willow that extended out over the Tubby. The branch was parallel with and only a foot or so above the water. About a couple of metres out from the bank, Jock stepped gingerly onto a short plank of wood that had been nailed to the top side of the willow's gnarled old limb.

'This is exactly what we used to do as well,' he grinned, his arms waving about as he struggled to keep his balance. 'The wee plank's like a kinda divin' board, see?'

In his enthusiasm to relive the reckless joys of his youth, Jock had forgotten that all the subsequent years of indulging his adult pastime of enjoying food had added considerably to his boyhood weight. Predictably, the plank complained with a short, grating squeak, then snapped.

Jock's yell of 'SHITE!' startled a heron that had been posing one-legged, round-shouldered and motionless on a half-submerged log in the middle of the river. I shut my eyes as I waited for the clumsy flapping of the bird's wings to be accompanied by the splash of Jock's unintended reacquaintance with the bottomless pleasures of the Tubby. But all I heard was the groaning of the willow tree, a slow, rhythmical creaking sound and a wheezed exclamation of, 'OOYA FUCKIN' BASTARD!'

Hesitantly opening one eye, I was presented with the image of a rotund and fully-clothed Tarzan figure swinging on a rope tied to a branch above what had been, until a few seconds before, the improvised diving board.

Jock started to laugh the unmistakable laugh of the gratefully reprieved. 'We used to have a rope hangin' from that very same branch as well,' he cheerily revealed. 'Yeah, I just kinda grabbed at the air instinctive-like just now, and there it was – like it always used to be. Amazin', eh!' With that, he lowered himself onto the horizontal branch and swayed back along it like a chubby tightrope walker – a stunt that he had performed many times before, I fancied.

Diagonally opposite the Tubby, a broad weir diverts the old mill lade from the main course of the river, along whose banks a pathway winds all the way round the southern perimeter of the town. In centuries past, the natural beauty of this riverside walk was enhanced by the planting of beeches and oaks along either side of the path. These mighty trees now form an impressive formal avenue to compliment the willows, alders and sycamores that grow in wild profusion on the banks of the river and provide a spreading canopy of shade over the little shingle and sand 'beaches' which occur here and there along its way. To add to Jock's obvious delight at being in the midst of this truly idyllic setting again, three families of mallard ducks appeared out of the undergrowth at the other side of the river and swam towards us, quacking keenly.

'I suppose they're lookin' for scraps o' bread or something,' Jock said.

'Yeah, they're really tame, aren't they?' I remarked.

Jock shook his head in disbelief. 'Jeez, how things have changed. When I was a kid, if ye were ever lucky enough tae see even one solitary duck here, it would fly away smartly wi' a white flag hoisted, thinkin' ye were a poacher about tae blooter it tae kingdom come wi' yer shotgun.'

I didn't doubt Jock's word, and we'd soon find out that ducks weren't alone in having had their lot change for the better in Haddington over recent years. A few hundred metres farther along, the river takes a wide sweep away from the footpath, which is now flanked by the mill lade on one side, with a broad 'haugh' fanning out on the other. Where the Haddington-to-Gifford road crosses this riverside meadow, the former Poldrate Corn Mill, complete with original water wheel, has been restored and converted into a community arts centre. It was at this point that Jock decided to make a short detour, and, to my surprise, it wasn't for another 'pit stop' at the mill's adjacent Tyneside Tavern either.

The fifteenth-century parish church of St Mary's sits on the banks of the Tyne where the mill lade rejoins the river. This imposing building, which is even larger than St Giles' Cathedral in Edinburgh, was gutted by an occupying English army besieged in the town by the Scots and their French allies for eighteen months between 1548 and 1549. Perhaps not too surprisingly, royalty and religion and their intertwined obsessions with self-promotion were at the root of this most ferocious of the town's many privations. At the end of this particular fracas, which was part of the continued 'rough wooing' of six-year-old Mary Queen of Scots for the future boy-king Edward VI of England, Haddington and its environs had been reduced to a wasteland. Even the church bells were stolen from the razed spire by the retreating English troops, and they were never recovered. For the next four centuries, less than half of the original area of this once magnificent church remained fit for use by the local faithful.

Now, however, after so much of it lying roofless and at the mercy of the elements for so long, all of St Mary's (except the spire) has been lovingly reconstructed and faithfully restored to something approaching its former glory, thanks to the determination and beneficence of its parishioners and sympathetic local organisations. Even a replacement peal of bells has been installed in the belfry, though not, as far as can be ascertained, with any financial contribution from the present-day successors of the covetous Tudor monarch whose soldiers made off with the originals.

Jock was patently awestruck by the sheer scale of the interior when we walked through the arched doorway. He hadn't been inside the old church since before its restoration, so his gasp of amazement didn't come as a surprise. Maybe it was the schoolteacher in him, or maybe there was a spiritual side to his nature that I'd never recognised before, but whatever the reason, Jock's interest in every detail of what we saw as we wandered round the interior of this ancient place of worship was clearly profound. I'd never known him to be so quiet before. What's more, he was visibly moved when he read the words that the renowned nineteenth-century Scottish writer and philosopher, Thomas Carlyle, had inscribed on the tomb of his wife. Jane Welsh Carlyle, the darling of Chelsea society during the time that her husband was known as 'the sage' of the same intellectual set, was born and brought up in Haddington, in a house now dedicated to her name in the town's Lodge Street. The grief-stricken Thomas Carlyle's elegy on his wife's grave describes her sudden death after the triumphs and tribulations of forty years of marriage as 'the light of his life as if gone out'.

Just what hidden emotions those simple words of Thomas Carlyle's had uncovered in Jock, I didn't know. His feelings were personal, he chose not to divulge them to me, and I didn't ask. But one thing was obvious – beneath his devil-may-care veneer, Jock Burns had a heart as soft as the one old Pep kept concealed behind his public image of the hard-bitten curmudgeon. Mid-Atlantic accents, John Wayne salutes and all the other devices of the dedicated extrovert may often amount to nothing more than a smokescreen for the real person to hide behind. The little boy within the man, perhaps?

It could be that Jock's stroll down memory lane with me that morning had done nothing more than release a temporary flush of nostalgia in him that was typical of the émigré paying a fleeting visit to where his roots will always remain. Whether that was the case or not, his genuine delight, however transient, in touching the symbolic green, green grass of home confirmed in my own mind that it was now time for me to start regarding my homeland in a different, less blasé light than I had since returning from Mallorca. There was still so much of Scotland that I hadn't even seen yet, so why hanker after an adopted home, where, like Jock, I may never have put down equally strong roots anyway?

I was the one to say, 'Jeez, how things have changed!' when we eventually left the serene ambience of St Mary's and walked through its churchyard into the Ball Alley, the easternmost of the three haughs that skirt the gentle curves of the river. At the other side of the Auld Brig, the same old bridge that I had looked out towards so often from my parents' house on the brow of a rise only half a mile away, a row of cottages that I'd remembered since childhood as always being on the verge of dereliction had now been transformed into a trendy watering hole for the upwardly mobile.

Many towns used to have a district, separate from the more 'select' residential areas, in which the less attractive, though nonetheless essential, businesses and trades were carried on. Americans would describe such places as being on the wrong side of the tracks. Haddington's version, the Nungate, was once regarded by the toffee-nosed element of the townspeople as being on the wrong side of the *river*. Accordingly, folk who lived in the Nungate were held by some to be a few steps lower down the social ladder than their neighbours on the more 'desirable' side of the Auld

Brig. And, in fairness, there's no doubt that, through its long and eventful history, the Nungate had been a melting pot for all the many types of people who were drawn to its crowded closes and anonymous alleyways, where few questions might be asked, but in which a certain toughness of character was a prerequisite of survival. Everyone from cattle drovers, peddlars, vagabonds, poachers, tinkers, itinerant Irish navvies and even Romany gypsies had contributed to the make-up of the Nungate's population at one time or another, and there is still a hook under one of the arches of the Auld Brig from which any miscreant among them was hanged if he or she behaved in a manner that displeased the upholders of the law on the 'right' side of the river.

Thankfully, those tough times are long past, and even the less attractive (and notably smelly) businesses, like tanning, slaughtering and brewing that were an integral element of Nungate life, had all disappeared by the time I left school. Yet the dilapidated state of some of its old buildings and a reputation for a lack of respect for authority among certain of its younger characters still existed when I eventually headed for Mallorca only three years previously. And now a group of these sadly neglected and occasionally vandalised buildings had become a fashionable eatery to which people travelled from far and wide to drink and dine in rustic respectability.

I'd found it hard to believe when first told about this transformation, but now that Jock was due for another 'pit stop', I'd have an opportunity to experience the Nungate's Waterside Bistro phenomenon for myself.

'You could almost be in Stratford-upon-Avon,' a man at an outdoor table overlooking the river said to his female companion.

'Absolutely,' she agreed, 'except that this is probably even more idyllic – and a damned sight less expensive, to boot.'

Listening to their accents, and to those of several others who were sitting beneath Martini parasols at neighbouring tables, we could indeed have been in Stratford-upon-Avon – or, for that matter, anywhere else four hundred miles south of Haddington. The career opportunities linked to Edinburgh's burgeoning financial sector, the flexibility of working locations offered by the Internet, the quality of local life and, not least, that new road to the city and the comparatively cheap property prices in the area had sparked a successful invasion from over the border that seemed set to counterbalance the movement of Scots to the south of England that traditionally had been the norm. And, as those new arrivals were unaware of any stigma that previously tainted this part of Haddington, there had been astute business method in the ostensible madness of the people who had gambled on turning this ramshackle row of cottages into a trendy watering hole after all.

'I'd never have believed it,' said Jock, casting an appraising eye over the interior of the bistro. 'A coat o' dark red paint and a load o' Sunday school furniture, and bingo! – ye've got a goldmine.'

Although it was true that the decor and furnishings appeared to have been put together to emphasise the 'cosy cottage' aspect of the place while also keeping costs down to a minimum, the result *was* altogether pleasing, nonetheless. A clever bit of thinking, in fact, and the total lack of pretension clearly appealed to the establishment's many patrons, whether having a drink and a simple snack in the bar, or opting for something a bit more opulent in the upstairs restaurant. As soon as he'd given everything the once-over, Jock opted to grab a table outside, however, and I offered no objection. On a sunny summer's day like this, the outlook was nothing short of magnificent, with not even the merest hint of traffic noise to detract from the tranquility. It was as if nothing had changed in centuries – except, of course, for the ambient smells of the neighbourhood and the affluence of the folk present.

'Poached?' Jock asked the waitress when she brought us the fillets of sea trout we had ordered from the bill of fare.

'No, sir – grilled,' was the girl's polite reply.

'Caught locally?' Jock probed.

'I believe so, sir.'

'Aye, well,' Jock muttered, 'if I know anything about the lads who run the black economy hereabouts, it *will* have been poached, no matter how ye've cooked it.'

The girl didn't rise to the bait, but went on to stress that all the accompanying vegetables were locally produced as well. Like the interior decor of the place, then, the food was wholesome and unpretentious, but well prepared and presented. This combination of fresh ingredients, straightforward cooking and friendly service had clearly proved to be a winning formula. But, for all that, the Waterside Bistro's biggest attraction had to be its location.

I had often passed this way as a schoolboy, but without taking time to dally and fully appreciate the stunning beauty of the view the old waterside properties commanded. Today, the river was drifting by at a lazy pace befitting such a fine summer day, while a small flotilla of swans glided regally under the arches of the Auld Brig to loftily pluck from the water chunks of bread thrown to them by a few of the Bistro's alfresco clients. On the other side of the Tyne, the green expanse of the Ball Alley drew the eye to the ancient doocot at the corner of a low-walled enclosure with the beguiling name of Lady Kitty's Garden. From here, the pathway that Jock and I had walked along earlier leads to the dominant feature of this captivating part of town, the old parish church of St Mary's.

Jock washed down the last of his sea trout with a goodly slug of Belhaven Best, then, his patriotism bolstered by the intake of such long-craved samples of local sustenance, he remarked in a broad Scottish accent and with but the merest sidelong glance at the original makers of the same observation, 'Aye, ye could be in Stratford-upon-Avon, right enough, except it's a damned sight cheaper here. And you better believe it, by the way.'

'Hear, hear,' the male half of his sideways targets concurred, while raising a genial glass of wine. 'And here's to your lovely old town, squire.'

'And lang may yer lum reek on other folk's coal,' Jock reciprocated. His offering of the old Scottish goodwill wish that its recipient's metaphorical chimney would smoke enduringly on freebie fuel caused this particular recipient's brows to gather into a puzzled frown.

'Lum?… Er, *reek*?' he queried, head cocked to one side. 'Don't quite follow, old boy. Gaelic, is it?'

That was all the encouragement Jock needed to launch into a schoolmasterly, one-to-one lesson on the differences between

Lallans, the Lowland Scots vernacular of which 'lum' and 'reek' are component words, and the Gaelic language of the Celts as spoken in the Highlands and Islands. Interestingly, his accent shifted further and further towards the mid-Atlantic the more he noticed the occupants of other tables eavesdropping on his lecture. They needn't have bothered. Jock's knowledge of Gaelic was about as thorough as his proficiency in DIY brain surgery. Not that this hindered him from fielding the volleys of questions that were soon being fired at him from all angles. Bullshit, on such occasions, is Jock's stock in trade, and I wondered that his production of it now didn't pollute the clear Nungate air with the same stench that once wafted from its long-demolished slaughterhouse.

However, as Jock's bad luck would have it, a hitherto silent fellow sitting with the Stratford-upon-Avon couple eventually put paid to his flanneling by revealing that he was a keen amateur student of Gaelic himself, as well as being an American, currently on a visit to Scotland in search of his ancestry. Although it seemed that Jock was about to be upstaged on two counts, he swiftly showed that he wasn't going to be cornered into a linguistic contest that he was almost certain to lose. Oh no, Jock would never allow himself to be caught out like that. So he skilfully changed tack and, reverting to his normal Scots accent, began a talk on a loosely related subject that he felt sure none of his audience of strangers to the area would know anything about – the mysterious old lingo of Haddington's Nungate.

Like me, Jock had picked up a handy smattering of the vocabulary of this peculiar way of speaking from Nungate kids at school, where it was frowned upon by the teachers as being nothing more than the common slang of tinkers and tramps. That didn't stop us from using it in the playground, of course – particularly as none of the teaching staff had a clue as to what most of the words meant. So, without fear of being understood by any of them who happened to be within earshot, we could make after-school plans in Nungate-ised English to 'chore yaps, then tober along the panny if any of the barrie gadgies deeked the stardies nashin' in'. Only polite interest was shown when Jock translated this random example as meaning to 'steal apples, then make a dash for it along the river if any of the lads saw the police coming'.

But at least Jock was off his self-baited Gaelic/American hook and, as I had long been fascinated by the history of this strange sub-language myself, I was happy to join him in revealing more about it. It was, after all, part of Haddington's unique heritage, so why shouldn't those from elsewhere who had now chosen to visit or make the town their adopted home be introduced to a little of its background?

'Gee, now that really is truly *awe*some, buddy!' the American student of etymology gasped when it was disclosed that, although some of the words in the Nungate lexicon doubtlessly were borrowed from the speech of peddlers, horsedealers, hawkers and vagabonds, others had a much more elevated origin. For many of the words once used as a matter of course in Nungate conversation are pure Romany, the language of the gypsies who arrived in Scotland some five hundred years ago, after another five centuries of wandering through Europe from their place of origin in northern India. And for those who, like some of our erstwhile schoolteachers, would pounce on this as confirmation that the words are only the vulgar jargon of travelling people (or whatever else one may choose to call them), the fact is that many of those words derive directly from Sanskrit, the ancient tongue of the gypsies' motherland and one of the oldest literary languages on earth.

Pockets of 'the cant', as it's sometimes called, had survived in other places in northern England and southern Scotland, though few, if any, retained it in such comprehensive everyday usage as in the Nungate of Haddington. But now, as we explained to those who were still listening, because of the gradual dispersion of the old Nungate families and the influx of people from other parts of Scotland and, more recently, from England as well, its use (to 'mang the cant', in local parlance) had all but died out.

The American was intrigued. 'But I guess you got some kinda museum place dedicated to all that gypsy stuff, huh? Sure, and maybe a theme pub about them good ol' boys – them apple-stealin' *barrie gadgies* – right here in the Nungate too, yeah?'

To his dismay and bewilderment, Jock and I shook our heads in unison, before going on to divulge that John Knox, the fervent driving force behind the sixteenth-century religious Reformation in Scotland, which was to develop into one of the most influential happenings in country's history, was born in Gifford Gate, a mere hundred yards along the riverside from where we were now sitting.

'Holy shit!' the American exclaimed. 'Wow, John Knox! Hey, I've heard of that guy. Kinda old-time Davy Crockett and Billy Graham all rolled into one, right?'

Without waiting to debate the accuracy or otherwise of that somewhat nebulous speculation, he stood up and requested to be directed immediately to Knox's birthplace. We duly obliged, and he marched purposefully forth along the river bank. He was back again within five minutes, looking particularly peeved.

'What the hell, you guys! Ah thought you'd been jivin' ma socks off when Ah got there. Ain't nothin' to see but a sad ol' tree and a little ol' plaque all half covered in goddam weeds. What kinda half-assed memorial to an immortal man of the cloth is that supposed to be, for Chrissakes!'

That was all there was, we shrugged – the property known as 'John Knox's House', which had once stood on the site, having been condemned long ago as unfit for human habitation and consequently demolished together with other old buildings in the vicinity. Feeling slightly embarrased, I pointed out that there was, however, a full-length statue of Knox perched high on the clock tower of the old school that bore his name, a neo-Gothic building now converted into a block of retirement flats. Oh, but there *was* one wee street in town named after him as well, Jock promptly reminded me.

'Yes, I'd forgotten about that,' I admitted. 'That'll be Knox Place, right in front of the old school.'

I laughed inwardly as I then recalled how, when I'd attended that daunting Victorian establishment as a young boy, some wag with a deadly aim had lodged an old tennis ball right in the crotch of Knox's stone pants. For the many years that this object of every pupil's delight remained in that delicate position, the 'father' of the Presbyterian Church was irreverently referred to by successive generations of the school's inmates as 'old Johnny three balls'. And, for some unknown reason, no one in authority ever bothered to send the school janitor up a ladder to remove the offending third testicle, which remained there, as far as I know, until it eventually rotted away.

To avoid the risk of causing offence, I thought it prudent not to tell this story to our new American acquaintance. He gave the impression of being a man with strong religious views, and he was already appalled that the town hadn't honoured this famous son in a way commensurate with his stature.

'Ain't ya even got a John Knox Day?' he enquired, squinting disbelievingly at us. He neither waited for nor needed a reply. 'Hell's bells, where Ah come from, we'd *really* do a local hero like that proud. Big neon sign sayin' "Birthplace of John Knox" at the entrance to town – flag-wavin' stuff like that, know what Ah mean? Yeah, and we'd have a feller in John Knox duds stompin' up and down Main Street every day, just a-preachin and a-hollerin' and a-thumpin his big ol' bible at all them tourists that'd come crowdin' in.' He shook his head in despair. 'Hey, you Scottish guys take too much of yer history for granted. No shit – unbelievable, man!'

We thought it best not to tell him about Scotland's oldest bowling green, lying unused, unsignposted and, to all practical intents and purposes, forgotten on the other side of the bridge. And we also decided to avoid mentioning the site of the early kings' palace, the town's status as one of the first Royal Burgh's in Scotland, the ancient abbey of the nuns by whose 'gate' we were now relaxing with our drinks, the bloody battles with the Auld Enemy, the bitter-sweet love story of Thomas and Jane Welsh Carlyle, the 'rough wooing' of Mary

Queen of Scots by King Henry VIII of England, the youthful Sean 'James Bond' Connery's one-time employment with the town's coffin-maker, and the many other events, people, intrigues, legends and locations that had contributed to Haddington's colourful past. To do so might have prompted our new American acquaintance to propose the creation of some kind of all-singing, all-dancing, all-jousting and all a-preachin' Disneyland right there on the bonny banks of the Tyne – designed, naturally, to pay just and fitting homage to the town's historic legacies.

Instead, we left him and his companions with thoughts of how the gypsy families of old had camped with their horse-drawn wagons on the green sweep of the Ball Alley on the opposite bank of the river, and of how they and their unsung, cant-speaking ilk had contributed so much to an almost forgotten culture that deserved to be preserved. Then we took our leave to continue our wander down a memory lane that was no longer just Jock's, but mine as well.

Indeed, it had taken Jock's brief visit home to truly open my eyes to so much about our town that I'd seen so often but had never fully appreciated. And, to be fair, there was also much truth in what the American guy had said, albeit that his idea of how to keep the memory of such things alive would never be an option in this unassuming old place. It was the same when Jock insisted that we go for a drive around the surrounding countryside and along the coast. Everything had a timeless and relatively unspoilt charm, which had always been understated in any tourism-related publicity about the county. It was a quality that had been known to the discerning visitor for ages, yet the area had somehow managed to remain comparatively undiscovered. The completion of that new road from the city had altered all that, though, and now such days of quiet constancy were coming to an end. East Lothian was about to become the playground and, perhaps, the 'stockbroker belt' of Edinburgh, with all the changes to the old social structures and traditional ways of life that this would entail.

'Anyway, son,' Jock said to me when I dropped him off at Edinburgh Airport a couple of days later, 'all this predicted flood o' incomers is bound tae get ye a right tidy profit when ye flog that old house ye're doin' up. So, as the sayin' goes, it's an ill wind that doesnae do somebody a wee bit o' good, eh?' He stopped at the entrance to International Departures, half turned and shouted back in mid-Atlantic mode, 'So, forget chasin' all yer dirt-scrapin' rainbows, good buddy, and hawl yer ass aboard that property-developin' train.' He threw me a US Marines salute. 'Way ahead, boy. Yeah, and you better believe it, by the way!'

★ ★ ★ ★ ★

The ironic thing about what Jock had said was that, if we'd wanted to make money from a little dabble in property speculation, we'd have been better off sitting in the house at Cuddy Neuk for the past three years instead of embarking on our orange-growing adventure in Mallorca, considering the upsurge in East Lothian house prices in the interim. My father had made that clear to me on the day we returned home. But our motivation had never been to make a fast buck from bricks and mortar, and it still wasn't. The reason for our move to Mallorca, our ultimate return to Scotland and now our renovation of Old Weston had been our desire to retain a foothold in our chosen way of life – farming.

Having said that, the route that we had found ourselves taking to achieve that goal had also led us into a requirement to learn quickly about the valuation of property and the practical skills required to maximise the returns from investing in it. And while we were still a long way from being proficient in any of these qualifications, at least Ellie and I were still doing what we enjoyed doing most, no matter what we were involved in to make a living, and that was working together.

As ever, Ellie was showing that she was no slouch when it came to getting on with the job, and the presence of qualified tradesmen fazed her not one bit, as Pixie and Dixie had quickly discovered. Their half-jocular warning to any workman who arrived in the house for the first time was, 'Dinnae stand in one place for too long when the mistress o' the hoose is aboot, mind – else ye'll either get papered or painted!' And the Dynamic Duo, or the Gruesome Twosome, as, depending on the mood, their fellow artisans secretly referred to our two main contractors, were never slow to offer us amateurs the benefit of their professional advice. However, one particular example of their sharing of trade secrets left me in no doubt that a generous pinch of salt usually had to be taken with it.

I had been standing in one of the refurbished attic rooms one day, looking at a newly-installed dormer window and trying to figure out how I'd ever manage to paint its exterior woodwork. The window protruded halfway up the steep slope of the roof, the eaves of which began two storeys above ground level – inaccessible, except by scaling a series of ladders, which would have been too risky (for my liking, anyway!), or by erecting scaffolding, which would have been too expensive. Pixie and Dixie had a simple solution to the problem, though.

'Dinnae even think aboot doin' a dangerous job like that yersel',' Dixie warned.

'Aye, just sit yer missus wi' her arse on the windae sill instead,' Pixie advised.

'That's wi' her feet and legs danglin' inside and her heid and arms and everything else ootside, like,' Dixie stressed.

'Just that, right enough,' Pixie agreed. 'She'll manage tae dae the paintin' fine for ye like that, ye see.'

I objected that this sounded a little dangerous to me, but both of my tutors merely laughed.

'Nah, nah, no even in the slightest wee bit dangerous,' Dixie chortled.

'No if ye follow the official health and safety regulations, like,' Pixie sniggered.

'Health and safety regulations?' I queried, scratching my head.

'Aye,' Dixie confirmed, straight-faced now. 'Once ye've got her sittin' comfy, like, ye just nail the legs o' her jeans tae the windae sill.'

Pixie nodded sagely. 'That's right. She'll never budge an inch. Safe as ye like, that system o' paintin' the ootside o' high windaes.'

'Absolutely,' Dixie affirmed. 'And then ye can go and make yersel' a nice cup o' tea and relax until she's finished the job and shouts for ye tae come wi' yer claw hammer tae pull the nails oot.'

Not surprisingly, Ellie vetoed that suggestion stone dead. And I totally agreed with her, on the grounds that it would cause too much damage to her jeans *and* the window sill. Yet there *was* some merit to what the Dynamic Duo had recommended. As a compromise, therefore, I did the gentlemanly thing and held on tightly to her legs inside the window while she adopted the Pixie-and-Dixie-prescribed painting position outside. The system worked a treat.

And so the improvements to Old Weston progressed. Naturally, there were times when we doubted the wisdom of ever having taken on such a demanding project. But, like so many things in life, if you jump in at the deep end you have to learn to swim pretty quickly, and once all the panicking and floundering about is over, you often end up enjoying the experience. That had been the case in Mallorca, and it worked out the same on this occasion as well. When the day finally came to shut the door on Pixie and Dixie and their cohorts for the last time, we not only breathed a huge sigh of relief that the worst was over, but really began to have fun putting the finishing touches to everything.

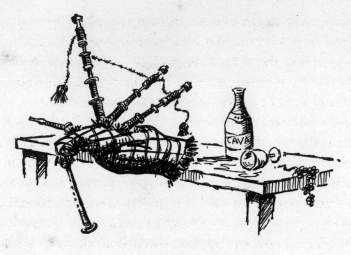

– EIGHT –

BAGPIPES AND BUBBLY

One of the great joys of restoring an old house involves repairing or replacing any of the original period features that have been damaged or lost. Architectural salvage yards that you previously wouldn't have given a second glance to now become Aladdin's Caves to be eagerly plundered for everything from the smallest window catch to doors and fireplaces and even bits of moulded guttering. Furnishing such a house in appropriate style is another adventure to be relished – if you're that way inclined, that is. We are, so we were soon scouring the ad pages of *The Scotsman* newspaper every day, looking for notices of forthcoming auctions that might yield 'just what we were looking for'. We'd even travel considerable distances to farm sales in the hope of finding that elusive item we needed among the household bits and pieces that came under the hammer once the tractors, combine harvesters and livestock had been disposed of. Such forays didn't always result in producing whatever we had set out to find, of course, but they did provide an opportunity to actually *see* some interesting places for the first time.

As a touring jazz musician earlier in my life, there were few corners of Britain that I hadn't been to, yet I'd seen comparatively little of any of them. The exhaust pipe of a diesel-belching truck in front of you looks exactly the same in Cornwall as it does in Caithness, and the scenery surrounding a greasy-spoon transport café at three o'clock in the morning is impossible to appreciate anywhere. But now, without the pressure of having to trek from one venue to the next on a tight schedule night after night and day after day, it was possible to take time en route to smell the proverbial roses. And it was a revelation just how near to home some stunningly beautiful countryside and delightful towns existed and deserved to be explored and enjoyed. Take, for instance, one trip Ellie and I made to attend an auction near the little Borders town of Melrose, less than an hour's drive south from Haddington.

The A68 road takes you over the Lammermuirs by way of Soutra Hill, from where you are presented with one of the most wonderful views in the south of Scotland. On a clear day, you could be forgiven for thinking that you really can see forever. Laid out before you is a vast panorama of farms, woodlands, villages, hills and vales, stretching all of thirty miles from Edinburgh in the west to the old fishing town of Dunbar in the east. In the middle distance, the waters of the Firth of Forth reach northward to the coast of Fife, and you look beyond to the far, purple peaks of the Highlands.

Once the summit of Soutra has been gained, the first thing to strike you is that the moorland covering the contours of the ancient landscape you are now traversing has been given a thoroughly modern makeover by the construction of one of the country's biggest wind farms. The towering white turbines of Dun Law stand like platoons of three-armed aliens, tilting their blades at the heather that extends away to the horizon on either side of the road. I'd probably join the ranks of objectors if one of these renewable energy sources were planned for anywhere within sight of my own back yard, no matter how eco-friendly the reason. Yet I have to admit that there is something strangely compelling about their presence in such a bleak and formerly featureless place as this. Like the working windmills of old, they have an almost hypnotic attraction, and these updated versions of what made Holland famous do possess a certain beauty in the sleekness of their lines – depending, admittedly, on the eye of the beholder.

Paradoxically, these monuments to modern engineering are located within a puff of the prevailing west wind from Soutra Aisle, a small stone building which is all that remains of one of the most important scientific institutions of medieval Britain. The Holy Trinity Hospital of Soutra was founded by Augustinian monks around AD 1160 on southern Scotland's most important highway of the time, almost halfway between Edinburgh and the great Border Abbeys. Dere Street was a legacy of the Roman occupation, and parts of its original line are still followed by the present-day road.

For three centuries after its creation, the hospital church at Soutra served as a refuge for the sick, a resting place for the weary traveller, a sanctuary for fugitives and a source of alms for the needy. But what marks its unique place in history is the pioneering medical work carried out by its monks.

Excavations in recent years have unearthed traces of herbal products procured from all over the then known world, as well as a skilfully concocted mixture of seeds that are believed to have been used as a general anaesthetic during the amputation of limbs. Evidence from skeletal remains also suggests that operations were done to repair fractures of the skull, and possibly even to perform some form of brain surgery. All of this took place five hundred years or more before chloroform, the earliest modern general anaesthetic, was first employed successfully by the Edinburgh obstetrician James Young Simpson. What's more, the groundbreaking monks of Soutra had devised herbal means of inducing childbirth and ridding the body of worms, although it isn't suggested that the same mixture was used! They also discovered how to cure scurvy and alleviate the miseries of hangovers, as well as anticipating the modern craze for slimming by using a preparation derived from the bitter vetch plant as an appetite depressant.

Yet three centuries of such momentous achievements were not sufficient to stop the religious hierarchy of the 1460s relieving the Holy Trinity Hospital of Soutra of its considerable assets and transferring them to Trinity College Hospital in Edinburgh. Alleged 'misconduct' by the then Master of Soutra had spawned Edinburgh's lasting status as a world-renowned centre for the advancement of medicine.

Although there is only the small 'aisle' of the original hospital church left standing at Soutra, the site (alongside the B6368 road) is still worth a visit, if for no other reason than to enjoy the unsurpassed views that it commands of Edinburgh, its coastline, the twin Forth Bridges and the guardian folds of the Moorfoot and Pentland Hills. In Spain, as I related before, many former monastic 'sanctuaries' – also located, as a matter of course, on the most spectacular of vantage points – retain a facility for selling food and drink to the present-day pilgrim or sightseer. In Scotland, though, no such commercially slanted amenities are provided in the old 'holy' places. A pity, I think, but just another example of the differences that exist between the two cultures, and doubtless exacerbated by the dissimilarity of the climates and consequent visitor numbers. Here, then, the weary traveller will have to trudge on a while yet to find rest and sustenance.

Back on the main A68 road, you soon clear the barren plateau of Soutra and descend into Lauderdale, a wide valley chequered with large farms famed for the quality of their cattle and sheep. The landscape of Lauderdale is typified by the fertile glens and sheltering hills that have made this part of the Borders coveted by man since time immemorial. It's a gentle countryside, graced by mature woods and blessed with a profusion of steams and rivers brimming with trout and salmon. It's a huntsman's and angler's paradise, in which the country estates of the nobility have historically boasted some of the finest stately homes in the land. It's an area of tranquil towns and sleepy villages, populated by friendly folk who reflect nothing of the violent times their forefathers suffered during centuries of battles between the Scots and English while warring over possession of this most desirable tract of country.

Today, the only coordinated strong-arm tactics evident in this region of Scotland are those employed by the rugby football teams that are the pride of its towns, the traditional producers of numbers of international players incommensurate with the modest size of their populations. And right in the forefront of these rugby-devoted townships is Melrose, nestling cosily in the lower slopes of the Eildon Hills, and our destination on that auction-seeking foray into the Borders.

Even more revered than the town's rugby players is a son of Edinburgh who, during the first quarter of the nineteenth century, enthralled the English-speaking world with such historically romantic novels and poems as *Rob Roy*, *Ivanhoe*, 'Marmion', *The Heart of Midlothian* and 'The Lady of the Lake'. Sir Walter Scott was so captivated by the serene beauty of this area that, with the fruits of his writing, he bought an old farm called Clarty Hole, overlooking the River Tweed near Melrose. In place of the original modest house and farmstead, he built Abbotsford, a mansion to rival the grandest in the Borders. The many Walter Scott aficionados who visit the former site of Clarty Hole now will realise that it must have been quite a transformation, considering that 'clarty' is the Scottish word for filthy!

For all that, a sharp lesson that all latter-day house-improvers can learn from Scott's experience is that you should never let your heart rule your head. So great was Scott's infatuation with Abbotsford that he did just that, and the cost of its ongoing enlargements and enhancements almost ruined him. But Scott's personal financial cloud contained a silver lining for his legions of fans, insomuch as he was obliged to increase his output of writing to unprecedented levels in a frantic attempt to pay off his creditors.

His deep love of the house and the surrounding area remained undiminished until his death, however. One touching anecdote relates how, during Scott's funeral procession from Abbotsford through Melrose to the graveyard of Dryburgh Abbey, the horses pulling his coffin stopped of their own volition at an elevated spot that had been the author's favourite place of muse and contemplation. And there they stood still for several minutes, ignoring all urgings to move on. That special place is still referred to locally as 'Scott's View'.

On driving into Melrose today, your immediate impression is of a trim and attractive little town, whose inhabitants clearly take a great pride in its appearance. The floral displays that abound have earned Melrose well-deserved success in both the Scotland and Britain In Bloom awards, and nowhere are these colourful adornments more effective than in the Market Square, the hub of this tight-knit little community. It would be hard to find a more instantly appealing town centre anywhere in the country, and it isn't because of its size, because the Market Square in Melrose is relatively small in comparison with those in other rural Scottish towns. But what it lacks in area it more than compensates for in the pleasing ambience created by its variety of well preserved buildings and the mix and quality of its shops. Ellie was quick to take notice of the latter.

'As good a selection as you'd get in any big city,' she smiled, eyeing up a classy-looking boutique. 'Better, actually, because everything's within easy walking distance *and* there isn't one chain store in sight.'

While I wasn't about to accompany Ellie on what I knew would be her mandatory rake around the shops, I had to agree that it was refreshing to see such a range of small retail businesses that were still independent and clearly thriving. Melrose already had me under its spell, a feeling of wellbeing instantly heightened the moment my eyes lit on a handsome whitewashed building, replete with flowery window boxes and positively oozing welcome, on the other side of the square. 'Burt's Hotel', the sign read.

'OK, Ellie,' I said, 'off you go on your rummage. There's a couple of things I want to check out myself. See you in Burt's over there in half an hour, right?'

Half an hour probably wouldn't be long enough for what I had in mind, but knowing Ellie's woolly concept of the passage of time, I reckoned I actually had a good hour to play with.

On approaching the square down the narrow East Port, I'd noticed an old building called 'The Ship Inn'. The name intrigued me, as Melrose is a good thirty-five crow's miles from the sea and without any navigable access to it. I was even more intrigued when I walked into the bar as, sure enough, the room was liberally festooned with seafaring knick-knacks. There was a large picture of a clipper in full sail on the wall beside the door, while behind the bar a ship's bell and helm wheel were prominently displayed. With the obvious exception of the pool table through in a side room, the pub had a decidedly nautical flavour to it.

I ordered a beer and sat at a table opposite the bar, weighing up the customers and listening to their chat. Interestingly, those standing at the bar spoke with the briskly lilting intonation of the Scottish Borders, while the accents of those sitting at the tables revealed that they were mainly from the south. However, any suspicion I may have been forming that there was some sort of ethnic segregation happening here was swiftly dispelled when I asked the Welsh-sounding couple sitting near me why this old hostelry, in a landlocked town like Melrose, happened to be called 'The Ship'. As if at the tap of an orchestral conductor's baton, the various individual conversations that had been in progress around the room halted abruptly, and within seconds, the origin of the pub's name had become the communal topic of discussion.

Unfortunately, it emerged that no one, native or otherwise, could throw any light on the subject. This prompted the barmaid to go to the trouble of fetching a book on the history of Melrose from a back room. But, despite a fairly comprehensive inspection of its most likely passages by a huddle of the bar-sitters, the book yielded no clues as to the reason for the inn's unlikely name. What the exercise did do, however, was to stimulate an outpouring of unassociated, though nonetheless interesting, details of Melrose's past from the folk present. I was soon in possession of all sorts of historical nuggets, ranging from the building and ultimate closure of the Waverley railway line from Edinburgh to how Thomas the Rhymer, a local thirteenth-century poet-cum-soothsayer, was 'inspired to utter the first notes of the Scottish muse' after being carried off by the Queen of the Fairies into the heart of the Eildon Hills.

'It's true,' an elderly chap in a scruffy blue suit and bright red socks told me as I stood up to leave. He had been sitting glumly nursing the dregs of his pint at the end of the bar, without contributing a word to the proceedings. Judging by his fairly decrepit appearance, I half expected him to say that he'd known Thomas the Rhymer personally. But all he wanted to assure me of was that the bard – real name Thomas Learmont of Ercildoune – had actually existed, and the remains of his tower house still survived in the nearby village of Ercildoune, now called Earlston.

It occurred to me that this old worthy, with some gentle persuasion, could yet cast some light on the origin of The Ship Inn's name. I duly bought him a persuasive pint of his nominated beer, then posed the burning question again, but for his ears only this time.

'Well, eh, Ah'm no' right sure,' he replied, 'but Ah seem tae mind somebody once sayin' it was 'cos an owner o' the property a long whiles back was a sea captain.' With that, he raised his new pint, winked at me, smirked and said, 'Here's tae ye're very good health, laddie. Aye, and safe sailin' tae us a'.'

I had no way of telling if the laughter that rang out from inside the bar after I left was the result of a quick joke somebody had just told, or because I had been the latest patsy to fall for the same scam that, in all probability, old Red Socks had pulled on many an inquisitive visitor to his curiously named local. And it didn't matter either way to me. I had thoroughly enjoyed my brief visit to a pub that I'd left a bit wiser than when I went in… I think. In any case, even if I had been the unwitting butt of an elderly local's droll sense of humour, it was nothing new. I'd experienced similar treatment often enough in Mallorca at the hands of old Pep, Maria and some of their Andratx cronies, and they had neither meant me ill will nor had they done me any. I'd accepted that it was all just harmless fun being poked at a *loco extranjero*, a crazy foreigner, who would either have to take it in good part or fail the initiation test.

Now I pondered that the 'pawky' character of the good folk of the Scottish Borders had probably been forged in an almost identical way to the one that had instilled a similar trait in Mallorcans. Both peoples, after all, had had to endure endless invasions by landgrabbing armies down the ages, and the development of a dry sense of humour (covertly aimed at the plundering incomer) had doubtless been a major contributory factor towards their long-term survival. Likewise, the modern influx of peaceful settlers would have revived and re-honed the same old instincts in the natives of both places. I reckoned that an ability to gracefully take such benign pills was a small price for the modern invaders to pay for acceptance into their adopted homelands.

Although I could have sat happily for hours in the company of both factions of The Ship Inn's regulars, there was one famous feature of this little town that I was determined to see before keeping my rendezvous with Ellie…

Melrose Abbey has been described as having been one of the most beautiful ecclesiastical buildings of the Middle Ages, and even in its present semi-ruined state, it is no wonder that it still attracts visitors by the thousands every year. Standing in its own grounds just a short stroll from the Market Square, it is a truly awe-inspiring example of the skills possessed by the craftsmen who built it for the first Cistercian monks in Scotland when they arrived from Rievaulx in Yorkshire during the third decade of the twelfth century. As usual, the monks had chosen the location for their monastery wisely, with particular attention being paid to the nearness of a river and the fertility of its surrounding land. However, in this case, they had fatally ignored one important point – the proximity of the border with England.

Like the other great abbeys of nearby Dryburgh, Jedburgh and Kelso, the fabric of Melrose Abbey suffered badly during the various Border Wars that raged for four hundred years after its construction. But the abbey survived and was always painstakingly restored, until, in 1545, an army led by the Earl of Hertford dealt the final blow in the name of his master, that arch-vandaliser of so many of southern Scotland's architectural treasures, King Henry VIII. But even the humblest of homes throughout the area were also laid waste and terrible atrocities committed to their inhabitants. This was all part of Henry's protracted 'rough wooing' campaign, through which he hoped to annexe Scotland to England by 'brokering' a treaty of marriage between young Mary Queen of Scots, of whom he was a great-uncle, and his own sickly son, Edward. He failed.

Nowadays, however, this old land of myth and legend basks in the tranquillity of a hard-earned peace, and, by a beautiful irony, it isn't any relic of Henry VIII's attentions that is the prime attraction for visitors to Melrose Abbey. Robert the Bruce, the legendary King of Scots, who defeated the occupying forces of the English crown at Bannockburn more than two centuries before Henry's abortive attempt to do what several of his predecessors had also failed to do, is recognised as the original champion of Scottish independence. Bruce's heart was buried, at his specific request, in a leaden casket beneath the floor of the chapter house of Melrose Abbey, and it is to pay homage to this unique symbol of a small country's patriotism that so many travel from all corners of the world every year.

Though, understandably, memories of the harsh treatment meted out by Henry's troops festered in these parts for generations, nowadays no animosity is shown towards anyone from south of the border… except, of course, on the rugby field, when the sons of Melrose and their fellow countrymen play against the Auld Enemy and do their utmost (though not always too successfully!) to knock the shit out of them. But, then, that's all just good-natured, sporting rivalry, isn't it? Well, *isn't* it? 'Aye, right!', as they say hereabouts.

All such mischievous insinuations aside, however, the welcome mat that the Borders country lays out for its visitors today couldn't be better exemplified than at Burt's in the Market Square of Melrose. Although at one time a temperance hotel (never the most universally popular of institutions in the homeland of whisky), Burt's now offers the best of Borders hospitality without any such abstemious reservations. As arranged, I met up with Ellie in the lobby, and the homely-yet-elegant feel of the place seemed all the more pleasant when she told me that she'd managed to stifle her temptation to buy a really *fabulous* dress that she'd seen in one of the really *marvellous* shops she'd rummaged through.

'I did get a boot-scraper for the back door at Old Weston, though,' she chirped. 'Just what we were looking for. And I picked it up in an antique shop for a lot less than we'd have had to pay for the one we were outbid for at the auction earlier.'

I was beginning to like this wee town more and more.

'Phew,' Ellie gasped, 'all that raking about the shops doesn't half make you hungry – especially when you haven't bought anything for yourself!'

'Well,' I said, 'no better way to celebrate your self-restraint than by having a bite to eat in here.' I pointed to a framed certificate on the wall. 'See – voted the best dining pub in Scotland.'

If it's possible to have understated opulence, then that's precisely what has been achieved in this charming country hostelry. The welcoming vibes that I had picked up from across the square came over even more strongly when we sat down in the lounge bar. And the fact that we were lucky to find an available table at all gave the clue as to why that best-dining-pub award had been won. The food was in a class that I'd never known to be equalled in any bar. The very best beef and lamb from those lush Borders pastures that had attracted the abbey-founding monks of old, wild salmon fresh from the sparkling waters of Tweed, venison and pheasant from the woods around the Eildon Hills, vegetables and fruit from local market gardens, and all prepared with a degree of culinary flair that you would sooner associate with flash, big-city eateries – but in which you could expect to pay several times the price.

We left Melrose that day with our hunger memorably sated, and, more importantly, our appetites well sharpened to see more of the gems of our history-rich native land. Excuses to drive off in search of old boot-scrapers and the like would not be too difficult to make from now on, I suspected.

★ ★ ★ ★ ★

The maxim that you should never buy furniture specifically to suit a house that you intend to sell was particularly pertinent in the case of Old Weston. In all probability, whoever eventually bought it from us would already have their own furniture, and even if they didn't, there could be no guarantee that they'd want to buy whatever we might think right for kitting out a period house like this. Yet, as the property dated back more than two hundred years, and since we had gone to great pains to restore as many as possible of its original features, we reckoned that we should at least buy a few *little* pieces of furniture that were in keeping with the character of the place. Then, by choosing larger items like lounge and dining room furniture carefully, we might be able to arrive at compromises that would look fitting here, without being too old-fashioned for our next home, which we hoped would be a newly-built house on the site of our proposed deer farm – wherever that might be.

With Edinburgh and its myriad of big-city retail outlets now only half an hour away along that new trunk road, it was for there that we headed one late August morning. We had been tipped off about a source of things that might just suit our needs – an establishment called Georgian Antiques. Paradoxically, though, Georgian Antiques' premises aren't situated within the elegant precincts of the capital's Georgian 'New Town', where the salerooms of upmarket international auction houses would have been unlikely targets for us in any event. 'Doing an Abbotsford', even on a miniscule scale compared to Sir Walter Scott's, was an indulgence that our limited financial resources strictly prohibited. So it was in Pattison Street, one of a labyrinth of equally nondescript backstreets bordering the docklands of Edinburgh's Port of Leith, that we found ourselves instead.

Try to imagine four football fields stacked on top of each other within the spartan interior of a former whisky warehouse, and crammed with everything from an ancient hickory-shafted golf club to the entire furnishings of the great hall of a Jacobean castle, and you have a fairly accurate picture of Georgian Antiques. If it isn't already one of Edinburgh's tourist attractions, it should be. Container-loads of antiques (by no means all of them Georgian) are regularly shipped from these anonymous-looking premises to every corner of the globe – and to the United States in particular. But the affable Irish owner is equally happy to let you rootle about all day without buying anything at all. It's hard not to yield to temptation, though, and there's no doubt that he's shrewd enough to know it.

To prove the point, our eventual purchases weren't quite as *little* as we had intended. After admiring them, deciding against them, walking on, swithering, going back for a second look, then a third, we became the proud owners of a huge, bleached-ash wardrobe with carved doors and matching dressing table. But the cost was surprisingly reasonable, and we decided that the two pieces would certainly blend nicely with the ambience of our bedroom in Old Weston. What's more, we agreed that they had a kind of timeless look that wouldn't seem out of place anywhere.

First mission accomplished, then, after a fascinating few hours of rootling. And, to Ellie's credit, she did heed my appeal (a tad too easily, I thought) not to splash out on a beautiful old pine dresser that, in all probability, had enjoyed pride of place for a century or two in the kitchen of some great country house or other.

'You're absolutely right,' she conceded. 'As wonderful and unique a piece of furniture as it is, and as much as I've always wanted a Welsh dresser just like that, we have to be sensible about what we spend – even though it *is* a bargain.'

'Nothing's a bargain if you don't need it, Ellie,' I stressed. 'I mean, I'd love to have that grandfather clock over there.' I pointed to it. 'It reminds me of the one my own grandfather had. Childhood memories could make it all too easy to yield to temptation.'

'Hmm, it *is* a beauty,' Ellie concurred. She walked over to take a closer look. 'And a fair price on the ticket, too.'

'But do I *really* need it?'

Ellie shook her head – a tad too enthusiastically, I thought.

'Correct,' I said, assuming the air of a paragon of virtue. 'So, the old grandfather clock stays where it is.'

'Just like the nice old dresser,' Ellie added, assuming the air of a willing martyr. 'Yes, we *have* to be sensible about what we spend.'

'Absolutely,' I said.

'And the old clock and dresser *will* find nice new homes,' she assured herself, assuming the air of a kid leaving the dog home empty-handed. 'In America!'

'Absolutely,' I agreed. 'Now, let's head up town and see if we can find some bargains in new three-piece suites.'

As an incurable hater of shopping, I was surprised by how much I enjoyed going round the furniture stores, surveying the stock, comparing prices and helping Ellie choose. Well, I was allowed to *think* I was helping with the choice. Ultimately, though, it was Ellie's eye for the 'classic' line in design that cast the final vote. Furniture was just the same as clothes, she told me. If you wanted things to outlast the fickle changes of fashion, you *had* to go for the classic look every time. I think I got the general drift, and it did appear to me that the stuff we ultimately bought would neither look out of place in Old Weston nor in a more modern setting.

Second mission accomplished, then, after another few hours of satisfying but tiring rootling.

Suddenly, I remembered what Ellie had come out with after her rummage through the Melrose shops. Now I knew exactly what she'd meant by it, so I quoted her, but with a slight variation.

'Phew,' I gasped 'You were right – all that raking round shops doesn't half make you, well, ehm... thirsty!'

'Yes, *especially* when you haven't bought anything for yourself,' she countered, quoting herself verbatim now, but with an added touch of acrimony.

'If you're referring to that old Welsh dresser you fancied, Ellie, you can forget it. We've already gone way over budget today. And anyway, we've bought some really super things for the house, so for Pete's sake just content yourself!' My feet were starting to hurt and I was doing my best to fight off the guilty pangs that, without fail, eventually invade the conscience of the thrifty man who has just spent a lot more money than he really intended to.

Ellie knew the signs. 'I know just the place to revive your spirits,' she said.

We were walking along Princes Street, unique among shopping avenues anywhere, having all its stores lined up along one side, with the manicured city centre 'glen' of Princes Street Gardens occupying the other. Punctuating the foreground are such imposing landmarks as the colonnaded National Galleries of Scotland and the Gothic 'space ship' that is the Sir Walter Scott Monument. Beyond them, the steeples and domes of the Old Town and the tall white gables of Ramsay Gardens step up towards the castle, which, seen from below, seems to grow directly out of its rugged pedestal of rock. One glimpse of this stunning view makes you appreciate why Robert Louis Stevenson, the venerated Edinburgh author of such masterpieces as *Treasure Island*, *Kidnapped* and *The Strange Case of Dr Jekyll and Mr Hyde*, wrote almost two hundred years ago that, 'No situation could be more commanding for the lead city of a kingdom; none better chosen for noble prospects.'

The clusters of present-day tourists aiming their cameras at that one particular prospect from Princes Street stand as ample testament to the lasting validity of Stevenson's observation.

We had been looking down on the city from the opposite direction the previous evening, however. For this was the Edinburgh International Festival season, and the annual arts extravaganza's most popular reciprocal attraction, the Military Tattoo, was our goal. The Royal Mile, that history-barnacled spine of the Old Town, which runs from Holyrood Palace all the way up through the High Street to Castlehill, is a hive of activity at this time, and the stretch by St Giles' Cathedral is the busiest of all. Every day, it teems with street performers, ranging in type from the ubiquitous solo bagpipers to clowns, fire-eaters, human statues, hairy poetry-spouters and transvestite unicyclists. This is an attention-grabbing spin-off from the official Festival's maverick and Topsy-like little 'sister', the Fringe, which keeps growing and growing so vigorously that its list of events now massively outnumbers the programme of its more refined sibling. So popular has the Festival Fringe become, in fact, that there isn't a venue, no matter how improbable, that isn't scrambled for by legions of would-be stars of tomorrow. The back of a delivery van, the bedroom of a student's flat and even an elevator have served as 'theatres' for some of the more determined (or desperate) participants.

Although it only lasts for a few weeks during August and September, all this uninhibited festivity has contributed to a permanent rejuvenation of Edinburgh, for so long regarded as the staid maiden aunt of urban Scotland. Nowhere is the city's smiling new face more apparent than in the cosmopolitan mix of restaurants, pavement cafés, trendy bars and nightclubs that have mushroomed in recent years, and continue to pop up with what seems like unsustainable regularity.

Ellie and I had certainly enjoyed the happy-go-lucky atmosphere that had the Old Town buzzing as we made our way that evening through the High Street's crush of Fringe hopefuls dishing out leaflets plugging their various events. We had been invited to the Military Tattoo as guests of its producer, Brigadier Melville Jameson, whom I'd known since producing the worldwide hit recording of 'Amazing Grace' with the Pipes and Drums and Military Band of his regiment, the Royal Scots Dragoon Guards, in the early seventies. At the time, Mel had held the comparatively modest rank of captain and, being a universally popular guy as well as an accomplished piper in his own right, he'd made an excellent president of the Scots Dragoon Guards' Pipes and Drums.

We worked together on several of the band's ensuing albums, mainly in Germany, where the regiment was stationed for much of the time. Mel and I became good friends during those happy days of chart-topping success, but the inevitable divergence of our career paths meant that we now hadn't been in each other's company for years. This was just one of the reasons I was glad he'd invited us to tonight's performance of the Tattoo. The other was that a reunion of some of the original 'Amazing Grace' band members had been arranged for before the show. It promised to be quite a night.

The last time I'd been on the esplanade of Edinburgh Castle was when I was a young piper myself, playing in the amalgamated pipe bands of local schools during a ceremonial 'beating of the retreat' to within the castle walls. Although the location was the same, the scene had been a lot different then. Our parade was watched by a few dozen spectators, mainly mums and dads and little brothers and sisters, while the banks of scaffolded grandstands rising high on three sides of the esplanade now indicated that, as on each night of the Edinburgh Military Tattoo, an audience of thousands would soon occupy every single seat. The feeling of anticipation was already building as we walked up the slope of the still-deserted parade ground and over the drawbridge into the inner wards of the castle.

Climbing up a cobbled walkway, you eventually arrive at a wide bastion enclosed by battlements that tower some eighty metres above the city. Here stands perhaps the most photographed of the castle's many attractions, Mons Meg, a massive fifteenth-century cannon that, in its day, was employed to encourage prospective raiders to keep a respectful distance. Nearby is one of Meg's modern descendants, the famous One O'Clock Gun, which blasts out a single volley at that precise moment every day, reminding Edinburgh folk to check their clocks, while making unsuspecting strangers waddle off to check the integrity of their underpants.

It was here that we dallied for a few moments to absorb the truly breathtaking outlook that these battlements command. Beyond the gardens directly below, the assorted frontages of Princes Street extend along the middle distance and provide an eye-catching forestage for the architectural precision of the New Town rising gracefully on the hillside behind. Then your gaze is drawn farther on towards the ever-present sweep of the Firth of Forth, and onwards still to the coast of Fife and the patchwork landscape of its fertile hinterland. In the words of Robert Louis Stevenson, 'noble prospects' indeed.

Our invitation stated that the pre-Tattoo reception was to be held in the castle commandant's personal quarters. True to his cavalryman's code of chivalry, Mel was at the entrance to extend a warm welcome to all of his guests. Resplendent in dress regimentals, he exuded the same gregarious air that had made him such a well-liked personality with his military colleagues, no matter how lowly or lofty their rank, when I first knew him those many years ago. Now he wore the badge of career success with equal informality, though with a quiet confidence befitting a man responsible for the annual presentation of what is justifiably rated as one of the greatest shows on earth. Mel, ever the latent impresario in my eyes, had finally blossomed into a producer of grand spectacles to whom even legendary showmen like Barnum and Bailey would have tipped an acknowledging hat.

Unstinting generosity had always been the hallmark of any social occasion that Mel had a hand in, and this get-together proved to be no exception. It was a real pleasure to be in the company of so many old acquaintances again, and the champagne endlessly on offer from a team of tray-toting stewards did no harm at all to the general mood of joviality. Mel had also invited along the leaders of the various bands and troupes of performers appearing in this year's Tattoo. Typically, they were from all corners of the globe, and it was fascinating to talk to them and to learn just a little about their countries and cultures. The occasion also revealed how much travelling Mel had to do in order to find and assess fresh attractions for each year's show. But, judging by the obvious pleasure he derived from seeing the product of his wanderings finally brought together in one place, it was a commitment he clearly revelled in.

The scenes in the castle yards as we eventually made our way back towards the esplanade were akin to what you might expect to see behind the set before the filming of an epic movie. While we had been sipping drinks and nibbling canapés in the commandant's residence, a stream of coaches had been ferrying in all the musicians, dancers and members of other Tattoo 'acts' from various barracks throughout the Edinburgh area – a logistical exercise of epic proportions in itself.

Here were a hundred pipers tuning their drones. There, about as many snare drummers practising paradiddles. Over by Mons Meg, a host of Highland dancers were limbering up, while somewhere out of sight, who knows how many display-team motorcyclists began revving their motors. Startled, a mounted fanfare trumpeter's horse kicked a kettledrum across the cobbles, scattering a troupe of Polynesian tribal dancers and creating barking bedlam among a pack of Royal Air Force performing guard dogs. Instant pandemonium. Soon, though, the entire cast of humans and animals would be mustered into their respective groups and assembled in designated areas ready to make their appearances on that huge arena with split-second timing. Perhaps only the army could put together such a massive event with the military precision required to make it run like clockwork night after night, no matter what the backstage dramas.

We followed Mel through secret passages of scaffolding poles enclosed in tarpaulin, to ultimately emerge right in the centre of the grandstand directly facing the castle. He showed us to our seats, which we could see had an unrivalled view of the entire esplanade.

'The royal box,' he grinned at Ellie. 'You'll be queen for an evening.'

Her expression was a mix of delight and disappointment. I knew what was going through her mind.

'Thanks for keeping it a surprise, Mel,' I said. 'You've saved me from having to buy her a tiara. Much appreciated.'

Ellie's attempt at laughing that quip off was far from convincing, but any regret that she may have had for not dressing up regally enough was soon replaced by her show of appreciation – along with the thousands of 'commoners' present – of the unfolding spectacle. That said, I did notice out of the corner of my eye that, when she thought I wasn't looking, she would occasionally mutate her applause into a discreet rotating of a limply-raised hand. The queenly wave, as routinely offered from a gilded coach to the flag-fluttering masses on the occasion of a royal wedding or like majestic pageant. Yeah, dream on, Ellie.

Strangely schizoid instruments are the bagpipes, their strident shriek being capable both of putting the fear of death into battleground adversaries and of stirring the soul in the most compelling of ways. Nowhere can the latter aspect of their contrary qualities be more evident than here at the Edinburgh Military Tattoo. The moment the lights go up on the dark esplanade and the first of the massed pipers appear through the portcullis archway, an electric thrill runs through the audience. You can feel it. The sensation builds as the pipers cross the drawbridge and fan out into rank after rank of kilt-swinging, plaid-billowing, sporran-swaying, drone-roaring, chanter-skirling swagger.

Then the drummers appear – waves of them: side drummers, tenor drummers and bass drummers – rattling, pounding and thumping out a driving beat to get even the least rhythmical of feet tapping in the grandstands. Now the maces of strutting drum majors twirl and fly in the vanguard of the massed pipers as they march and counter-march up and down the esplanade, churning out selections of well-known Scottish tunes that have the audience clapping in time and singing along. Against the floodlit backdrop of Edinburgh Castle, this is a feast for the eyes and ears that quickens the pulse and sets the blood surging. What's more, the phenomenon appears to apply to everyone, no matter what their nationality, or, I mused, how prejudiced against the bagpipes they may previously have been.

As the rearguard of the Massed Pipes and Drums marched back over the drawbridge into the castle, the floodlights faded and all fell eerily silent. During the gradual decline in temperature following sunset, a thin veil of mist had been drifting in from the coast and had gathered, almost unnoticed, above the esplanade. Now, with the outline of the Tattoo's magnificent backdrop silhouetted against the night sky, the sound of distant bagpipes pierced the expectant hush that had descended on the blacked-out scene. Then a searchlight picked out the figure of a lone piper on the uppermost ramparts of the castle, his feet shrouded in swirling wisps of white. It was as if he were standing on a cloud – a ghostly figure, playing a slow air charged with pathos and longing. The strains of this haunting melody seemed to evoke the very essence of the Highlands. A place of majestic mountains and lonely glens, of great lochs and misty islands, of tumbling waterfalls and winding rivers, of bloody battles won and lost, of humble though proud people robbed of their birthright and condemned to exile in far-off lands, never to return.

As the piper played on, I looked around me, and there wasn't a face that didn't show signs of being deeply moved. Such plaintive musical expressions of human feelings come from and touch the heart. And, in this setting and on such a night, no instrument but the bagpipes could ever express those sentiments more emotively. The hairs rise on the back of your neck, and strange feelings that swing between melancholy and elation fill your chest.

It's irresistible and inimitable. It's also totally irrational, in the opinion of some people who were discussing the phenomenon as they made their way down Castlehill with the rest of the crowds at the end of the Tattoo. I felt like telling them that that's the bagpipes for you. Love them or loathe them, in skilled hands, there's a lot more to their sound than the wailing of a tomcat in the throes of being castrated, as some of their unenlightened mockers are wont to suggest. But my temptation to intervene in defence of the pipes was mercifully thwarted by a yell from a nearby doorway –

'Hi, Kerr, ya stuck-up bugger ye! Are we no good enough for ye now, after all yer lordin' it up in the royal box back there?'

It was one of the former Royal Scots Dragoon Guards pipers, with whom we'd been exchanging polite chat at the pre-show reception. I could see that he had the rest of his old pipe band mates with him, and they were now clearly intent on loosening the strings of restraint that they'd felt obliged to keep respectfully tied in the presence of their one-time officer-in-command, Brigadier Mel.

The Ensign Ewart pub is located just down from the castle at the top of the Lawnmarket, and stands on what is reputedly the site of one of the oldest taverns in Edinburgh. Such luminaries of Scottish writing as Robert Burns, Sir Walter Scott and Robert Louis Stevenson are said to have supped within its welcoming old walls during their respective eras. But it wasn't any literary connection that had attracted my piping pals, now about to make their way inside. Nor was it simply because it happened to be the first bar they'd come across after exiting the esplanade. Well, not *entirely* for that reason, anyway. For Ensign (or Sergeant) Charles Ewart, after whom the pub is named, also happens to be the greatest hero in their regiment's long and illustrious history.

Before comparatively recent government policy dictated that many old British regiments be amalgamated in the interests of economy, the Royal Scots Dragoon Guards were known as the Royal Scots Greys, Scotland's oldest regiment and its only cavalry. The most notable of the many acts of bravery attributed to them in far-flung theatres of war was the single-handed capture of Napoleon's standard by said Ensign Ewart at the Battle of Waterloo. The eagle insignia of the defeated French Emperor's flag was duly adopted as the Scots Greys' regimental emblem, and remains that of the Royal Scots Dragoon Guards to this day.

'Aye, so that's why we like tae pop in here for a wee dram or two if we're ever in the area,' said one ex-stalwart of the 'Amazing Grace' pipers as he shepherded Ellie and me into the packed bar. 'Kinda payin' our respects tae the memory o' our old regimental hero, like.'

I noticed Ellie rolling her eyes. 'Any excuse for a drinking session,' she muttered to herself with the holier-than-thou dismissiveness of the near-teetotaller. 'I mean, there's an

Ensign Ewart statue in Princes Street, so why don't they go and give a quick salute or two to that instead?'

'They probably will, when they're in *that* area,' I hissed, hoping the lads hadn't heard her. 'Come on, Ellie, just try to look happy.' I surveyed the heaving mass of humanity crammed into the low-ceilinged confines of the pub. 'We won't hang about for long, I promise you. Jeez, there's hardly room to breathe in here!'

Then the live music started up somewhere behind a sea of heads. Fiddles, tin whistles, guitars, banjos and melodeons began belting out old Scottish folk tunes as if there was no tomorrow. Even if, like me, you usually don't drink whisky, it's hard to resist when you're in a historic hostelry in the ancient heart of Scotland's capital city, and especially if you're in the company of a bunch of committed dram-downers when the 'heederum-hoderum' tunes are ringing in your ears. It's a phenomenon that – in a more high-spirited way – is just as compelling as the plaintive sound of the lone piper on the castle ramparts. Nevertheless, painful past experience should have taught me that it's fatal to get suckered into matching ex-army bagpipers whisky-for-whisky, no matter how exhilarating the atmosphere.

And that's precisely why, at the end of our furniture-buying jaunt the following day, I was feeling totally knackered. Moderation-in-all-things Ellie, meanwhile, was still as fresh as a daisy as she swung me left off Princes Street. I was expecting no sympathy from her, and I didn't get any.

'Serves you right,' she said when I complained of having a thumping sore head. 'You should've stuck to your word when you first told your old pals we were leaving. But no, we were still in the pub at closing time, and you were last to leave, as usual. Yes, and even then the barman had to almost carry you out.'

'Well, I was tired,' I feebly mitigated. 'All that champagne earlier, then the whisky. The grape and the barley. Bad mixture. I'm not used to it.' I countered the look of impending attack in Ellie's eyes with a swift, proactive defence submission. 'But at least I keep myself to myself when I'm tiddly. Not like some people – making a bloody fool of themselves in public.' I was grasping at straws now. Ellie knew it and she snatched them away.

'Tiddly! Did you say… *tiddly*?'

'Of course, and everybody's entitled to get a wee bit merry on occasions when –'

'*Tiddly?* A wee bit *merry*?'

'Uh-huh, and –'

'*Tiddly? Merry?*' She stopped walking, grabbed my arm and looked me square in the eye. 'Listen, you were absolutely plastered, blootered, blitzed, stotious, pie-eyed, pissed as a fart – whatever you want to call it – but certainly nothing as middling as *tiddly*!'

I kept my own counsel. It's hard to argue when you only have a hazy memory of your accuser's allegations. In this case, hazy meant blank, and I knew that Ellie knew it too.

She likes nothing better than taking a well-timed, psychological kick at the afflicted male; particularly *her* male, and especially if his affliction has been self-inflicted. She had saved the following verbal boot until she sensed my defences were at their lowest ebb.

'And as for not making a fool of yourself...' She paused to exhale a puff of derision down her nostrils. 'What's grabbing the folk group's tambourine, prancing about and doing an impression of Mick Jagger during their rendition of 'Flower of Scotland' if it's not making a fool of yourself? Just tell me that!'

I knew when I was licked. I recalled the theme of an obscure American record called 'Little Bits and Pieces'. The lyrics recounted the mental agonies of a guy who had become the victim of a sadistic friend, intent on drip-feeding him the ever-worsening details of his drunken misdemeanours at a party in their boss's house the night before. The payoff line, whimpered by the mortified culprit was, 'Did I take off *ALL* my clothes?'

I held up my hands. 'OK, OK, Ellie – end of post mortem,' I pleaded. 'Just, uhm, just lead me to that fountain of revived spirits you mentioned. Yeah, and don't take any detours.'

★ ★ ★ ★ ★

Hanover Street is one of several that run equidistantly northward from Princes Street and cross over the pub-crawlers' mecca of Rose Street, then on to George Street at the top of a gentle rise, before commencing downhill towards Queen Street, its eponymous gardens and the shores of the Forth in the far distance. This is the graceful, ordered heart of Edinburgh's New Town, universally recognised as the finest surviving example of neo-Georgian town planning anywhere. It has the architecture to match in the fine commercial and residential buildings that line its long, straight streets, each intersecting the other at right angles, and at intervals perfectly calculated to best exploit the superb visual qualities of the hillside location.

No more than fifty paces over the 'summit' of George Street, the red-white-and-green *Bar Napoli* sign beckons on the right. I could smell the enticing aroma of freshly baked bread as Ellie led me down a short flight of steps from the pavement to the door.

'I've popped in here a couple of times when I've been shopping,' she said. 'The businessman's lunch selection is fantastic, and the value's every bit as good as the fixed-price *menús del día* we used to go for in Mallorca. Unbelievable. You wouldn't have credited it in Scotland a few years ago.'

I could see the evidence of this the moment we walked in. At almost four o'clock in the afternoon, it was already well past the time that any conscientious, clock-watching Edinburgh businessman should have returned to his desk. This wasn't Spain, after all, yet the arched, white-walled basement was still full. And, as I was pleased to note, the mood was anything but businesslike. Not, I should add, that there was anything *un*businesslike about the way the business was being run. On the contrary, the shuttle service of waiters breezily dispensing food from the open-plan kitchen suggested that this was the slickest of catering operations. It's also fair to say, in defence of all conscientious, clock-watching Edinburgh businessmen, that none of their diligent fraternity now appeared to be occupying any of the tables.

This, remember, was Edinburgh at Festival time, so the place was alive with an international congregation of tourists with time on their hands and a will to enjoy every second of it. One whiff of the lively atmosphere already had the cobwebs clearing from my head. Ellie had chosen well – and shrewdly too, as time would prove.

'*Ciao*, Signora Kerr!' a smiling young man with a distinctive Italo-Scottish delivery called out to Ellie as he beckoned us into the body of the restaurant. 'Hey, nice to see you again, eh! This way, *per favore*. I gotta special table for you up-a the back here a wee bit.'

'That's Giorgio,' Ellie whispered. 'The boss's son. Nice boy. The Crolla family. Well-known Italian food people in Edinburgh. I was introduced to the mum and dad in here a while back. Nice people.'

Ellie seemed to have established herself as a recognised regular in the Bar Napoli surprisingly quickly, considering she'd only been in the place 'a couple of times' before. But, as I then deduced, that would be mainly down to the gift that Italian folk possess of not just welcoming the stranger but remembering the face and name as well. And I couldn't deny that another contributory factor was Ellie's ability to make a lasting impression without even trying. It's called presence, and you either have it or you don't. I fall into the latter category myself, and that suits me fine – although my Mick Jagger impersonation in the Ensign Ewart the night before might have given the opposite impression to those present.

'I thought that, since we'd skipped lunch,' Ellie said to me once we were comfortably seated up-a the back, 'that a quick wedge or two of pizza would help recharge your batteries.' She gestured towards the laughing, wine-quaffing occupants of the adjacent tables. 'And I reckoned the lively company in here would perk you up as well.'

It did, and so did the waiter whose patch included our table. Giorgio introduced the dashingly handsome Latin fellow as Salvatore, but after he'd spoken a few words, it was obvious that his accent wasn't Italian, but Spanish. We got chatting, and it transpired that he came originally from Madrid, and his name wasn't really Salvatore, but Salvador. Both words mean 'saviour' in their respective languages, which was very apt, as Salvador's insistence that I should forget the mineral water I'd ordered to wash down a couple of headache-curing paracetamols and have a hangover-chasing glass of wine instead turned out to be a life-saver. Or so I thought.

It can happen all too easily when you resort to taking the hair of the dog when you're dying on the day after the night before. As soon as you begin to feel that little bit better, one hair leads to two, or three, or even more. I ended up in the 'even more' camp. Salvador's happy banter about his homeland and our comparing of notes about the noisy Sunday lunches that are such a feature of its culture saw to that. Those boisterous gastro-social occasions, surrounded by huge Spanish families that extend from babes in arms to grandparents in their dotage, had been a highlight of our weekends in Mallorca, and we'd missed them a lot since leaving the island.

So when we eventually said our goodbyes to Giorgio and Salvador, it was with a promise that, although it was Italian, the Bar Napoli would be our Mallorcan home from home every Sunday lunchtime from then on.

'Nice to see you looking so happy,' Ellie said as we drove out of the multi-storey car park at the top of Leith Walk. 'I had a feeling that place would do the trick.'

With Ellie at the wheel, I sat back and heaved a wine-induced sigh of contentment. 'Yes, it was an inspired decision of yours to get me into such a lively atmosphere, Ellie. And all that talk about Spain with Salvador was just what the doctor ordered to chase away the booze-and-bagpiper blues.'

Ellie smiled sweetly, but said nothing. I should have taken that as a warning. But I was feeling so mellow now that it didn't even strike me as particularly odd that she continued straight on towards Leith instead of turning right for Haddington. By the time we drew up outside the Georgian Antiques warehouse again, the multiple hairs of the dog that Salvador had plied me with had really kicked in. I was totally at peace with the world – euphemistically speaking.

Taking my arm, Ellie steered me straight to the old Welsh dresser she had drooled over earlier in the day.

'You've got to admit that it's a real beauty,' she purred enthusiastically, but with a tinge of despair blended in.

My mellowness had now graduated into mindless magnanimity. I gave her shoulder a patronising pat. 'Pieces like this aren't an extravagance, Ellie, they're a gilt-edged investment.'

Her face lit up. 'You mean we can *buy* it?'

I shrugged sagely. 'It would be a crime not to.'

She planted a kiss on my cheek. 'I *knew* you'd eventually come round to my way of thinking.'

She also knew what she was doing.

My mindless magnanimity now rushed headlong into profligate prodigality. I nodded towards a matching pair of antique oil lamps on an adjacent table. 'Buy those as well,' I said with a devil-may-care flourish of my hand. 'They'll sit perfectly on the dresser.'

'And, uhm, the grandfather clock over there?' Ellie stealthily ventured. 'The one that brings back childhood memories for you?'

'The most rock-solid investment of them all,' I declared. 'Oh yes, my dear, I knew that from the very first moment I clapped eyes on it. Absolutely, and it'll sit perfectly in the front room at Old Weston.'

I ignored the knowing winks that Ellie and the Irishman exchanged as I settled the bill. It had been a long twenty-four hours, and it was as much as I could do to focus on the cheque-book.

– NINE –

OF GHOSTS, WITCHES AND PIRATES

Although we had learned a lot during the renovation of Old Weston, and had enjoyed most of the related experiences as well, there was as much relief as satisfaction in finally seeing the work completed. Month after month of living in a building site is hard to remain enthusiastic about, and the perpetual upheaval of moving one room ahead of the work in progress doesn't do a lot for family life either. We had hardly seen Charlie, except at mealtimes, of course, and even then the conditions in the kitchen hadn't really been conducive to relaxed conversation. It's difficult to be chatty when you're sitting at a folding table surrounded by piles of timber and bags of cement.

Meanwhile, though, Charlie was growing up fast, as thirteen-year-olds do, and the yodelly breaking of his voice was coinciding with the usual adolescent experimentations with things that aren't *necessarily* good for you. Ellie, the way mums do, had a knack of 'stumbling upon' the tell-tale signs. The soft-porn magazine on top of Charlie's wardrobe that he reckoned 'one of the plumbers must have left there'. The matches and half-smoked fag in the bottom of his schoolbag that he claimed he was 'just keeping for a friend'. The empty beer can under his bed that he could 'only imagine one of his mates must have planted there for a laugh'.

We couldn't recall any of this stuff happening with his brother Sandy when he was the same age. Maybe he'd been of a less 'inquiring' nature, or, as Charlie was quick to allege, just a lot smarter at hiding the evidence of his misdemeanours. Whatever, Sandy had come through that awkward age unscathed and without causing us any worry, so we had no reason to delve into the implications of Charlie's leading remark now. All things considered, though, what was perhaps significant was that Sandy had spent his childhood living on a farm, whereas Charlie, at an impressionable stage of his life, now found himself living in the centre of a town, surrounded by an entirely different set of potential distractions and temptations. There are no corner shops where you can buy magazines, cigarettes and beer on a farm, and peer pressure from the more streetwise kids in a town is all an easily-led kid needs to encourage him to get up to things that he shouldn't. For instance, walk through any municipal park on a Saturday or Sunday morning and the chances are you'll see a scatter of booze bottles and cigarette ends marking the place where the wayward-inclined members of the local youth had gathered for a puff and swig under cover of darkness the night before.

So did Charlie really spend all of each weekend evening he visited his chums safely ensconced inside their homes, or did he (and they) join the ranks of the park reprobates when the opportunity arose? As concerned parents, all we could do was keep encouraging him to behave in the way he'd been brought up to, whilst also leaving him a reasonable amount of freedom to use his own spare time as he saw fit. It's all a matter of mutual trust and respect, and we certainly believed that Charlie had enough respect for us to allow us to trust him. And we did. All the same, I couldn't resist the temptation to somewhat mischievously put the basis of that trust to the test one evening.

I had been left an old double-barrel shotgun by my grandfather when he died, and although it had seen better days, it was a keepsake that I would never have dreamt of parting with. Even though I never used the gun, the law required that I had a licence for it, and each time I renewed the permit, the police would dutifully pay us a visit to check that the gun was being stored in a secure place. In Old Weston, it just happened that I'd fixed the locking gun cabinet inside a cupboard in Charlie's bedroom – my idea being that it wouldn't be the most obvious place for a potential thief to look. It would have taken a brave burglar indeed to venture into such a midden as that.

'We've come with the renewed shotgun licence,' one of two police constables said when I opened the door to them at ten-thirty one night. Old Weston is located next-door-but-one to the Haddington police station, so it didn't strike me as being strange that they'd come at such a late hour. I assumed that they'd been on their way back from doing a bit of routine beat-bashing round the streets. They apologised for disturbing us, nevertheless, then asked if they could check the gun cabinet. That would be no problem at all, I assured them, the shoots of a wicked little idea sprouting in my head.

I led the constables upstairs, then stopped outside Charlie's room and listened. Perfect. He was snoring. I threw open the door. 'This is the lad you're looking for, officers,' I declared at the top of my voice. 'Take him away!'

Not even Edinburgh's One o'Clock Gun going off immediately behind the back of an unwitting sightseer could have evoked a more startled reaction. Charlie sat bolt upright in bed. 'Oh, shit!' he warbled, his eyes almost popping out of their sockets when he noticed the uniformed policemen staring down at him. His jaw dropped so far that, if he had been standing up, I swear it would have hit the floor. It was impossible to tell if there was any element of guilt in his expression, because the look of sheer terror contorting his face masked every other emotion. I laughed so much I thought I was going to wet myself, and even the two dour constables allowed themselves a brief chortle. Charlie, his face ashen, leapt out of bed and dashed past us to the bathroom.

Only after the policemen had left and Ellie and I had gone to bed ourselves, did I hear him returning to his bedroom, but that wasn't before he'd gone down to the kitchen to chuck something in the washing machine. I started to chuckle delightedly, but Ellie didn't see the fun in any of this.

'That was a terrible thing to do, frightening him like that,' she snapped. 'Honestly, it was really cruel. Childish, too. You should be thoroughly ashamed of yourself.'

'Nonsense!' I laughed. 'It'll teach him what it would feel like if the long arm of the law ever did have reason to collar him. Yeah, he won't forget that experience as long as he lives, and that can only be a good thing.'

There was no way of telling if the practical joke really did teach Charlie a lesson about staying on the right side of the law. But he did, and Ellie never 'stumbled upon' any further evidence of teenage 'research' that she could pin on him. Nevertheless, her view was that the entire silly episode had probably served no other purpose than to encourage Charlie to be a damn sight more careful about keeping his little peccadillos better concealed in future – an outcome which, of course, flew in the face of her motherly inquisitiveness.

Anyway, even Charlie eventually saw the funny side of his bedroom brush with the beat bobbies, and now that he had a room of his own that was fit to bring his friends into, we saw a lot more of him *and* them. We couldn't have been more pleased about that. Once again, family life was returning to normal, and we took great delight in being able to enjoy the charms of the lovely old house that each of us, in our own way, had contributed towards restoring. I think that Ellie probably loved Old Weston more than any of us. She revelled in the unpretentious charm that a typical Scottish town house of the period simply oozed. Whether sitting in the window of the upstairs living room, having a cup of tea while looking out at the town going about its daily business, or taking time at last to pretty up the courtyard garden at the back of the house with flower boxes and hanging baskets, she was in her element. One way or another, domestic disruption had been an all-too-often recurrence since leaving Cuddy Neuk four years previously, so she was right to make the most of this interlude of normality, which she knew wouldn't last long.

I was still determined to find a piece of land on which to set up the deer farm, and now that the task of doing up the old house was out of the way, I'd have more time to devote myself to that priority. But this didn't stop me from enjoying our period of living in Old Weston as well. Its proximity to the facilities of the town wasn't what appealed, however, as I was really itching to get back into the country again. Yet, although located near the centre of town, this house had an unmistakably rural feel to it. That may seem like stating the obvious to many city dwellers who, understandably enough, might regard having a home anywhere within an old market town like Haddington as 'living in the country' anyway. Well, equally understandably, to a yokel like me, it isn't. Looking through your window onto a street instead of fields and woodland for as far as the eye can see is the difference. All that aside, though, what gave Old Weston its rural feel had less to do with its location than to that intangible 'character' that comes out of the very fibre of an old house. It's there in the ghosts or spirits of the people who have lived within its four walls before.

One night, after dark, I was sitting alone by the fireside in the downstairs front room, which, in times past, would have been called the parlour – the 'best room', kept neat and tidy for the reception of visitors. To the sleepy ticking of the grandfather clock, I was reading through the yellowed pages of the property's title deeds – the first time I'd had a chance to do so since receiving them from our lawyer some months earlier. The only light, apart from the flickering of the flames in the hearth, came from the glow of a table lamp beside my armchair. It was the mellow sort of light that might just as well have come from a similarly-placed candle a couple of centuries ago.

Looking down the list of the house's previous owners was akin to studying a family tree, with the names and occupations of every member carefully recorded for posterity. It was fascinating to learn, for instance, that the house had once belonged to the local doctor, who had lived in one of Court Street's 'mansions' himself, and had made a bit of extra money on the side by renting out each room in Old Weston to separate tenants. Many years before that, the house had been the home of the proprietor of one of the town's first newspapers, and earlier still to the owner of Haddington's livestock market.

Reading this latter entry in the soft lamplight had me imagining this old character sitting by the same fireside, perhaps with a glass of whisky in his hand, going through his sales legers after a profitable day of auctioneering at the mart. Then I pictured him in daytime, sitting behind a big desk in this same room, cheerfully welcoming a procession of farmers lining up to settle their accounts – in cash, of course. The banter about cattle and sheep prices and the occasional bawdy joke would have been little different, I mused, from that heard at livestock markets to this day – except for the value of the cattle and sheep, of course.

The sound of a throaty chortle quickly followed by a girlish giggle caught my ear. At first I assumed it was coming from outside – a couple having a bit of slap and tickle on their way home from the pub, no doubt. That was a fairly normal occurrence at this time of night. Then it happened again, and this time it seemed as if the sound was coming from *inside* the house – from somewhere upstairs. But it couldn't be, I told myself. Ellie and Charlie had been asleep in their respective bedrooms for ages. In any case, Ellie didn't have that sort of tinkling laugh, and although Charlie's voice was in the process of breaking, it hadn't yet reached the gruff baritone of this one. A shiver ran up my spine as the laughter rang out again. I tried to persuade myself that, after thinking so much about the 'ghosts and spirits' of the old house, my ears were just playing tricks on me. But they weren't, and the muffled sound of male and female hilarity repeated itself as if to prove it.

Curiosity overcame my natural coward's reluctance to investigate, and I made my way *very* hesitantly upstairs, being extra careful not to step on any squeaky boards. Whistling softly, I checked the bedrooms first. Sure enough, both Ellie and Charlie were sound asleep. No sign of anyone in the living room. Nobody lurking in the bathroom, either. A narrow, winding staircase led up to two large attic rooms. Could the sound have been coming from there? No, I was just being silly, I said to myself as reassuringly as I could. It had only been my imagination – surely. Then that eerie sound of giggling and chuckling echoed out again, and it *was* coming from above. I was convinced of that now. I was sorely tempted to awaken Ellie and Charlie and ask them to accompany me up to the attic. But that would only have proved to them what a complete wimp I was, and a hallucinating one at that.

I made my tentative way up the stairs, still whistling softly. I opened the first door. It creaked, sending another nervy shudder scurrying up my back. I felt for the light switch and flicked it. Silence. I poked just enough of my head round the door to allow me to peek inside with one eye. Nobody there. I took a deep breath. Only one more room to go. My heart thumping, I followed the same routine again. Open door sl-o-o-ow-ly, switch on light, peep cautiously inside. Nobody there again.

I started to laugh. It was the near-hysterical laugh of the true whistler in the dark who has just twigged that the bogeyman he thought was staring at him through the window had been nothing more sinister than his own reflection in the glass. Just as I was starting to congratulate myself on my extreme bravery, my eyes were drawn to a little trap door in the centre of the attic room's ceiling. Funny, I thought – I'd never noticed *that* before. It was only about six inches square, just big enough to put a hand through, which, for some unknown reason, was what I immediately did.

My fingers explored this way and that. Then, among the dust and cobwebs, they lighted on something cold. I took hold of it and pulled it out into the light. It was an empty whisky bottle, or rather a flat half bottle – a handy shape and size for slipping into your coat pocket. It was obviously very old, but it still had a label attached. Although faded and mouse-nibbled, I could just make out the figure of a man in Highland dress, with the distiller's name emblazoned underneath. Intrigued, I poked my hand through the opening again and found another whisky bottle, then another and another, until I had a collection of ten sitting on the floor. A few of them bore the name of Maltman, a wine and spirits merchant, who, according to the labels, had owned a shop in Haddington's High Street at some stage back in the mists of time.

My thoughts returned to the old owner of the livestock market, whose name on the house's title deeds had fired my imagination just a few minutes earlier. In his day, an attic room like this would more than likely have been the maid's quarters. I wondered if the maid and the collection of empties stashed away in the roof cavity might have had a connection. Maybe she'd been a secret tippler. And why not? Life would have been hard for a young girl in household service back then, and perhaps getting a bit tipsy occasionally would have been one of her few simple pleasures.

Then an even more juicy possibility entered my mind. Maybe the old auctioneer had been in the habit of having furtive liaisons with the maid up here while his wife was safely asleep in bed downstairs. Yes, that was it – the randy old bugger would have crept up here, bottle of whisky in his pocket, got the lassie half drunk, then –

My mental meanderings were brought abruptly to a halt by that ghostly sound again. An old man chortling and a girl tittering. What surprised me, though, was that the sound wasn't coming from inside the house after all, but from outside. Directly outside, in fact. I ran to the window and, tugging it fully open, stuck my head and shoulders out. But the street was completely deserted. Not a solitary soul in sight. My flesh began to creep as it dawned on me that, if the laughter had neither come from inside the house nor outside in the street, the only other place it could possibly have emanated from was within the very walls of the old building itself. Two spirits of times past, happily lubricated on the spirit from one of those old bottles now lying empty at my feet.

I slept uneasily that night, waking every so often to listen in the darkness for evidence of further whisky-fuelled capers echoing out from... somewhere. But all I heard was the striking of the town clock down at the bottom of Court Street, and the whining and spitting of two tomcats feuding over scraps in someone's capsized rubbish bin.

Ellie scoffed at my ghost story when I told it to her next morning, preferring to believe that I'd been hearing things after having a late-night beano on the contents of the booze cabinet myself. I knew very well that that wasn't the case, but I let the matter rest, as I knew equally well that Ellie wouldn't change her opinion. Images of my Mick Jagger take-off in the Ensign Ewart pub were still too fresh in her mind. Give a dog a bad name.

I never did hear the spectral laughter again, and the more I thought about it, the more I convinced myself that I'd been the victim of my own over-fertile imagination. The source of the laughter would have been outside – probably a nearby doorway, where the slapping-and-tickling protagonists were tucked safely out of sight of nosey eyes like mine peering out of nearby windows. Still, there was no harm in believing that there was more to the old house than met the eye, and I felt that any spirits of previous occupants that did live on within its walls were happy ones. That was certainly the atmosphere that pervaded Old Weston, and it wouldn't have taken much persuasion for us to have put down permanent roots there

– though maybe with the proviso that we could somehow transport it intact to a countryside location.

That could never be, however, and the reality of the situation was that we would now have to recoup the money we had spent on the house's restoration, with, we hoped, a tidy profit attached. Accordingly, the 'For Sale' sign was posted – yet again. As Ellie rather wryly commented, it would soon reach the stage when we'd have to consider adopting those two fateful words as the motto on the Kerr Clan crest.

I managed a sheepish laugh. 'Yes, eh, many a true word spoken in jest, as the, uhm, old saying goes.'

She pursed her lips, raised a cynical eyebrow and shook her head. 'Except I wasn't jesting.'

In an ideal world, a piece of land for the deer-farming enterprise would have become available before a buyer for Old Weston emerged. But, regardless of my best efforts, none did – and that despite the fact that it took a lot longer to sell the house than we'd presumed it would. The increased demand for homes in this area that the opening of the new road from Edinburgh had sparked certainly existed, but, as we soon discovered, not yet to an extent that had potential buyers lining up outside the door of every house that came on the market. What's more, like everyone else in our position, we'd assumed that our lovingly-restored old property would have viewers swooning at its charms the moment they stepped over the threshold. Some did, but by no means all. Tastes differ and, as we had learned when selling Ca's Mayoral back in Mallorca, 'For Sale' signs attract as many rubbernecking time-wasters as they do genuine prospective purchasers.

In our position, with no other source of income, the longer it took to sell our current home, the more our finances diminished, courtesy of daily living expenses – or weekly, monthly, or even, as transpired in this case, multi-monthly living expenses. By the time that elusive buyer for Old Weston did emerge, it didn't take very close inspection of our bank balance to discover that, rather than having made the tidy profit we'd hoped for, we had just about broken even. In truth, the only additional 'moveable' assets we had to show for our efforts were the wardrobe, dressing table, grandfather clock and Welsh dresser we had bought from the Georgian Antiques warehouse in Leith. They, at least, were already increasing in value, and they'd be going with us. Ellie had been right again when she foxily cajoled me into buying them on the afternoon of my hangover-chasing treatment at the hands of Salvador, the Bar Napoli's Spanish waiter.

'What are we going to do next?' I now asked her, repeating a question that I had put to her more often than I cared to remember during the course of our roller-coaster life together.

'Well, you either get an honest job like normal people, or...'

Now it was my turn to purse my lips, raise a cynical eyebrow and shake my head.

'Or,' Ellie continued, 'we buy another run-down property to do up and sell on.'

'OK, then,' I swiftly came back without recourse to unnecessary debate, 'let's make the rounds of the estate agents. If you're game to do it all over again with your wallpaper scraper and paintbrush, I'll be right behind you with my hammer and saw.'

★ ★ ★ ★ ★

Again, in a perfect world, we'd have found just such a ripe-for-renovation house to move into on the same day that we moved out of Old Weston. Instead, we were obliged to rent somewhere to live in while the search went on. This time, it was a rambling old farmhouse in the back of beyond, where we spent a chilly winter trying to keep warm in the evenings without actually sitting *in* the fire. Once you've become accustomed to central heating, you forget what it's like to fight a losing battle against draughty doors and rattly windows that turn the condensation from your breath into frosted glass during the night. Just to see out, you even have to fetch the de-icer spray from the car on the coldest mornings.

And there's the dilemma of what to do about a shower, if there's only a vintage bathtub so big that the clapped-out old boiler can't heat enough water to fill it. You have to improvise, because it isn't your house and you aren't going to spend any of your own money on fixed improvements. So, you sit on your knees in the bath, trying to convince your chattering teeth and goose-pimpled flesh that the ancient paraffin heater in the corner really is keeping the temperature above freezing, while one of those hose-type hair-washing sprays with rubber orifices that fix over the taps dribbles tepid water over your tortured, puzzled body.

'Just think of it as character-building,' I said to Ellie and Charlie round the dinner table one windy night, when the draughts whistling over the kitchen floor were attempting to turn the rug under our feet into a magic carpet.

Their silence said more about their opinion of that futile statement than words could tell. For all of us, the balmy climes we had enjoyed in Mallorca had never seemed more like a distant dream. But, I then reminded them, as Jaume, old Maria's avuncular son-in-law, encouragingly told me when I was despairing about our prospects after he'd revealed that our orange orchards were disease-ridden, everything would come right in the spring. No one was more surprised than I was, however, when the adage actually came true back here in Scotland. Well, at least *partly* true.

★ ★ ★ ★ ★

'Merryhatton Roselea' may sound more like the name of a vaudeville-era striptease artiste than a pantiled country cottage. But a cottage is what it is, located in the heart of the rolling East Lothian countryside, about halfway between Haddington and the picturesque little seaside town of North Berwick. We managed to buy the house for a price that was extremely reasonable for a property in such a pleasant and convenient area, not because it was in a poor state of repair, but because it was just a tad on the small side for many families' aspirations these days. The learning curve that we had been scaling since buying Ca's Mayoral was about to take another upwards turn. 'Home Extension' would be the title of our next lesson in personal property development.

Deciding on the scope and layout of the extension was the first task we had to tackle, followed by getting an architect to draw up the plans and submit them to the planning department of the local council for approval. The first two tasks were a pleasure. If you have any kind of creative bent, there's a load of fun to be had in juggling permutations of room sizes and positions relative to each other, then learning the practicalities or otherwise of each idea from the architect. We eventually arrived at a plan to build on a new living room, bedroom, bathroom and utility room at right angles to the original building which, consequently, would end up being L-shaped. So far so good. Enter the man from the planning department.

Having spent eighteen months as an executive officer in the civil service after I left school, I knew something about how the bureaucratic brain is expected to work – which is one of the reasons I left the civil service. There's always a rule somewhere in the endless book of official commandments that must be obeyed, no matter how superficial it may happen to be within a specific context. Again, if you have any kind of creative bent, you'll find a way to circumvent the anomaly while satisfying the *spirit* of the regulation. Unless you're at least a cabinet minister, such devious imagination is not encouraged in the corridors of government, however, and the carrot of a rock-solid pension at the end of the road is dangled to remind the potential miscreant not to wander from the well-trodden path of compliance. The result is that a minor matter that could quickly be resolved by a bit of discreet rule-massaging can end up in irritating delays for Joe Public and in even more paper-chasing for the already 'overworked' civil servant. On such eccentricities is the voracious appetite of the tax monster fed.

That said, in fairness to the planning officer who was dealing with our Merryhatton Roselea plans, the first hurdle he threw in front of me was one that I should have seen coming even before we bought the cottage. I hadn't employed the services of a property surveyor to evaluate the place, but had relied on 'my eye being my merchant', just as we had done when buying Ca's Mayoral and Old Weston. Our septic tank would have to be replaced, the planning man said. It was located within the boundary of the next-door cottage, the effluent from which also flowed into it, making it too small for what was being asked of it at present, even before taking into account the 'product' of our proposed new bathroom and utility room.

As the neighbouring house was much younger and had been built on land originally belonging to ours, why, I asked him, had the sharing of an inadequately-sized septic tank been sanctioned by his local authority colleagues in the first place? A noncommittal shrug was all I got in reply, but it went without saying that, if I took the council to task over that, then I'd have a fat chance of achieving anything but a long delay in the processing of our planning application *and* an unbargained-for legal bill to boot.

Damned septic tanks! They had been the bane of my life at both Cuddy Neuk and Ca's Mayoral, they'd had me knee- and elbow-deep in 'organic matter' trying to unblock their pipes so often I could write a thesis about most aspects of human sludge, and now yet another smelly pit had bubbled up to blight me. Just agreeing to install a brand new septic tank wasn't to be the end of the matter, though. Oh, no – nothing as straightforward as that.

Because of the geography immediately surrounding our house, the only feasible location for a new cesspit would be on a piece of land that currently belonged to our neighbours. Being reasonable folk, they offered no objection to that, provided I bought the piece of land from them, at *their* price. Not open to negotiation. Fair enough – we'd all probably do the same in those circumstances. They had me over a barrel, nevertheless, and they knew it. Another condition of obtaining their cooperation was that I would restore their long-overloaded septic tank to perfect working order. More knee- and elbow-deep poking and plunging of drains beckoned, and this time I wouldn't even be fishing about in our own muck. The joys of country living.

No sooner was one planning permission problem solved, however, than another was presented to me, and this one ratcheted up the slope of our learning curve even more steeply. The L-shape of the proposed alteration to the form of the house meant that the new part of the building would reach the present boundary of the front garden, which was really quite a narrow strip of land. Anyway, regulations dictate that you can't build to the absolute extremity of your site. Our architect had forewarned me about that, and I fully understood the logic behind it. The solution, I thought, would be simple. All I'd need do was buy a bit of land from the owner of the field in front of the house and extend our garden into that. The farmer whose field it was had proved amenable, so a price had been agreed and the deal closed even before our planning application was submitted. Be prepared in good time – that was my motto. Fine, but don't try to second-guess the planners – that was the lesson I was about to learn.

'You'll have to apply for change-of-use permission,' the official told me, and it was plain from the *fait accompli* look on his face that he thought he'd finally managed to throw a wrecking spanner in the works.

I was suitably nonplussed. 'Ehm, that would be permission to change the use of... what?'

I cocked my head apprehensively while the planning man smiled a self-satisfied smile, then twirled his trusty hank of red tape into a verbal lasso.

'The land you bought from the farmer,' he replied. 'It's designated as agricultural, and the rules come down heavily against it being used for any other purpose.' Noting that I was now even more nonplussed, his smile mutated into a smirk as he added, 'You can apply for change-of-use permission to make it into a garden if you want, but...'

'But what?'

'But that piece of farmland has to be protected as part of our heritage.'

By now, I was starting to see as red as his tape. 'Part of whose heritage?'

'The people's.' Now he was sounding as red as I was seeing.

'But that piece of land doesn't belong to the people. I paid good money for it, so it now belongs to me, as does its heritage. Agreed?'

He chose not to be drawn on that, so I tried another approach – a slightly less provocative one.

'Look, we're talking about a postage stamp of land amounting to about a third of an acre here. Are you honestly suggesting that it's going to make one blind bit of difference to the millions of acres that comprise the United Kingdom if that piddling little scrap is used as a lawn instead of a cabbage patch or whatever?'

He half-closed his eyes and gave me an accusing look. 'We know your type. We know you're fully aware of the advantage of having that third of an acre designated as garden land on your title deeds.'

'The only advantage I'm aware of is that it'll give me a *bigger* front garden. Do you have a problem with that sort of thing?'

'I *beg* your pardon?'

I should have known better than to direct a jibe like that at a bloke who hadn't exactly been blessed with the stature of a basketball player, but my mouth was now working without too much advice from my brain.

'What are you trying to say?' I snapped. 'Stop talking in riddles. I'm self-employed, so, unlike you, I don't get paid for standing around playing word games with a clipboard under my arm!'

He looked at his watch. I looked at mine. Just after four o'clock. Time for him to head back to the office and prepare for going home. No surprise there, although what he said next did knock me back on my heels.

'For your information, I don't get paid nearly enough for what I do. Neither do my local government colleagues throughout the country, and that's why our union has called for industrial action, starting tomorrow.' He got into his car, slammed the door, then informed me through the window, 'Your planning application will go on hold until such time as we're awarded a just pay rise.'

Fortunately, he drove off before I could ask him who the hell he thought paid his bloody wages, anyway. Future experience would teach me that crossing swords with such strict 'thou shalt, thou shalt not' upholders of town hall doctrine can be a rough sport, and the chances of you winning are invariably slim. That doesn't stop some of the more impetuously dogged of us from having a go, though.

We eventually did get permission to extend the house, but not without a frustratingly long wait while every official 't' and 'i' was meticulously crossed and dotted. There were also two firm provisos – the boundary of the garden could only be moved forward by precisely the same distance from the front of the extended building as had existed in front of the original house, and what remained of the extra land we'd bought could never be used for any purpose other than agricultural.

Could I still sow grass on it? I asked the planning official. Yes, that would be permissible, he said, provided I remembered that it, in law, would be regarded as grazing land and not a lawn. And, I further enquired, if I chose not to put animals to graze on the grass, but kept it neatly mowed instead, just as I would a lawn, would that still be permissible? Yes, he replied, but it wouldn't *officially* be a lawn, but a paddock. And the difference would be? I politely enquired. The difference, he smugly told me, would be that regulations would *not* allow me to build houses on a paddock, whereas precedents existed for building houses on a lawn.

So, that had been his suspicion all along. And my assertion that people like me actually choose to live in the country so that we have a bit of space around us instead of other houses didn't convince him of the innocence of my reasons for having bought that extra piece of land. To him, I remained a potential defiler of the nation's heritage – a sly blackguard, whose evil, capitalist intentions had been foiled by a vigilant white knight in official armour provided at the tax-payers' expense.

The final irony was that, while the white knight had been making such a song and dance over the nominal use of a tiny corner of a field, the government was paying the nation's farmers *not* to grow anything at all on vast swathes of productive land. This was the infamous EU's Land Set-aside Scheme, intended to reduce grain mountains, wine lakes and the likes, while keeping produce prices artificially high. It was a fantastically extravagant piece of bumbledom that's been called everything from ridiculous to obscene. Still, it all amounted to more jobs for bureaucrats, and, when all's said and done, what better use could there possibly be for Joe Public's taxes?

★ ★ ★ ★ ★

If, like we were, you're rookies in the so-called 'self-build' game, you need an expert you can trust implicitly to guide you through the maze of unforeseen problems that invariably occur from the day the first sod is dug for the foundations of your new building. Wee Bob lived just a few miles away in the coastal village of Gullane, more noted for its fine links golf courses, like the world-famous Muirfield, than for its highly skilled builders, perhaps, but Bob was up there among the best brickies and stone masons around, nonetheless. What's more, he wasn't just a skilled craftsman, but a scrupulously honest bloke as well. That's an important quality in the person who advises you on what quantities of building materials are needed and where best to buy them at the most favourable prices. Wee Bob did all that, and he also gathered round him a team of equally experienced and trustworthy experts in the other trades that would be needed on site as work on the project progressed.

But don't kid yourself that just because you're paying the bills, you're going to be regarded as site foreman or clerk of works or anything highfalutin like that. You're a glorified gofer, and if you don't see to it that the required materials are right there when they're called for, then you're the one who's going to be doling out money to pay for skilled men to sit about waiting until you get your act together. However, once they see that you're happy to dance to their tune *and* are willing to get your own sleeves rolled up as well, then a happy working relationship quickly develops. Pretty soon, you're also on first name terms with the guys at the builders' supply yards, and picking up a whole new vocabulary of trade jargon. One thing that does take a bit of getting used to, though, is seeing truckload after truckload of bricks, cement, sand and timber disappear into what seems to be a fairly small building in comparison with the amount of materials it's gobbling up while it grows. But for us, it was all part of the learning curve, all a matter of accumulating useful experience for what we still hoped would one day be the building of an entire new house on that elusive block of deer-farming land.

The one big difference between the Merryhatton Roselea project and the one we had been involved with at Old Weston was that this time we weren't obliged to actually live our daily lives among all the paraphernalia, clutter and muck that is an inevitable feature of any building site. We could exist comparatively comfortably and undisturbed in the original part of the cottage while work on the extension continued on the other side of the gable wall, which wouldn't have a connecting doorway 'slapped' through it until almost the end of the whole job. And, although there was plenty of work for us to do in the old cottage by way of redecorating every room and completely refitting the kitchen, Ellie and I also made a point of making time to enjoy the charms of the beautiful landscape that surrounded us whenever the opportunity arose.

Just as we'd done back in Mallorca, we would scour the countryside for signs of any available land that might do for our next farming enterprise. In Mallorca, the dream had been to rear Aberdeen Angus cattle, whereas back here in Scotland the plan, as I was determined to call it, was to breed deer. No matter what terminology I'd used to label either aspiration, however, it was becoming ever more evident that the common denominator was likely to be failure to find what we were looking for. The reality is that large-farming areas like East Lothian aren't the same as Mallorca, where you see individual fields with 'For Sale' signs posted. That doesn't happen in Britain, where such sales are either advertised in the farming press or they're done by word of mouth within the farming community. But (to go the extra mile) we did occasionally cruise about looking for fields that we might approach a farmer about selling. Ever the optimists, we were getting accustomed to being patient in such matters, and if ever a little cloud of despondency did appear above our heads, Ellie always came up with the same idea for blowing it away. Her well-tried panacea of 'Let's eat out!' turned out to work just as well in Scotland as it had under like circumstances in Mallorca.

These days, East Lothian isn't short of eateries of the most popular international denominations, but on our land-hunting travels, we would invariably end up in one of the traditional Scottish inns or pubs that are to be found in most of the county's historic towns and villages.

Following the course of the River Tyne five miles eastwards from Haddington, you arrive in East Linton, now a sleepy commuting backwater just off the old A1 highway, but once a thriving market town, with fifty shops and scores of other businesses, including a distillery and a dozen or so bars. You won't find such a wide choice of hostelries in East Linton these days, but the Drovers' Inn and Crown Hotel are two that retain much of the character of olden times in their cosy public rooms.

On the banks of the river just outside the village is the chocolate-box-pretty Preston Mill, the last surviving of seven that once provided for the corn-grinding needs of the rich surrounding farmlands. It's a tiny building that looks like a pop-up picture in a nursery rhyme book, and is said to be the oldest working water mill in Scotland. Its riverside location and its crooked, conical roof, clad in pantiles and topped by a windvane known locally as the 'long arm of friendship', have made Preston Mill a magnet for generation upon generation of artists and photographers.

Another of the village's visual attractions is the miniature gorge through which the Tyne flows at this point. Here may be seen massive rocks and a waterfall up which strange, large fish perpetually try to jump, without ever seeming to reach the top. The riddle of the fish's identity has been exacerbated by the fact that no angler has ever claimed to have landed one – not, at least, by conventional means. Poachers, whose catching methods may be less principled, have been known to whisper that close inspection of the fish will reveal that, contrary to popular speculation, they are neither larger-than-normal sea trout nor are they salmon. They call them 'bull (pronounced as in 'lull') troot', exotic cousins of the brown trout that grow to their great size while feeding on 'something' in the dark, mysterious waters of the Linn Pool at the foot of those insurmountable falls. Broach the subject of the bull troot with local worthies over a nip or two of whisky in one of the village bars on a Saturday night and you're liable to elicit even fishier tales, however.

Just five meandering miles south of East Linton, you'll find the hamlet of Garvald, crouching shyly in one of the lower folds of the Lammermuir Hills. The focal point of this drowsy huddle of houses is the Garvald Inn, a hillfoot haven that's as welcoming as the warm, red sandstone of its outer walls. This is stock-rearing country, and as you order up your sirloin steak or lamb chops in the homely atmosphere of the inn, you may well be sitting along the bar from the very farmer who produced them – unless, of course, the animals were reared on the monastery lands above the village. I presume that the holy brothers' sale of their farm produce to the outside world wouldn't be accepted by their abbot as an excuse for frequenting the local pub to see how it was going down with the punters.

The Cistercian monks who, in 1952, started to build their new Sancta Maria Abbey at Nunraw, Garvald, were establishing their first monastery in Scotland since John Knox's Reformation of the church four centuries earlier, and 814 years to the very day after their order began the construction of their first *ever* monastery in Scotland – Melrose Abbey. At Nunraw, they turned what previously had been a tract of barren moorland into a productive farm, and the impressive results of their labours, both as builders and farmers, can be seen from the hill road above. There are also sensational views northward over the turtleshell dome of Traprain Law to the distant hills of Fife and, when weather permits, you can even see as far as the summit of Ben Lomond, some eighty-plus miles away to the west. So, fortune and favour may have wavered for the monastic orders over the centuries, but it seems that one thing that never changes is their predilection for high living – literally.

For me, however, as stunning as the outlook from the Lammermuir Hills may be, there is nothing quite to match the views that regale you back down along East Lothian's coastline, and nowhere more so than from the two sandy bays of the ancient royal burgh of North Berwick.

'From pilgrim port to golf resort' is how the history of this old fishing town has been potted, and while it's an accurate enough précis, much of interest took place in this delightful spot on the map in the interim. Throughout the Middle Ages, as many as ten thousand pilgrims a year were ferried over the Firth of Forth from North Berwick on their way north to the Fife town of St Andrews, where the relics and bones of the eponymous apostle, Scotland's patron saint, are believed to have been enshrined. As less pious times evolved, both towns became synonymous with the origins of golf, and it's claimed that, in the sixteenth century, first Mary Queen of Scots and later her son, King James VI of Scotland (I of England), played the fledgling sport of *gowff* on the seaside links of North Berwick.

It was during the reign of James that one of the most ill-famed events in the contemporary history of Scotland took place within the precincts of the town, then still little more than a cluster of fishermen's and artisans' cottages nestling in the seaward lea of 'The Law', a cone-shaped volcanic 'plug' that dominates the town and surrounding countryside. On Hallowe'en, 1590, up to two hundred witches and warlocks gathered in the Auld Kirk (old church) down by the little harbour, some of them, according to a later account, having sailed over the wide expanse of Aberlady Bay 'in sieves and riddles and freshened by flagons of wine on the way'. With the Devil himself directing proceedings from the pulpit, a right unholy shindig took place, the night of satanic merriment culminating in everyone kissing the Devil's '*ers*' (arse), before opening three graves for the purpose of obtaining bones as aids to further 'evil-doing'. Almost two centuries later, the legend of this heinous happening was to form the blueprint for Robert Burns' poetic materpiece, 'Tam o' Shanter'.

The object of the black mischief in North Berwick was, in fact, King James, and the 'Devil' none other than an appropriately disguised Earl of Bothwell, who claimed to have a right to the Scottish throne himself. Bothwell's idea was, through the power of witchcraft, to summon up a storm in the Firth of Forth that would shipwreck and drown King James on his voyage back from Denmark with his new bride, the Danish Princess Anne. The ploy failed, but once James got wind of it, he had the suspects arrested and personally attended a series of witch trials that resulted in those confessing (usually under torture) being hanged and burned at the stake on Castlehill, Edinburgh. Bothwell got away with it, but for a century after King James wrought his 'legal' vengeance on the witches of North Berwick, thousands of innocent people throughout Scotland were convicted of witchcraft and put to death, their 'crime' being ratified by the ignorance-riddled church of the time. Once more, the self-interested forces of royalty and religion had conspired to treat the population with contempt and cruelty.

But less controversial days were to come for North Berwick. The beauty of its location, the health-giving properties of its brisk sea air and the coming of the railway age eventually began the town's gradual transition from fishing village to holiday resort and playground for the better-off folk of Edinburgh. Robert Louis Stevenson spent his summers here as a young boy in the late 1850s and early '60s, and descriptions of various local landmarks were later to be included in his writing. For instance, in 'The Lantern Bearers' he describes the Bass Rock, yet another of East Lothian's old volcanic 'plugs' and the most dramatic of the four islands that lie off the North Berwick shore, as 'tilted seaward like a doubtful bather, the surf ringing it with white, the solan geese (gannets) hanging around its summit like a great and glittering smoke'.

Coincidentally, it is North Berwick's new Seabird Centre, from where you can view live, interactive TV pictures of the gannets nesting on the Bass, that has become the town's most popular visitor attraction (apart from golf) in recent years.

Yet it was another of those four islands, the Isle of Fidra, that made the greatest impression on young Robert Louis Stevenson's already fertile imagination. As his grandfather's engineering company designed, built and maintained the lighthouse on Fidra, it's possible that he knew the otherwise uninhabited island intimately. In any case, it's believed that Fidra provided the inspiration for what is arguably his greatest book, *Treasure Island*. If that's true, then it's also likely that many of the book's seafaring characters, including the pirates Long John Silver and Ben Gunn, were actually caricatures of salty North Berwick worthies who frequented a scruffy drinking den called The Bluebell Inn, located (of all places) in Quality Street, where The Ship Inn now stands. This old hostelry was, they say, Stevenson's model for The Admiral Benbow Inn, which he later immortalised as the home of young Jim Hawkins, the hero of *Treasure Island*.

By the start of the twentieth century, however, word of North Berwick's charms had spread much farther afield than Edinburgh, and its reputation as a holiday resort of distinction was such that it had become known as the Biarritz of the North. A coterie of royalty, nobility and London socialites had adopted the town and, on its western approaches, had built a 'suburb' of fine villas and mansions, which they would occupy, with their large retinues in tow, during their North Berwick 'season' of August and September.

Although those 'high society' days are long gone, North Berwick is still regarded as *the* coastal place to live in south-east Scotland, and the value of its property reflects the demand that seems to increase by the year. However, much of the bustling old High Street still remains as it would have been in Robert Louis Stevenson's time, except for the cars that crowd its narrow confines, and the cosmopolitan range of eating places that abound. A choice of kebabs, Thai curries, canneloni ripieni, vindaloos, chop sueys, escargots or deep-fried Mars Bars would most certainly not have been on his mind as he wandered back to his parents' holiday home after an evening of observing the local worthies through the window of North Berwick's version of The Admiral Benbow Inn.

The wide variety of restaurants suited Ellie and me, though, and although we could never have hoped to find land at a price that would have been viable for deer farming around affluent North Berwick, we were never short of an excuse to drive into town. And again we made the Italian connection. Living in Mallorca had given us a taste for things Mediterranean that wouldn't go away, and the Mastrocinque family, the genial owners of North Berwick's Ristorante Bella Italia, satisfied it nicely. But, for me at least, it wasn't only Papa Giovanni's wonderful, 'just-a like Mama used to make' food that pleased so much, but also the knowledge that he had dragged his wife and kids around even more than I had done before finding his rainbow's end. The search for his metaphorical pot of gold had taken them from Italy to Australia, back to Italy, then to Edinburgh, back to Italy again, and finally to North Berwick. Yes, listening to tales of Giovanni's wanderings made me feel like a stay-at-home, slippers-and-pipe man, and that eased my conscience no end.

In fact, all things considered, we could happily have stayed in the vicinity of North Berwick for ever, especially after all the building work at Merryhatton Roselea had been completed and the little house had been transformed into a family home that was spacious, had every modern comfort and convenience, yet also retained its cottage-like cosiness. As at Old Weston, we took much satisfaction and enjoyment in seeing our plans materialise, but the rub was that, once again, the cost of completing the project had been much more than we'd bargained for. In addition to all the other unforeseen outlays that we had now learned were part and parcel of doing up houses, the expenditure involved in replacing the septic tank and extending the garden had taken its toll on our bank balance.

The house would have to go on the market – and quickly.

Whilst stoically accepting the inevitable, Ellie did allow herself the satisfaction of rather caustically suggesting to me that, instead of just altering the Kerr Clan motto to 'For Sale', we should now go the whole hog and change the family name entirely – to a Bedouin one!

– TEN –

MONARCH OF THE GLEN... ALMOST!

The Fermer's plan to organise a Bolton 'Festival' materialised a few weeks after we put Merryhatton Roselea up for sale. It was just after harvest time when I got the phone call. The Festival, The Fermer said, would be a one-night affair, to be held in the farmhouse garden, with his wife Rona cooking up the grub in the kitchen and his four young sprogs acting as waiters, bar attendants and musical directors. As none of his kids could play musical instruments, my hunch that the Edinburgh International Festival of the Arts wouldn't be under threat from its Bolton counterpart seemed likely to be proven correct. Sandy and Charlie would be welcome to attend, The Fermer informed me. In fact, he added, it would be *essential* that they turn up, as the number of likely participants among the residents of the village would hardly comprise a festive throng of any size at all. With this in mind, he had also roped in some of the stalwarts from the public bar at the Goblin Ha' Hotel in Gifford to swell the numbers and, as he put it, 'to add to the cultural tone'.

Ellie knew what to expect. 'Still,' she said, 'at least the Bolton farmhouse garden will make a lovely setting for the display of formation vomiting after The Fermer's chums have gorged themselves on free booze all night.'

It rained. It not only rained, it blew a gale as well. In fact, the afternoon of the Bolton Festival was one of those October days when nature posts fair warning that winter is waiting round the corner – one of those October days when the wind takes hold of trees clad in glorious autumn leaves and strips them naked.

Ellie was relieved. 'Phew!' she smiled, looking through the window at the rain passing horizontally by. 'That'll mean The Fermer's cultural ceilidh is off. Can't honestly say I was looking forward to it. All the men getting pie-eyed and their poor wives trying to drag them off home long after the party's over. All that drunken hand-shaking and laughing at nothing and back-slapping and everything. Just like Hogmanay. Never fails.' She thought for a moment. 'I just hope Rona hadn't prepared too much food in advance. All that trouble for nothing.'

Then the phone rang. I answered it. It was The Fermer. Ellie's face fell as she watched a grin spreading over my face.

'You needn't have worried about Rona going to all that trouble for nothing,' I told her after I'd hung up. 'The Fermer made contingency plans in case the weather turned bad. The Bolton Festival will now be an indoor extravaganza.'

Ellie sighed.

'And,' I added, 'The Fermer said to tell you not to bother dressing too formally now.'

Ellie sniffed a cynical sniff. 'So, I can put away my Royal Ascot hat and Queen's Garden Party frock, can I?'

'Yeah, I reckon jeans, wellies and a duffle coat with a hood would be more appropriate. Oh, and better include a pair of fur-lined gloves in your ensemble as well.'

Ellie sighed again, but said nothing. As usual, she knew what to expect.

The marvellous thing about the traditional Scottish farm steadings is that they always had a large grain loft, usually located above a row of arch-fronted cart sheds. It was in such lofts that the 'harvest home' *kirns*, or barn dances, were held. The low ceilings and thick stone walls ensured that, no matter how cold the outside temperature, a good, steamy fug soon built up inside the loft once the floor was shaking under a hundred pairs of feet stomping about doing Highland 'schottisches', 'dashing white sergeants', 'eightsome reels' and all the other favourite old country dances.

The Fermer's venue was nothing like that. It's difficult to build up a good, steamy fug inside a modern agricultural shed the size of an aircraft hangar, even with the help of a hundred pairs of stomping feet. And there weren't a hundred pairs of feet – only about twenty, The Fermer's afternoon telephone offensive to ginger up support from his friends having proved that many of them were of the fair-weather variety. However, those who did turn up *were* stomping their feet, although it was in an effort to keep them warm, not in the course of tripping the light fantastic. It's difficult to get into the mood for Scottish country dancing when the music blaring out of the cassette machine inside a tractor cab has a distinctive rock flavour. But that's what The Fermer's kids fancied and, as official musical directors, that's what they dished up.

The roar of two industrial space heaters provided evidence that The Fermer had been thinking of his guests' comfort, even if the heaters' noise, combined with the thump of the rock music, did result in conversation being in the hundred decibel range. But the beer was flowing freely, and by the time Rona and the few other wives present retreated to the warmth of the farmhouse kitchen, a fairly festive atmosphere *was* building up in the corner of the vast shed that the Goblin Ha' stalwarts and the rest of us festive bravehearts had huddled into. That we hadn't headed for the farmhouse kitchen with the women was an indication that we wanted to show our appreciation of the effort The Fermer had made to salvage his rain-ruined plans. It was also an indication, as Ellie had muttered to me before leaving the shed, that we were all off our bloody trolleys. Such sacrifices of personal comfort in the cause of male bonding are beyond the realms of female comprehension, it seems.

Despite The Fermer having cobbled together a charcoal-fired hotplate out of an old oil drum and a drain cover, the heap of sausage rolls that Rona had made for the occasion ultimately succumbed to the icy draughts rampaging about the shed. The sausage rolls just sat there on their tin tray, cold as the grave, waiting to be consigned to the wheelie bin of fate. However, as Jock Burns often said, it's an ill wind that doesn't blow someone a bit of good, and that certainly proved to be the case in relation to the chill blast that howled through the shed door when it was opened around midnight by a group of Festival late-comers. It was a bunch of some more of The Fermer's Goblin Ha' cronies, their resistance to cold suitably fortified by a long evening in the public bar, from which, at closing time, they decided to make their way by taxi to the big shed at Bolton for a late-night intake of culture. Consequently, The Fermer's stock of beer was soon diminishing rapidly, as was the pile of dead sausage rolls.

'Mm-m-m-m, sausage rolls!' wee Bertie, a farming colleague and portly best pal of The Fermer, drooled. 'Next best thing to a curry when ye've had a gutful o' pints, them. Aye, pity Rona never laid on some baked beans, though.'

At this point, I had no notion of the good wind that wee Bertie was the embodiment of. And I'm not alluding, even obliquely, to baked beans. He scoffed a few sausage rolls, then sat down beside me on a straw bale, a can of beer in one hand, two more sausage rolls in the other.

'I hear ye're in the market for a bit o' land,' he said. 'Twenty-odd acres, maybe?'

My heart skipped a beat.

Bertie rammed one of the sausage rolls into his mouth. 'Well, I could have just what ye're lookin' for,' he mumbled. 'Possibly perfect for your purpose, Pete.'

I flicked some flecks of cold pastry from my face. 'Yeah?' I prompted, half suspecting that he was about to deliver the punchline of a joke.

But he didn't. He took a leisurely slug of his beer instead, then sunk his teeth into the remaining sausage roll.

The Fermer's musical-directing young sprogs had been shooed off to their beds hours ago, so Sandy and Charlie had taken over disc jockey duties inside the tractor cab. Vintage

Jerry Lee Lewis was now competing with the loud roar of space heaters – and winning.

Wee Bertie burped luxuriantly after washing down the final chunk of sausage roll with the dregs of his beer, then strolled over to the bar table for a replacement can. He dallied to pick up another sausage roll on his way back to rejoin me on our straw bale seat. By now, I was beside myself with apprehension. Was he or was he not pulling my leg about having a piece of land for sale? I didn't want to give the impression of being overly keen to find out, though, so I tried to appear convincingly nonchalant while he enjoyed his latest cold course of curry substitute.

'Anyhow, about that bit o' land,' he eventually said. 'Well, ye see, I've just bought another farm – a fair distance away from the present one, and there's an outlyin' field away on its own. Twenty-five acres, cut off from the rest. No' too handy for travellin' to wi' the machinery when we've got so much other land to work now, ye see. Aye, could be better just to sell it.'

'Aye?' I said, doing my best to control the grin that was tugging at the corners of my mouth.

'Aye,' replied wee Bertie, deadpan, 'and it's yours for the goin' rate, if ye want it.'

The sweet sound of angels singing almost drowned out the pounding jangle of Jerry Lee's 'Great Balls of Fire'. And the good news got even better. Bertie was happy to close the deal on a handshake, with no money changing hands until I'd obtained the required planning permissions for our deer-farming project. In this way, he'd have enough time to take a crop of barley from the field while I waded through all the red tape that doubtless would be laid in my path.

'Would that be OK wi' you?' he enquired, casually.

I shook his hand, enthusiastically. 'Done!' I said, standing up. 'And please allow me to treat you to another sausage roll. In fact, I'll make it two.'

'HEY, PETE!' wee Bertie shouted after me. 'Make that four, eh! Aye, and ye'd better grab me another coupla cans o' beer while the goin's good.' He took a quick look around the gathering of fellow culture vultures. 'Some right greedy bastards in here!'

★ ★ ★ ★ ★

The field known as Howe Knowe is situated about four miles from the village of Gifford, on a south-facing rise in undulating land at the foot of Lammer Law, one of the highest of the Lammermuir Hills. There's a stream called the Howe Burn at the bottom of the field and a strip of mature woodland running down the western edge, affording some shelter from the prevailing wind. And *any* form of protection from the wind at Howe Knowe makes sense, as I would find out in due course. Look at any map of the area and you can see that, centuries ago, when all the big farms were created, a sheltered location for the farmhouse and steading was a priority. Significantly, there were no old farmsteads within sight of Howe Knowe.

For the present, though, all that concerned me was the suitability of the place for a deer farm, and it appeared to fit the bill just fine. It was a bit off the beaten track, but I saw that as a plus point, as you don't want nervy animals like deer to be spooked by heavy traffic noise or gangs of unruly kids on their way to and from school. There were no motorways or schools *any*where near Howe Knowe.

OK, the land's relative remoteness did present a few practical problems, primarily the unavailability of electricity and telephone lines and a source of water, but I wasn't about to let such paltry considerations put me off now. Preliminary checks with the respective authorities revealed that the first two of those essential services could be brought in from a road about half a mile away. Not cheap, but possible. So far, so good.

Laying on a water supply proved to be a bit more difficult, though – apparently impossible, in fact. The only feasible source of mains water was at a farm about a cross-country mile distant, but the pipes there were so old and furred-up that there was only just enough pressure in them to supply the farmer's own needs, far less travel all the way to Howe Knowe. Any water that did make it that far would arrive as no more than a miserable trickle, if at all. But that particular problem transpired to be purely academic, as the farmer concerned decided that he wasn't interested in sharing his already unreliable supply of water with anyone. I couldn't blame him, yet I'd been under the misguided impression until then that I'd left all such water problems behind in sunny Mallorca.

I'd already learned enough about planning regulations to accept that, without adequate drinking water being available at the location, an application for permission to build a new farmhouse wouldn't be entertained for a moment – and quite rightly so. Neither man nor beast can exist without water. So, it appeared that the sun that had risen over wee Bertie's sausage rolls at the Bolton Festival had turned out to be a false dawn after all. And, by this time, I had already signed the papers for the sale of Merryhatton Roselea. In two months' time, we'd be nomads again.

Ellie gave me one of her long-suffering smiles when I broke the news to her.

'Please, oh mighty one, do not concern yourself,' she monotoned with a little bow of subservience. 'I, your faithful camel herd, will follow your caravan to yet another oasis of dreams.' She dipped her head again, more deeply this time. 'Yes, sire, and I will diligently gather up the dung along the way.'

Ellie, as I mentioned before, has a knack of kicking a man when he's down, though I have to admit that she'd already had plenty of opportunities to make perfect the practice. That made me feel even worse about our current predicament. I had led the family into yet another blind alley, and this time there was no obvious way out – until, that is, I thought back to what that old fox Sebastià had told me when he was trying to flog us his dry farm near the town of Algaida back in Mallorca:

'If you want water,' he'd bluffed, 'you just drill a hole in the ground and pump it up.'

Eureka! All might not be lost *just* yet.

I immediately dashed off a letter to the British Geological Survey office in Edinburgh, giving them map references for the Howe Knowe field and asking if they could advise if there was likely to be a source of underground water there. A few days later, I received a reply informing me that, in their opinion, there *could* well be. The geology of the area suggested that an aquifer (a water-holding layer of rock) which supplied a borehole at a maltings in Haddington might extend in the direction of the field in question. The only way of finding out for certain, however, would be to drill a test hole to approximately one hundred and fifty feet – their estimation of the depth of the water source, *if* indeed one did actually exist. Understandably cautious people, those British Geological Survey folks. Boring holes in the earth's crust can be an expensive business, and they don't want to be sued for providing over-optimistic forecasts of what may or may not lie underneath. By a similar token, I wasn't particularly keen about splashing out for a test bore on such inconclusive advice.

I phoned them up and asked if there was any way at all that I could shorten the odds before stumping up money to a drilling company. The geologist chap on the other end of the line was both sympathetic towards my dilemma and keen to help, but told me that he was obliged to advise that there was no alternative to sinking an exploratory borehole... or two... or three... or more. Sensing my sinking spirits, he then added – off the record, I would understand – that there was *one* comparatively inexpensive thing I could try. There was absolutely nothing scientific to back up what he was about to suggest, he stressed, but he had to admit – in the strictest confidence, I would understand – that it was a process that he'd found to have a surprisingly high success rate in the past.

Edwin Taylor, an instantly likeable man in his early sixties and a farmer himself in the north-east of England, arrived at Howe Knowe equipped with only a Y-shaped 'twig', made out of whalebone. If the fellow at the Geological Survey office had been right, Edwin and his divining rod would provide 'reasonably reliable' evidence of any aquifer present underneath the field. I wanted to believe that, of course, but

I couldn't help being sceptical. Accordingly, I said nothing to Edwin about the Survey office's scientifically calculated depth of whatever subterranean water source *might* exist.

'Oh yes, yes, yes,' he declared as soon as he'd climbed over the fence, 'there'll be plenty of water under here.'

Edwin had a friend with him, and he responded to my questioning frown with a reassuring smile and a nod of his head that implied that Edwin knew what he was talking about.

'Where in the field would be your first choice for having a well?' Edwin asked me.

I indicated roughly where the ideal location for the farmstead would be.

'OK,' said Edwin, 'that shouldn't be a problem.'

With that, he took an end of the two 'Y' arms of his divining twig in each of his hands, with the leg of the 'Y' pointing horizontally ahead. He then strode off in the appointed direction, telling me to follow close behind with the hammer and clutch of wooden stakes he'd instructed me to bring along. He had walked no more than thirty yards into the field when the point of his twig twitched and dipped to the vertical.

'Knock one of your stakes in here,' he told me. 'That'll mark this edge of the aquifer.'

I looked at his friend, half expecting him to be sniggering behind my back. But he wasn't. He gave me that reassuring smile again and motioned me to do as Edwin said.

'I'm getting a really good message here,' Edwin called over his shoulder as he strode on across the field. 'Plenty water down there. Plenty water. More than you'll ever need.'

About fifty paces farther on, his twig began to twitch again.

'That's the other extremity of the water course,' he said. 'Bash another stake in here.'

I did as instructed, still wondering if the mickey was being taken. This whole divining business seemed too simple to be true.

Somehow, Edwin knew what I was thinking. 'It's all right, I've been water dowsing all of my life,' was all he said. He then walked back over the field to where we had started, and he got exactly the same response from his twig. 'That's it, then,' he declared. 'Job done. All you have to do now is put a stake halfway between the other two and that'll be the centre of the aquifer. That'll be where you'll drill your well.'

He went on to tell me how deep the bore hole would need to be – just ten feet more than the depth estimated by the people at the British Geological Survey office. Uncanny. I then revealed to him what their estimation had been, and he merely shrugged and said that they were wrong. Near enough, but wrong all the same. The proof of that would be provided by the drillers, he predicted, and there wasn't the faintest hint of doubt about the way he said it. He must have sensed that there was still an element of doubt in *my* mind, though.

'OK,' he said, 'follow me again. We'll make another pass over the field.'

His twig reacted in exactly the same way as before. This time, though, he stopped on the way back and turned to face me. He indicated that he was only holding the twig with the minimum of pressure – just enough to stop it falling through his fingers.

'Right,' he said, 'take hold of the point of the twig and try pulling it up.'

'It – it's fighting back,' I chuckled, scarcely able to believe what was happening.

'And you can see that I'm still holding it *very* lightly. It's not me that's causing the resistance, right?'

'Absolutely right,' I gasped, totally mystified. 'But how – I mean, what's making it, you know – where's the energy coming from?'

Edwin shot me a wily wink. 'Ah well, that's the magic of water dowsing for you.' He said no more until he'd climbed back over the fence, when, as a sort of casual aside, he offered me his prediction of the number of gallons of water per hour the well would deliver.

This only added to my confusion. I didn't know what to make of this amiable, apparently genuine man. I still wasn't sure if the entire exercise had been a leg-pull. Then it dawned on me that he had driven more than a hundred miles to do what I'd asked him to do, yet hadn't even mentioned a fee. I drew his attention to this as he got into his car.

'Tell you what,' he smiled, 'on the way here, we dropped our wives off to have a wander around Gifford. If you give me enough to buy them a bar lunch in the Goblin Ha', that'll do fine. We've had a nice day out.'

'Well, even if it was some kind of trick, at least he wasn't doing it for a fast buck,' I told Ellie when I got home. 'Yeah, he was a really nice man, but I *still* can't bring myself to accept that he could get all that technical info out of a twig.'

'Nonsense!' Ellie came back. 'I believe in these mystic things. The supernatural. Mediums and everything. Some people have strange powers like that, and you can't go pooh-poohing their gifts just because you don't understand them.' She went over to the phone table and picked up the Yellow Pages directory. 'Now then,' she said, 'you've had an encouraging forecast from the rock boffins *and* an almost identical one from the water diviner man.' She handed me the phone book. 'So, let your fingers do the walking and then ring the hole-boring company of your choice – right away!'

★ ★ ★ ★ ★

On the drilling of the very first test bore, an aquifer was located precisely where Edwin Taylor had said it would be, and his prediction about its depth proved to be accurate, almost to the inch. Preliminary pumping through a flow meter confirmed his forecast of the borehole's potential yield as well. I was now a believer in the magic of water dowsing, and the prospects for setting up that deer farm were looking really good at last. One vital matter still had to be attended to before our way would be clear to approach the planning authority, however. The purity of the well water would have to be officially approved, and no analysis could be undertaken until it first *looked* clear.

The drilling process had churned up a gritty sludge at the bottom of the borehole, with the result that what was coming up looked more like thin, brown porridge than drinking water. It took a week of pumping, twelve hours a day, before the water began to run bright and clear. By now, it was late January and we were experiencing the worst weather of the winter so far. I would drive up to the field at the crack of dawn every morning, and I'd have to hand-crank an old diesel generator into grudging life before I could start the pump. That was when the wind blowing down from the snowy summit of Lammer Law brought it home to me why no one had built a farmstead on the face of this hillside before. That damned wind was truly cold enough to freeze the marrow in your bones. Many a time I believed I would either die from that or from a heart attack brought on by struggling for half an hour to fire up the stubborn old generator. But at least I didn't have all that far to travel home for a thawing-out session by the fireside, as we had rented a farm cottage about a mile away after moving out of Merryhatton Roselea.

We were now in our fifth house since returning from Mallorca less than three years earlier, but the ever-improving prospects of starting our deer-farming enterprise provided the stimulus to make us believe it would all prove worthwhile in the end. With the well water finally having been certified as fit for human consumption, we were ready to apply for planning permission in principle. It was turned down flat.

The local authority had no objection to the proposed deer farm. Truth to tell, they gave the impression that they couldn't have cared less if we filled the field with trombone-playing elephants. What they were opposed to, and with a vengeance, was any notion we might have about building a house there. That sort of thing was totally taboo. We were told that planning regulations came down clearly and firmly against house-building on agricultural land, other than in *very* exceptional circumstances, and even then permission would only be granted with rigorous conditions attached. In their opinion, the circumstances pertaining to our case didn't even come close to being exceptional. And that, they said, was that.

And so began what was to develop into a long, tough and expensive battle with officialdom. I could have given up at that first rebuff, and I'm sure I was expected to, but years of dragging my family about while chasing that elusive rainbow of mine had made me absolutely determined not to be defeated now that I had come so close to finding its end. I knew from our brush with bureaucracy at Merryhatton Roselea what we were likely to be up against, though it was obvious that I now faced a much bigger struggle. It was one that I could well have done without, but the gloves were off and I was ready for the fray. Some of us never learn!

Our appeal against the planners' decision prompted them to ask why there was any need for a deer herder to live on his farm anyway. Obvious considerations like the necessity, as on any livestock farm, to tend continually to the animals' welfare apparently hadn't occurred to them, nor had the need to maintain security by guarding against poachers. Farmed deer make a tempting target, and even if the rustlers only bag one, once the fence is cut, your entire herd could be gone in the blink of an eye. It struck me as odd that the planning officials couldn't see any of this in relation to deer, when they had recently approved the building of a house on the site of a proposed snail farm. Did they really imagine that, without constant supervision, the snails might batter down the door of their shed and gallop off into the distance in a cloud of dust? Or did the aspiring snail farmer have strings to pull that I hadn't? Either way, my resolve was strengthened and I battled on.

I called on the British Deer Farmers Association to confirm the necessity of my living on site, which they did, and the planners countered by requesting the Ministry of Agriculture to define what they judged to be the minimum size of a viable farming unit in East Lothian. Anything less than an optimum of five hundred acres, the Ministry opined, would not be regarded as potentially profitable, so any request to build a farmhouse on a lesser area should not be considered. Our twenty-five acre field, therefore, wouldn't enter the equation. This was getting serious – and silly.

While something like five hundred acres would be a reasonable minimum for an arable farm, the same rule of thumb has absolutely no bearing on more intensive agricultural enterprises. Pig and poultry farming, for example, can be successfully operated on a couple of acres or even less, while a deer farm (according to experts in the field) could be established perfectly feasibly on twenty-five acres of suitable land. A snail farm, conversely, can be set up in a garden shed, and I made that very valid point to the local planning department. They didn't like it, but I had found a chink in their regulatory armour and I re-submitted my planning application accordingly.

The Americans have a much-quoted saying that you can't fight city hall. I was masochistic enough to keep trying, although there would be many times in the ensuing months when I'd ask myself why I was so hellbent on bashing my head against such a solid brick wall. The planning officials reaffirmed that they would continue to oppose the building of a house at Howe Knowe, and they would advise the elected planning committee councillors, who had the final say, to do likewise. I was up against formidable opposition, as only one of those councillors had any practical experience of farming, and he came down on the side of the officials. His opinion, as a large farmer, was that to sanction such a development as the one I proposed would open the floodgates for the countryside to be littered with townies keeping horses or ponies on similar 'small estates'. That, he declared, would never do. Strange, elitist logic and an irrelevant analogy as well. I was neither a townie nor a 'weekend countryman'. I was a farmer, albeit a small one, who was seeking to invest his own hard-earned money in a new livestock holding that didn't qualify for any government subsidy or any form of financial aid from the local authority. I was trying to start an agricultural business that would inject some new life into the countryside at a time when the farm-related population was melting away like snowflakes on a river. To my way of thinking, that was the type of enterprising attitude that should be welcomed by officialdom, instead of being vigorously discouraged. But, regulations are regulations, and if it's your job to enforce them, then no one should question why you're doing what you're paid to do. I recalled the mindset vividly from my own short career as a civil servant.

Once you challenge the system, you soon realise that it's designed to wear you down, little by little, as technicality after technicality is thrown in your way. It becomes a war of attrition, and if you're one man against the forces of bureaucracy, they are always strong favourites to win, if for no other reason than that they continue to draw their salaries while your bank balance takes a hammering.

It took a long time to persuade enough councillors on the planning committee to support our proposal, yet – hallelujah – we were eventually granted planning permission. However, this was only after we'd appealed to the Secretary of State to overrule the local planning department's machiavellian condition that Howe Knowe, with its new house, could never be sold to anyone, but would have to be passed down in perpetuity within our family. I had to hand it to them – they'd put up a spirited fight. And, as subsequent events would reveal, they still had a couple of potential knockout punches in their armoury.

★ ★ ★ ★ ★

Four years had now passed since the day we began our search for a bigger farm in Mallorca. We had come a long way from Ca's Mayoral and had made many home-comfort sacrifices in the meantime, but all the domestic disruption we'd experienced was soon forgotten as the buzz of making our plans a reality finally kicked in. Old Jaume had said in Mallorca that everything would come right with the arrival of spring, and it looked as though he would be proved correct, given that he hadn't predicted precisely *which* spring he was talking about. But the sun was shining on the April morning Ellie and I set out for Inverness, the capital of the Scottish Highlands, to make preliminary arrangements for buying our first deer. We still had a house and farm steading to build at Howe Knowe, and we still had to sow grass on the land and construct a two-metre-high deer fence all the way round the perimeter, but first things first. Without stock, the deer farm wouldn't exist, so the sooner we made arrangements to create the nucleus of a herd the better.

On the way north, the twin Forth Bridges looked even more spectacular from the car than they had from the air.

The rolling countryside of Fife seemed even more appealing than usual, the green hills and glens of Perthshire even more enchanting. It's amazing what an escape from a tangle of red tape can do for your perception of the world around you. Such rose-tinted specs couldn't make Pitlochry any more attractive than it actually is, however. Situated in the very heart of Scotland, this is a town whose charm was first made famous by Queen Victoria after staying at the turreted, fairy-tale Blair Castle nearby. Her words of praise sparked an attraction to the area that persists with discerning visitors to this day. Anyone who has an image of Scotland that's limited to bleak moors, redundant shipyards and sideways sleet should pay a visit to Pitlochry. It is the epitome of Victorian elegance, set in a sheltered, wooded landscape that Mother Nature has endowed with a combination of breathtaking beauty and priceless tranquillity. Popular with hill walkers, pony trekkers, anglers, golfers and the more adventurous types who take to rafting on the dramatic Tummel River, the town also has its own cultural Mecca, the Festival Theatre. For over half a century, Pitlochry's 'Theatre in the Hills' has presented a year-round programme of plays, concerts, art exhibitions and now even a star-studded 'Winter Words' book festival.

This little Highland town is also handily placed for anyone travelling by road from the south of Scotland to the north who feels like making a halfway stop for a leg-stretching stroll and, perhaps, some sustenance. Which is precisely what we did. Looking for all the world like a rambling Victorian farmhouse, the Westlands Hotel is set back from the main street in its own grassy grounds. It fairly radiates welcome. The easy-going proprietors, Robert and Johan Cowan, add a personal touch of Highland hospitality when you step inside. No fuss, no fawning, just an unobtrusive attention to detail that sets the caring hotel owner apart from the ordinary.

It was a Sunday, and the sunny Westlands dining room was quickly filling up with customers for the 'Special Carvery Lunch', which we'd noticed advertised on a sign as we walked past. The reason for this buffet's popularity was easy to identify – large joints of roast beef, lamb and pork sitting succulently side by side on hotplates, flanked by trays of roast, boiled and mashed potatoes, and a selection of vegetables that the Cowans were at pains to point out were, like the meats, all the very best of locally produced fare. Simple food, apparently, typical of a British family's Sunday lunch, admittedly, but perfectly cooked and generously served in elegant yet homely surroundings. An example to all similar catering establishments that aspire to welcome visitors to this country, in fact.

Ellie and I could happily have sat on after lunch, relaxing by the window and looking out over the captivating Perthshire countryside, but we still had a long drive through the Grampian Mountains ahead of us before we'd reach our destination, twelve miles west of Inverness, the capital of the Highlands.

This is an area that has visual charms ranging from gentle coastal braes through steep, wooded glens roaring with waterfalls to the starkly magnificent mountaintops of the Scottish wilderness that stretches away to the west and north. It's a land of folklore and legend, of ancient battles, romance and adventure. Loch Ness, with its lucrative monster, the bashful Nessie, lies just over the mountain of Meall na h-

Eilrig to the south, and all around the more docile parts of the landscape are peppered with pretty Highland villages. It's the type of country in which you expect to see red deer roaming wild on the mountainsides, and they do. But we had come to view the majestic creatures at closer quarters, and we did.

Archie Crawford's deer farm occupied a large expanse of hilly pasture near the picturesque little town of Beauly, which snuggles at the head of the firth of the same name. What Archie delightedly referred to as his 'Heavy Brigade', a dozen or so young stags in full antler, came charging down the slope towards us on hearing Archie's Land-Rover approach. Here were naturally wary animals that had obviously been reared with both respect and fondness, and perhaps even a measure of adulation. They showed no fear of us humans at all, to the extent that the snorts and, as Archie put it, 'playful head gestures' they were making at us through the fence had me considering myself lucky not to be on the other side of it. An uppercut from just one of those multi-pronged horns could do serious mischief to the backside of a bloke trying to outrun its 'playful' owner.

Regally handsome though these red deer were, however, and justifiably proud of them as Archie was, it was smaller cousins of his 'Heavy Brigade' that we had come to talk to him about. At that time, his farm was the only one in Scotland that ran a herd of fallow deer in addition to the more common red. Used for centuries to stock the large deer parks of the huntin' and shootin' nobility in England, fallow deer had gained a reputation for being flighty and difficult to manage within the closer confines of a farm. Yet I had seen them farmed successfully in Spain, and on a unit substantially smaller than the one we planned for Howe Knowe. The other possible advantage I saw in them was that their meat (the ultimate object of the exercise) was reckoned to be less strong than red deer venison, thus giving us an opportunity to create a niche market for those not keen on eating anything too 'gamey'.

An honest and open man, Archie didn't pretend to be able to either confirm or deny any aspect of the fallow deer's reputation, as his experience of them had been fairly limited. I would be ploughing a lone furrow if I chose to farm them commercially in preference to red deer, but if that was what I ultimately decided to do, he would be glad to sell me sufficient animals to start our herd.

Fallow deer could be described as the Bambis of the deer world – delicately attractive little animals, with white spots speckling the back of their coats, and flat, 'palmated' antlers rising from neat, doe-eyed heads. It would take the most hard-hearted of livestock farmers not to have pangs of conscience about rearing such cute creatures for meat. But that's the way of the human carnivore, and to prove that beauty is in the eye of the beholder, I've even known pig producers to have lumps in their throats when sending their bonny wee porkers off to market.

Archie's fallow deer, like everything else about his farm, were in prime condition, and we had no doubt that a selection of them would indeed make ideal foundation stock for Howe Knowe. Our short but highly informative visit was rounded off by Archie showing us an aspect of his enterprise that he thought we might like to consider as a potentially profitable sideline ourselves. His farm shop sold not just venison, but also all sorts of tourist-attractive Scottish food and souvenirs, while the adjacent 'mini farm' allowed the customers' kids an opportunity to hand-feed a few of his more docile red deer hinds, as well as to hold and stroke rabbits, guinea pigs and various other small animals. It was certainly a diversification that appeared to be doing nicely for Archie, and although our farm was going to be much farther off the beaten tourist track than his, the idea was one that I decided there and then to emulate when the time came.

We left Beauly filled with even more enthusiasm than when we'd set out, and Archie's parting recommendation that we should stop off a few miles along the Inverness road, 'to pick up a wee drop of what's good for what ails you', proved to be as well considered as his business advice.

Successive generations of the Fraser family have lived in Moniack Castle since it was built in 1580, and doubtless its thick stone walls will have witnessed many an intrigue and inter-clan tussle during the ensuing centuries. Now, though, there's nothing more threatening for Philippa, the present Fraser incumbent, to worry about than coping with invasions of people seeking to carry off (at a fair price) bottles and jars of her family's unique Highland concoctions. Wild flowers, berries and fruit gathered locally are the main ingredients of several alcoholic beverages and a score of sauces and jams. After a tour of the castle kitchens and cellars, where the delights of Moniack are either prepared and cooked or mixed, squeezed and fermented, Ellie concentrated on sampling the chutneys and jellies, while I committed my taste buds to checking the alcoholic beverages.

It's difficult to remain totally objective after you've sipped your way through consecutive nips of honey mead, sloe liqueur and six different country wines that owe nothing to the sun-loving grape, but are no less enjoyable and potent for that. Resourceful folks, those Frasers of far-north Moniack. I finally plumped for a take-home purchase of their fascinatingly named 'silver birch wine', having been told by a nervous-looking American in the nip-sipping group that it possessed amazing calming qualities. He could vouch for that from long past experience, he assured me with a twitch. Although he didn't come over as a particularly convincing ad for what he professed, I elected to go along with his advice anyway. If nothing else, the liquor did have a pleasantly dry taste, and the idea of drinking tree juice with a percentage-proof rating had a weird kind of primeval appeal to it. Maybe I'd even plant a birch grove of my own in a corner of Howe Knowe.

A jovial lady, with the lilting Inverness accent that is credited with being the purest and most unaffected of all varieties of spoken English, wrapped my chosen two bottles in brown paper, while educating me more expansively about their contents. Silver birch wine, she said, is made from the rising sap of the ubiquitous Scottish *birk* tree, the bark being tapped in early spring to harvest the basis of what Queen Victoria once divulged was her husband Prince Albert's favourite tipple, when the royal household was in residence at Balmoral. If that's the case (and I have no reason to doubt that it is), Albert's preferred Highland snort didn't do much to promote his longevity, given that he popped his clogs at the age of forty-two. However, this sad thought didn't deter me from looking forward to enjoying the wine myself – when the right occasion arose.

It wouldn't be long, though, before I wished I'd bought two *cases* of the soothing sap, instead of just two bottles.

★ ★ ★ ★ ★

Time really does fly when you're enjoying yourself, and there can be few things more time-consumingly enjoyable than sitting down with a blank piece of paper and designing your own house. Ellie and I went through a mountain of paper. Nevertheless, when we finally presented our layman's lay-out to the architect, we felt that our minor contribution to the deforestation of the planet had been converted into time well spent. We had come up with a sketch plan for a single-storey house that had something of a country cottage look to its front, yet had sufficient depth to accommodate all mod cons in a deceptively large area of living space. The experience gained in putting together our plans for the extension at Merryhatton Roselea had stood us in good stead for what was going to be a significantly larger project here. That said, we weren't without our apprehensions about taking on such a daunting venture as organising and supervising the building of an entire house in the middle of a remote field, but our rookies' enthusiasm for the challenge overcame all else – initially.

The first blow to our confidence came some time after the architect had presented his preliminary drawings to our old sparring partners in the local authority's planning department. They reminded us that the elected councillors on the planning committee had only granted us planning permission 'in principle', but final decisions on the acceptability or otherwise of the design details of our proposed building would lie with themselves, the local authority officials, and with them alone.

The pitch of the roof as depicted in our plans, they then informed us, was unsuitable for a house in the East Lothian countryside. It would have to be increased from thirty to forty-five degrees to comply with the roof angle of traditional farm cottages in the county. Our response was that the width-to-depth ratio of this house was totally different from that of a typical local cottage, and the architect's decision on the angle of the roof pitch had been made accordingly. I maintained that the angle he had suggested *looked* right, was in balance with the dimensions of the building and, in any event, was identical to the roofs on other houses built recently in rural East Lothian. But the official assigned to our case wouldn't be budged. He was adamant – the roof pitch would have to be changed as instructed, or there would be no rubber stamp for our plans.

To say that our hearts fell would be to put it mildly. The imposition of this ostensibly minor adjustment to the architect's drawings amounted, in reality, to a major and correspondingly expensive increase to the overall size of the house. The roof cavity would now be so vast that it would be able to accommodate a replication of the three public rooms and four bedrooms on the ground floor. We would now be building a de facto two-storey house, with a roof so high that it would make the building twice as conspicuous as before. Our constant aim had been to keep the house's presence in the surrounding landscape as discreet as possible, on the assumption that this would automatically meet with the planners' approval. So why had they now turned that piece of logic on its head? It surely couldn't be that they genuinely preferred to have a building standing out like a sore thumb when a much more subtle proposition had been put to them.

'It could just be their way of reversing an outline planning decision that they didn't approve of in the first place,' the architect told me when I asked him what he thought the bureaucrats were up to. 'Could just be that they hope you'll be put off by the additional cost involved. You know, they maybe think you'll take cold feet and call the whole thing off.'

I felt my hackles rise. 'Well, they've got another think coming!' I snapped. Then I thought about the implications of this new turn of events for a moment, which is all the time it took me to decide that it didn't bear thinking about. 'Can we fight it?' I asked.

The architect shrugged and said that we could, *if* I could afford the time. Such things could drag on and on, and the chances were that, in the end, the planners' decision wouldn't be reversed anyway.

The old adage that time is money never rang truer – or louder. When we first started down this route, I had thought, in my naivety, that we would have had the deer farm up and running by now. Instead, we were still locked in a war of attrition with officialdom, and our bank balance continued to take a battering. We had already paid wee Bertie for the land, which would be of absolutely no commercial use to us if we walked away from our project now. Dammit, I thought – those power-mad buggers may think they've managed to deliver a knockout blow at long last, but we're not down yet, and *certainly* not out.

'OK,' I said to the architect, 'alter your plans to include the new roof pitch, then re-submit them as quickly as you can. The project goes ahead!'

He cleared his throat. 'Ehm, wouldn't you like me to give you a ballpark figure for the extra cost of materials and labour first?'

I didn't even attempt to answer him. I knew very well that the word 'no' would probably stick in my throat.

★ ★ ★ ★ ★

Though the full story of building that house at Howe Knowe could fill a book on its own, by and large, the experience was a wonderfully rewarding one. We called on the expert services of wee Bob and his Merryhatton Roselea team again, and as the months passed, it was a thrill to see the building rise from its foundations to what was now turning out to be (thanks to the planners' insistence on that additional roof pitch) a large and imposing house. It was going to be much larger and a whole lot more imposing than we had ever envisaged, which had an associated effect on our budget, but at least it was there, and our goal was getting ever nearer. What's more, we hadn't had to resort to borrowing from the bank, so the unforeseen strains on our finances hadn't reached the critical stage yet. Then the planning department dealt us another blow, and this promised to be the knockout one that we had doggedly managed to dodge so far.

'All the outer brickwork will have to come down,' the council's building inspector stated flatly on what I presumed would be one of the last of his regular visits to the site.

'Down?' I queried, scarcely able to believe my ears. 'Did you say… *down?*'

'Down, demolished, razed to the ground – whichever way you want to put it.'

My blood ran cold. It was common knowledge that this go-by-the-book martinet had recently insisted on a new house down on the coast being demolished because of some minor technicality not having being observed to the letter by the builder. Also, the inspector had the reputation of being totally devoid of a sense of humour, so I knew he wasn't joking.

'But why?' I pleaded. I gestured towards the almost completed house. 'I mean, you've inspected every stage of the construction work from day one without finding a single thing to complain about, so what the hell's the big problem now?'

He nodded towards some narrow lengths of wood lying on the ground nearby. 'These are fire stops. Your architect was advised to include them on your plans, and that's why, I presume, your builders' supply people delivered them here along with the rest of the materials. They should have been fixed at regulation intervals between the outer and the inner skins of the house as the bricks were laid.'

I was livid now. 'Fire stops? These bloated matchsticks? What kind of bloody fire are they supposed to stop, for Pete's sake?'

I was treated to what I presumed was a verbatim account of a building dictate that had only recently come into force. The gist of it was that the inclusion of these slim wooden strips in the wall cavity of a house would delay the spread of a fire by a few vital minutes. It sounded like bureaucratic bullshit to me, and I told the inspector so. I also asked him if he was related to the sadistic bastard in the planning department who had tried to scupper me with all his roof-angle crap. Big mistake.

The martinet was seriously miffed. 'I don't bullshit,' he said drily. 'Regulations are regulations, I'm empowered to enforce them, and you're in blatant breach of them.' There was a triumphalist smirk on his face as he pointed directly at the house and declared, 'Without fire stops, that building is illegal, so all the outer brickwork will have to be removed to allow them to be fitted.'

'But that'll weaken the rest of the structure. The whole lot could collapse.'

'Which will teach you to stick to the rules next time.'

'And why, pray, didn't you tell me about your precious damned fire stops long before the brickwork reached the top of the gables?'

His smirk morphed into a supercilious scowl. 'You employed an architect and an experienced builder to advise you on technical points, so ask *them* why they missed this one.'

I took a deep breath, counted silently to ten and thought of the taste of silver birch wine. It was all I could do to stop myself from taking this self-important control freak by the throat. 'You do realise,' I said, my voice shaking with rage, 'that by enforcing this piddling regulation, you're going to put an end to this entire project? The fact of the matter is that I simply can't afford to rip it all down and start again – which, in effect, is what you're asking me to do, right?'

He replied with a not-my-problem shrug.

I gestured towards the bundle of fire stops. 'So, for a few bits of wood that are worth next to nothing, and which didn't even feature in your book of rules until recently, I'm going to lose all that I've invested here. You understand that, do you?'

He repeated his shrug.

'Don't you think that's taking *official* nit-picking a bit too far?' I asked.

He shook his head dismissively. 'I don't make the –'

'Yeah, yeah, yeah,' I cut in, 'you don't make the orders, you only obey them. Enough bloody said! That just about sums your type up, doesn't it?'

'You know what you have to do,' he countered, 'and if you don't do it, a demolition order will be issued. It's as simple as that.' He then turned on his heel and swaggered off to his car.

It finally looked as though our long roller-coaster ride had taken a terminal plunge into the buffers. There had been some scary moments along the way at times, but we'd survived them all and had always managed to come out smiling. But now it really did seem that we'd come to the end of the line. And there would be no good in my pointing the finger of blame at anyone other than myself. In the so-called 'self-build' business, you are your own main contractor, so the buck stops with you, not with anyone you hire to help you. It was just unfortunate that wee Bob the builder hadn't come across the new fire-stop strips before this job, and it was a pity that the architect hadn't drawn his attention to them on the plans. But that was all water under the bridge now, and the bottom line was that I simply hadn't been up to the job I'd taken on.

A gloomy silence engulfed our rented cottage that evening, and I didn't sleep a wink that night. I had ploughed the bulk of our assets into a dream that had turned into a nightmare, which became all the more real the longer I lay awake, trying to think of a way out of it. But there was none. We were facing ruin, and I'd brought it upon my family by selfishly chasing that damned rainbow of mine – with a little help, of course, from that conniving planning official and his mate, that heartless bloody dictator of a building inspector. By the time morning finally came round, I was feeling exhausted, dejected and, I'm ashamed to admit, more than a wee bit sorry for myself as well.

Conversely, Ellie was well-slept, bright-eyed and bushy-tailed. 'I've been thinking,' she chirped as she poured the breakfast coffee, 'and I reckon I've solved your problem.'

I was gazing blankly down at a slice of toast, which I'd gone through the motions of buttering, but had no inclination to eat. 'Nah, there's no way of solving it,' I mumbled. 'I've gone over and over it in my head all night, and there's just no answer. Let's face it, the red tape merchants have had it in for me from day one, and they've finally –'

'All you need to do,' Ellie interrupted, 'is make holes in the brickwork at regular intervals up the four corners of the house and stuff the fire-stop thingies through. You can make other holes here and there along the four sides of the house to guide them along and fix them through.' She gave her hair a *fait accompli* toss. 'Problem solved! Simple!'

I looked up blearily from my toast, a chink of light appearing through the fog of dismay that had been clouding my brain. 'Just, uh, run that past me again,' I muttered.

She did, and, by God, what she said was right. There would be no necessity to demolish anything. Her solution was perfect. Suddenly, the roller coaster was back in motion and heading optimistically upwards again. It gained momentum after I'd checked the idea with wee Bob, who agreed it would work. All right, it would be a fiddly, time-consuming operation, he said, but the main thing was that the building would be saved and the new fire regulations covered. Bingo! Happy days were here again.

If the council's building inspector was pleased for us, he made a convincing job of disguising the fact when I put the suggestion to him. After much deliberation and consultation with colleagues, he finally conceded that our proposed method of inserting the fire stops would be acceptable, but with one condition. We would have to provide him with photographs of every detail of the operation, to serve as proof – should his superiors ever require it – that he had properly enforced the requisite regulations.

I assured him that I would not only provide photographs but, if it would do him a bit of good with his superiors, would frame them for him as well – with bells and whistles on.

To quote one of old Maria's Mallorcan proverbs, 'A fig out of reach tastes all the sweeter for the climb', and she never said a truer word.

– EPILOGUE –

HOME IS WHERE THE HEART IS

By the time we eventually moved into the house at Howe Knowe, Sandy had completed his course at college and planned to develop an agricultural contracting business with a couple of his friends. Charlie, meanwhile, had recently done a work-experience stint at an advertising agency in Edinburgh and had been offered a position in their design department when he left school in a few months' time. Although Ellie and I had hardly had time to notice, both boys had grown up while we travelled a road that had been longer, rougher and with higher tolls to pay than we could ever have anticipated. Now, however, we had almost reached the end of that chosen road, if not the end of a rainbow, and we were proud owners of a superb new home – albeit one with enough empty floor space upstairs to play roller hockey in.

Wee Bertie, from whom we'd bought the land, had taken his last crop from the field, and we were ready to sow the grass on which our new herd of deer would be grazing next spring. In the intervening months, a deer fence would be built round the property, along with handling pens and an all-purpose agricultural shed. We were also thinking about where we should eventually locate our farm shop and 'mini farm', modelled on those we'd seen on Archie Crawford's inspirational enterprise up near Inverness. Apart from the fact that our finances had suffered badly due to the additional building work and related delays that resulted from our contretemps with officialdom, we could hardly have been happier to be in this position at last, and the future looked bright.

★ ★ ★ ★ ★

Then the Berlin Wall came down and fell on our best-laid plans like several tons of proverbial bricks.

One may well ask how on earth such a political development in a distant land could have any effect at all on a nascent deer farm in Scotland. The answer is that West Germany, as it was then, just happened to have the highest per capita consumption of venison in the world. Consequently, the country had become a vital and lucrative market for the produce of British deer farmers. Now, with the sudden demise of Communism, the floodgates to West Germany were opened for an influx of cheap wild venison from the east. The event sent shock waves through British deer farming, which was still in a fairly early stage of development itself and vulnerable, therefore, to such a significant downturn in demand. The UK farming press was full of predictions of doom for the country's deer farmers, except the best established and most securely capitalised of them. But, according to some pundits, all but the largest of them could be hard-pushed to survive as well.

Once again, then, we were faced with a scenario in which 'big is beautiful' and 'bigger still is even more beautiful' were going to be the bywords. And we hadn't even started to trade yet. Also, the depleted state of our finances meant that, for the first time, we would be obliged to borrow in order to develop our new farm, so the crucial question we had to ask ourselves was whether such a commitment would be prudent in what had become an extremely uncertain line of business. The advice from the bank was, as anticipated, in the negative, and, downhearted and disillusioned as we were, we had to concede that their advice was sound. We had to face the hard fact that all our efforts had been in vain.

Ironically, the wind of change that breathed favourably on millions of people in communist Eastern Europe had also blown away the commercial aspirations of at least one family in free-enterprise Britain. But, in the larger scheme of things, our predicament amounted to little. Such is life. Yet would our situation have been any different had red tape not delayed the setting-up of our deer farm? In all honesty, I can't claim that it would. For all I know, the bureaucratic interference that so frustrated me at the time may even have spared us from complete financial disaster. Not, I should add, that I'd be sending any messages of thanks to the perpetrators of those obstructive shenanigans.

'So, what are we going to do now?' Ellie asked me one August evening, when we were sitting sipping after-dinner drinks with the boys on the verandah of our new house at Howe Knowe.

'That used to be our family motto,' Charlie quipped before I had a chance to answer.

'Yeah, but it was changed to "For Sale" a while back,' Sandy put in.

There was an apprehensive look on Ellie's face as she waited for my reaction to Sandy's loaded observation.

I didn't take the bait, though. 'You know,' I said, 'this evening was the first time the four of us have sat down to eat together in our own home since we left Ca's Mayoral almost four years ago.'

'Just seems like yesterday,' Ellie muttered, 'although nobody would guess it from the amount of extra lines on my face.'

A few moments of pregnant silence followed while the boys and I thought our own thoughts about the significance of Ellie's aside. Then Sandy came out with something that opened the lid on what I then realised I'd been keeping bottled up subconsciously all along.

'I, ehm… I hope you won't take this the wrong way, Dad,' he said, a note of hesitance in his voice, 'but don't you think that maybe all you've been doing – I mean in Mallorca as well as since you came back here – has been trying to find what we left behind at Cuddy Neuk?'

'Yeah, I'd give anything to be back there,' Charlie said. 'All the millionaires' villas and swimming pools and yachts and Rolls Royces and stuff in Mallorca were great while we were there, and I wouldn't have missed getting a chance to sample it all. But, well, there's been nothing to touch Cuddy Neuk.' He looked at me with a maturity in his eyes that I hadn't seen before. 'I know you always tell me never to say never, Dad, but we all know deep down that we'll never find another Cuddy Neuk again.'

I looked out towards the age-softened outline of Lammer Law, its heathery slopes reflecting subtle shades of mauve and green in the glow of the setting sun. It presented a magnificent picture, just as it had in a notably less benign way on those freezing cold mornings when I'd been cranking up that old diesel generator to test our newly-prospected water supply. Yes, this house that we'd built on what had then been a bleak and empty hillside had the makings of being a fine family home in a truly beautiful setting. Yet there was no arguing with what the boys were telling me – for us, it would never be Cuddy Neuk, and the twenty-five Howe Knowe acres would never now earn us a living. In fairness to Ellie in particular, it was time to put the past behind me once and for all – time to find a new path to follow in life.

'You're absolutely right, boys,' I said. 'There's no point in chasing that same old rainbow any more.'

Ellie gave me an apprehensive look. 'So, what *are* we going to do next, then?'

'Well, if the days of the small family farm are over,' I replied, 'and I think we're all agreed that they are, right?'

'Right,' they replied in unison, their eyes fixed on me.

'Then I've decided that there's only one thing I can do as a substitute.'

'Uh-huh?' they chanted expectantly.

'And that's to write about it.'

'*Write?*' Ellie exclaimed. 'Write what?'

'A book,' I smiled. 'A book about our experiences in Mallorca.'

Another pregnant silence, this time accompanied by unbelieving stares in my direction.

'Yeah,' I continued, undaunted, 'and I've even dreamed up a great name for it – *Snowball Oranges*. You know, taken from our first day at Ca's Mayoral, when that freak blizzard turned the orange groves into –'

'Yes, yes, I get your drift, if you'll pardon the pun,' Ellie butted in, 'but writing a book could take you years, and even more years to get it published – if ever. How do you propose to keep the wolf from the door in the meantime?'

'Aha, but I've thought about that as well, and I've come up with the perfect solution.'

Ellie raised her face heavenward and closed her eyes, mouthing what I took to be a silent prayer.

'And the way we'll make a living while I write my book,' I breezed, 'is by doing up and selling old houses again.'

Charlie groaned.

Sandy burst out laughing.

Ellie faked a faint.

I poured her a glass of silver birch wine.

THE END

www.summersdale.com